BUNKER

BUILDING
FOR THE END TIMES

BRADLEY GARRETT

SCRIBNER

New York London Toronto Sydney New Delhi

Scribner
An Imprint of Simon & Schuster, Inc.
1230 Avenue of the Americas
New York, NY 10020

First Scribner hardcover edition August 2020

SCRIBNER and design are registered trademarks of The Gale Group, Inc.,
used under license by Simon & Schuster, Inc., the publisher of this work.

For information about special discounts for bulk purchases,
please contact Simon & Schuster Special Sales at 1-866-506-1949
or business@simonandschuster.com.

The Simon & Schuster Speakers Bureau can bring authors to your live event.
For more information or to book an event, contact the Simon & Schuster Speakers
Bureau at 1-866-248-3049 or visit our website at www.simonspeakers.com.

Interior design by Erich Hobbing

Manufactured in the United States of America

1   3   5   7   9   10   8   6   4   2

Library of Congress Cataloging-in-Publication Data has been applied for.

ISBN 978-1-5011-8855-8
ISBN 978-1-5011-8857-2 (ebook)

"Everybody wants to own the end of the world."
—Don DeLillo, *Zero K*, 2016

Contents

Author's Note

Some names, locations, and identifying details have been altered and certain events have been reordered. In making some of these changes, I was mindful of the words of one person who wishes to remain anonymous: "What's the point of prepping if everyone knows you're prepping?"

This research was generously funded, in part, by a Sydney Fellowship from the University of Sydney in Australia. However, the university did not sanction, condone, or fund the journey undertaken in the book's coda—that wholly irresponsible adventure was undertaken entirely of my own volition.

Acronym and Argot Glossary

4K—A high-resolution screen with a horizontal display of approximately four thousand pixels.

#10 Can—The most ubiquitous long-term food storage can. Each can holds about a gallon.

ADF—Australian Defence Force.

AFP—Australian Federal Police.

After Time—The time after an "event" (see PAW).

Agent BZ—3-Quinuclidinyl benzilate nerve gas.

AI—Artificial Intelligence. Intelligence demonstrated by machines.

American Redoubt—An area in the northwestern part of the United States designated by survivalist James Wesley, Rawles as the best place in the world to ride out TEOTWAWKI.

APC—Armored Personnel Carrier.

Armageddon—The eschatological notion of a literal or metaphorical gathering of armies for a battle during the end times.

ATF—Bureau of Alcohol, Tobacco, Firearms, and Explosives.

BBB—Better Business Bureau. A nonprofit established in 1912 to enhance consumer trust.

BLM—Bureau of Land Management.

Bolthole—A survival retreat. Also called a "doomstead."

Bug-In Bag (BIB)—The essentials for "hunkering down."

Bug Out—To leave quickly.

Bug-Out Bag (BOB)—A bag with enough supplies to survive on the move for seventy-two hours. Also called a "go-bag."

Bug-Out Location (BOL)—The place you retreat to in an event.

Bug-Out Vehicle (BOV)—The vehicle you will use to escape, and/or your mobile bunker.

Button Up—Seal the bunker.

BVP—Bioengineered Viral Pandemic. A human-engineered viral contagion that is let loose on the world.

CCTV—Closed-Circuit Television.

CDC—Centers for Disease Control and Prevention.

CERN—The European Organization for Nuclear Research. The largest particle physics laboratory in the world.

CFC—Chloroflourocarbon.

CGI—Computer-Generated Imagery.

CGWHQ—(United Kingdom) Central Government War Headquarters. Colloquially known as the Burlington Bunker.

CME—Coronal Mass Ejection. A significant release of plasma and a magnetic blast from the sun's corona.

COG—Continuity of Government.

COVID-19—A strain of coronavirus pathogen that emerged late in 2019 from Wuhan, China, and grew into a global pandemic in 2020.

CRISPR—A technology used to edit genomes in organisms, including humans.

CROWS—Common Remotely Operated Weapon Station.

Cryonics—The low-temperature freezing and storage of a human corpse or severed head, for potential future resurrection.

CUT—Church Universal and Triumphant.

DARPA—Defense Advanced Research Projects Agency.

Deep Larder—Enough food for an individual, family, or community to survive for months or years.

DHS—Department of Homeland Security.

DIY—Do It Yourself.

DNA—Deoxyribonucleic Acid. The self-replicating main constituent of chromosomes, the building blocks of life.

DOD—Department of Defense.

DMZ—Demilitarized Zone. A strip of land separating North and South Korea.

DRT—Disaster Response Team.

DUMBS—Deep Underground Military Bases.

EDC—Everyday Carry. Basic tools like a pocketknife, flashlight, lighter, or phone always to hand.

ELE—Extinction Level Event.

EMP—Electromagnetic Pulse. A burst of gamma rays from a solar flare or nuclear explosion that could disrupt or destroy electronic equipment.

Event—A serious event that has the capacity to shift social and/or political order. The trigger can be environmental or anthropogenic.

(the) Fall—The collapse of civilization.

FBI—Federal Bureau of Investigation.

FCDA—Federal Civil Defense Administration.

FEMA—Federal Emergency Management Agency. Some preppers say it stands for "Foolishly Expecting Meaningful Aid."

FIFO—First In First Out (system for food storage).

FSB—(Russia) Federal Security Service.

FTD—First to Die.

Generational Theory—A theory that every eighty years there is an inevitable, and necessary, period of turmoil in United States history.

Geoengineering—The deliberate and large-scale intervention in the Earth's climate system.

GFC—Global Financial Crisis (of 2007/2008).

GOOD—Get Out of Dodge.

GSA—General Services Administration. An agency established to support the function of federal agencies by managing real estate, services, and products.

HAARP—High Frequency Active Auroral Research Program. A $290 million installation built by the United States Air Force and Navy to study Earth's ionosphere.

Hard Reset—A localized event of major impact, like the Chernobyl nuclear reactor explosion.

Hardened Architecture—Engineering and constructing a building to be more resilient against external threats.

HARTS—(North Korea) Hardened Artillery Sites tunneled into the sides of mountains.

HEMP—High-Elevation Electromagnetic Pulse.

HEPA—A popular, and very effective, air filtration system.

HI-EMA—Hawaii Emergency Management Agency.

Homestead Preppers—Preppers focused on self-sufficiency and off-grid living. They often craft, make, and repair items rather than buying them. Also called "prepsteaders."

ICBM—Intercontinental Ballistic Missile.

ICO—Initial Coin Offering (of cryptocurrency).

INCH Bag—I'm Never Coming Home bag.

Intentional Community—A planned residential community designed around a common social, political, or religious ideology.

IRIS—NASA's Interface Region Imaging Spectrograph observation satellite. Built to observe the sun's atmosphere.

ITV Growler—US Army Internally Transportable Light Strike Vehicle.

JLTV—US Army Joint Light Tactical Vehicle.

LDS—(The Church of Jesus Christ of) Latter-Day Saints.

MAD—Mutually Assured Destruction.

MAG—Mutual Assistance Group.

MAGA—Make America Great Again. A favorite slogan of US president Donald Trump.

MAV—Mormon Assault Vehicle.

MERS (illness)—Middle East Respiratory Syndrome. A strain of coronavirus pathogen first reported in Saudi Arabia in 2012.

MERS (program)—Mobile Emergency Response Support (a FEMA initiative).

MERV—An air filtration system one step below HEPA.

MiG—The Russian Aircraft Corporation. Often used as a shorthand for any Russian-produced fighter jet.

Millenniarism (or Millennialism)—From Latin *millenarius*, "containing a thousand." A religious, social, or political belief in a future ideal society created by catastrophic change.

MoD—(United Kingdom) Ministry of Defence.

MRE—Meal, Ready-to-Eat combat rations.

MTA—Mormon Transhumanist Association.

NASA—National Aeronautics and Space Administration.

NASCAR—National Association for Stock Car Auto Racing.

NBC—Nuclear, Biological, and/or Chemical.

NGA—National Gardening Association.

NIH—National Institutes of Health.

ACRONYM AND ARGOT GLOSSARY

NORAD—North American Aerospace Defense Command. The aerospace control and defense hub for North America.

NRA—National Rifle Association.

NSF—National Science Foundation.

NWO—New World Order. An alleged emerging clandestine centralized world government.

OPSEC—Operations Security.

PAW—Postapocalyptic World.

PHEIC—A Public Health Emergency of International Concern, declared by the World Health Organization.

PLA—(China) People's Liberation Army.

POW/MIA—Prisoner of War/Missing in Action.

PPE—Personal Protective Equipment, such as masks and gloves.

Practical Prepping—Prepping for everyday emergencies.

Prepping—The practice of preparing for a range of future crises by bolstering self-sufficiency through community organization, stockpiling, skill development, and the building of defensible space.

PTSD—Post-Traumatic Stress Disorder.

RAND Corporation—The Research and Development Corporation. An American nonprofit think tank created in 1948 to offer research and analysis to the US Armed Forces.

RFID—Radio-Frequency Identification. Uses electromagnetic fields to track tags attached to, or embedded in, objects.

Ripple Effect—An event that triggers another event, descending into chaos like dominos falling. Also called "cascading impact."

SARS—Severe Acute Respiratory Syndrome. A viral illness caused by a coronavirus pathogen strain that manifested in 2002 from the Guangdong province in China.

SHTF—Shit Hit the Fan.

SLOAP—Space Left Over After Planning.

Solastalgia—A sense of grief and existential dread caused by rapid environmental change.

SPAM—Canned cook pork produced by the Hormel Foods Corporation. The acronym is thought to mean "spiced ham," but during World War II it was often called "Special Army Meat."

SPLC—Southern Poverty Law Center. An American nonprofit legal advocacy organization that monitors extremism.

Stalkers—Explorers of, and guides into, the Chernobyl Exclusion Zone around the exploded Nuclear Reactor No. 4.

SWAT—A Special Weapons and Tactics law enforcement unit.

Tacticool—Clothing and accessories that offer a ready-for-action aesthetic.

TEOTWAWKI—The End of the World as We Know It.

THC—The main psychoactive compound in marijuana.

Transhumanism—The belief that science and technology can assist us in evolving beyond our current physical and mental limitations.

UN—The United Nations. An intergovernmental organization that aims to maintain international peace and security.

USAF—United States Air Force.

Ute—Australian shorthand for a "utility" vehicle.

WHO—World Health Organization.

WROL—Without Rule of Law. When the police or military have lost control.

YOYO—You're On Your Own. For instance, when the government isn't providing essential services.

BUNKER

Private Arks of the Underground

"The immediate cause of World War III is the
preparation for it."
—C. Wright Mills, *The Causes of
World War Three*, 1958[1]

For a decade I've been carrying around a small stack of empty notebooks pilfered from the library of the Central Government War
Headquarters, a thirty-five-acre Cold War bunker buried deep under
the English countryside just outside the city of Bath. The books are
pulpy and sallow, and their spines have two spots of radiating dis-
coloration from where the staples holding them together have bled
rust into the paper. Each is emblazoned with the royal emblem of
Queen Elizabeth II: the letters "ER," separated by a crown.

Each book is also stamped "S.O. Book 111." I've always assumed the "S.O." stood for "Special Operations" and that 111 must be a government code for the type of notebook it is: forty-eight pages, ruled. I could never confirm this, because the internet provided no answers as to their production or provenance. What I can tell you is that if, during the Cold War years, World War III had unfurled and London had been obliterated by a nuclear strike, the thoughts of the survivors might have been recorded in those pages. I often wonder about the words that might have been written in them, and I ponder that if those words *had* been written, I might not be alive to read them.

The bunker itself is larger than twenty-five football fields combined, but this didn't make getting into it any easier. The early dusk of winter provided cover for a dozen of us, dressed in black, to squeeze through a long-broken iron gate and descend some sixty-five feet down a ramp into a pitch-black underground Bath Stone quarry, which on our tattered map was labeled, simply, "Box Mine." Each of us—all seasoned urban explorers—had long relished the opportunity to investigate what we colloquially knew as the Burlington Bunker. None of us anticipated the scale of what awaited us on the other side of the massive red blast doors we wrenched open with rods ferried from the broken iron gate.

This massive subterranean space could be "buttoned up" to seal off and shelter four thousand people for months. More than sixty miles of roads, strung with a hundred thousand lights, interconnected an industrial kitchen, sleeping quarters, a bombproof radio broadcasting station, laundries, a drinking water reservoir, and of course, the government library where I pocketed the books. As we drove hot-wired electric buggies through the complex, it was possible to imagine a small, elite tribe enduring here in the first months of a postapocalyptic period. What those residents would find when they finally opened the blast doors and walked back up the ramp was more difficult to envisage.

I'd seen astonishing places with that crew of urban explorers—and spent some time in court and jail as a result—but nothing rivaled finding a subterranean city. For a decade after visiting the

Burlington Bunker, I kept the notebooks with me, still unfilled, waiting for a story worthy of them. I finally saw my chance in 2016, when the secret city was put on the market for £1.5 million ($1,717, 278).

One of the prospective buyers was an American named Robert Vicino. Founder and CEO of the Vivos Group, Vicino was a property developer with a difference: his pitch was both doomsayer and savior. Convinced that the collapse of civilization was imminent, he was all over the internet, speaking in a booming register of pandemics, floods, riots, and war; the end of the world as we know it. He lambasted skeptical journalists who sought to interview him for their naïveté and unpreparedness and suggested the government would leave us behind to fend for ourselves when things began to fall apart.

In the face of this catastrophe, the Vivos Group offered buyers a chance at survival: a "life assurance solution," as Vicino described it, a way to cross through those hazardous troughs. In Burlington, he saw an opportunity: a perfect venue for constructing a private bolt-hole to ferry a small percentage of the world's population through that collapse. Imagining the bunker filled with paying clients, rather than government officials, was the beginning of my descent into prepper culture. As I would find over the next few years, there were many like Vicino with similar visions: a group of doomsday capitalists I came to call the dread merchants.

For much of my life, the word "bunker" conjured up a mental image of a crumbling concrete World War II monolith, a pillbox on a beach somewhere in Europe, slumped in the sand, covered in graffiti. Or, sometimes, I envisaged a windowless room under a German city, with a map table and a red telephone, curling cigarette smoke emanating from a huddled group debating taking action with serious consequences. In other words, I imagined a bunker as a generic government-built military refuge. There's no doubt that during the twentieth century the bunker became a ubiquitous architecture in response to the threat of airpower. Its precedents, however, have deep roots in human history.

Though the word "bunker" originates from the Old Swedish

word *bunke*—originally meaning "boards used to protect the cargo of a ship"—the earliest examples of bunkered space long predate the term. In Cappadocia, in the Central Anatolia region of what is now Turkey, the Hittites began carving into its soft volcanic tuff as their empire was fragmenting, around 1200 BCE. They hollowed out spaces for living, storage, and industry inside subterranean systems that were only accessible through small entrances sealed with weighty three-foot-tall millstones. The design allowed for the stones to be rolled open and closed only from inside the bunker.

There are twenty-two known large-scale ancient subterranean cities in the region. Many still exist. The most sprawling is Kaymakli, a network of hundreds of constructed tunnels connecting areas for earthenware jar storage, kitchens, public space, and stables. Archaeologists believe that a five-mile-long passageway links Kaymakli to Derinkuyu, the deepest of the twenty-two cities, which at some points stretches two hundred feet below the surface. Derinkuyu sheltered as many as twenty thousand people, along with their livestock and food stores, and consisted of more than eighteen floors of bedrooms, halls, churches, armories, storage chambers, wells, and toilets. As a matter of necessity, the Derinkuyu network is punctuated by more than fifty vertical ventilation chimneys: snorkels to Earth's surface.[2]

These bunkers appear to have been used throughout history for extended periods during wars, raids, massacres, and times of social unrest. In 370 BCE the Greek scholar Xenophon wrote about the underground cities of Central Anatolia—more than eight hundred years after they were first carved out. In the first century of the Common Era, persecuted Christians hid from Romans in these subterranean cities.[3] It's possible, I would suggest, that the story of Jesus's resurrection in the New Testament, in which the rock was rolled from the cave at Calvary, was based on experiences of rolling the millstones from the Cappadocia bunkers, or spaces like them.

Meanwhile, the persecutors were also building secure spaces. In the Roman city of Pompeii one resident, Quintus Poppeus, a wealthy in-law of Emperor Nero, had constructed, under his block-sized villa, a hidden chamber with thickened walls and secured subterranean access chambers. The only reason we know about it is because it was preserved by the eruption of Mount Vesuvius in 79 CE.[4] The notion of a Roman bunker seems odd, but that's precisely what it was.

As an architectural space, the bunker developed in tandem with sedentism. To remain in one place, sustained by collected resources necessary for survival, is to make oneself into a target, to invite disaster or social conflict, making defense necessary. It was in this context that the bunker came into being: first adapted from caves whose entrances were blocked up, and later as human excavations.[5] There can't be an accidental bunker. Constructing one requires an awareness of the future and of our own mortality. Just as a hole in the ground isn't a cave unless it's large enough to be entered by humans, an underground space doesn't become a bunker until it's transformed into one through our intervention.[6]

Bunkers have always been existential places: earthly wombs from which to be reborn. When resurrection becomes impossible, bunkers become tombs.[7] Safe crossing through periods of danger and instability requires having a destination plotted in the future and making it to that destination by weathering the psychological and social hurdles of lockdown. Although you aren't guaranteed resurrection if you build and stock a bunker, you're seriously diminishing your chances of making it through these periods of turmoil if you don't.[8]

Just as bunkers are older than we often imagine, their function and form have changed much over time. In recent years, bunkers have become not just spaces for human bodies but spaces from which to revive the things we care about. Part of what makes our species unique is our desire to transmit culture—ideas, beliefs, symbols, artifacts—from one generation to the next. Bunkers, those "boards used to protect the cargo," are where we now store what we most cherish as a species.[9] The more we have to protect, the greater the urge to "bunker up." It's no wonder we now keep all of our virtual data on servers in bunkered sites. The Library of Congress, for instance, has adapted a massive bunker in Virginia and filled it with all of the library's movie, television, and sound collections. The goal is to prevent another catastrophic loss of human knowledge like the torching of the Great Library of Alexandria two thousand years ago.

There is more. Twenty-first-century experiments in bunkered living involve melding the body and data in the form of DNA and cryonics storage facilities. If death can potentially be forestalled by building a bunker, why not also use it to store biological data—or, even better, the heads and bodies of the dead, who may have hope of being reanimated at some point in the future?

Back in the nineteenth century, the Russian philosopher Nikolai Fedorov was convinced that through science we'd one day learn how to resurrect the dead.[10] Today, the thinking among some in Silicon Valley is that death is a disease that can be cured. Among them is PayPal founder Peter Thiel, who has become convinced that computation will soon be brought to bear on death, eventually reducing it from a mystery to a solvable problem.[11] He has invested in a company called Unity Biotechnology that is working to slow, halt, or reverse the aging process. These experiments in transhumanism, or the belief that science and technology can assist us in evolving beyond our current physical and mental limitations, often take place in bunkers: spaces of protection for the fragile human body; spaces to sequester information; subterranean time ships.

The southwestern United States, where I was raised, seems to be the epicenter of such plans. Perhaps this is because private bunker-building and bug-out activities have historical precedent in a place whose indigenous cultures have long sought *terra subterranea* as shelter from extreme environmental forces and social conflict. As a result, these underground spaces became places of power and transformation. The Native American traditions of retreating into the underground kiva, cliff-dwelling, and cave, sites where ancestral forces emerge from the Earth rather than descending from the stars, is part of the character of the Southwest, which blends survivalist and apocalyptic beliefs, often to weird effect. One of those effects is the emergence of a subculture of preppers like Robert Vicino, people who are building bunkers underground to survive every eventuality.

As a teenager who grew up on the eastern edge of Los Angeles, I would regularly pack a four-wheel-drive with supplies and head into the Mojave Desert looking for prehistoric remains, foreshadowing an eventual first career as an archaeologist with the United States Bureau of Land Management (BLM). In Colorado, I once hiked for three days into a gulch over flint-knapped glass and pot-sherds, until I found myself standing at the rim of a thousand-year-old kiva, a stacked-stone structure dug into the ground. Though it was long abandoned, it was easy to imagine descending into it down a ladder in the roof, and then through a hatchway in the floor called a *sipapu*, a Hopi word meaning "humanity's emergence place." Having grown up surrounded by such underland sanctuaries, when I first encountered people burying architecture in the ground for ostensibly very different reasons, it was obvious to me that they weren't just functional, they were hallowed spaces. As I researched this book, I wandered through many places west of the Mississippi, from California to South Dakota to Texas. In each, I dipped into people's underworld spaces, seeing in them reflections of our past.

It didn't take long before I was seeing bunkers everywhere: in Europe, Canada, the Korean Peninsula, Thailand, and Australia. Today, like many of the technologies we use, the bunker has achieved "escape velocity" from its origins. The "hardened architecture" of the bunker now takes physical form in the infrastructure of our everyday lives: in malls, airports, gated communities, "shooter-proof" schools, even the vehicles we drive.[12] Each of these is an element of an architecture of dread, a conflict mentality transposed onto everyday life. In this respect, the bunker is a metaphorical space as much as an architectural one: an expression of our twenty-first-century anxieties and insecurities, a reflection of the way we see the world and each other.

The withdrawal of the rich and powerful into fortified and hidden bunker-enclaves—whether for individuals, families, or communities—is the logical endpoint of the atomization of social life, in which we build armored redoubts to keep wealth and possessions inside and potentially hostile forces out. Hollywood and Wall Street are filled with wealthy preppers hedging against collapse by buying space in private bunkers.[13] Their actions, as those historical precedents make clear, herald the end of an era of abundance and the beginning of an age of austerity, rationing, and retreat. In the process, the social inequality we experience on the level of the everyday takes on existential significance.[14]

As I wrote this book, there was a swirl of rumor about the Silicon Valley elite burying bunkers on ranches in New Zealand, wealthy Russian oligarchs buying whole Pacific islands to bug out to, and bunkers being subcontracted by the wealthy (notable examples including Bill Gates, Kim Kardashian, and Shaquille O'Neal). According to a *Wired* magazine article from 2007, Tom Cruise poured $10 million into building a bunker under his 298-acre ranch in Telluride, Colorado.[15] Ten years later, Reddit CEO Steve Huffman made it clear in a *New Yorker* interview that he felt contemporary life was founded on a fragile consensus that was crumbling, and that he was ready to escape at any moment when it all kicked off.[16] In Los Angeles, a porn production studio even decided to build their new headquarters in an underground bomb shelter—you know, just in case.[17]

Meanwhile, Donald Trump spent much of his time during his presidency at his Florida resort of Mar-a-Lago. The golf course there is undergirded by a bunker built in the early 1950s by breakfast cereal magnate Marjorie Merriweather Post. Back in 2004 Trump told a journalist for *Esquire* magazine that he'd spent $100,000 "fixing up" the bunker. He explained that in the event of a nuclear, chemical, or climactic calamity, Mar-a-Lago is where he'd want to be. "We did tests, and the foundation is anchored into the coral reef with steel and concrete," Trump crowed. "That sucker's going nowhere."[18] It was in his private bunker in Mar-a-Lago that Trump made the decision with his top foreign policy advisers to assassinate Qassem Soleimani, one of Iran's top military commanders, in a January 2020 drone strike.

In the Spring of 2020, public frustration over police brutality led to civil unrest in cities across the United States, including Washington, DC. At one point, President Trump hid in a bunker underneath the White House as protesters clashed with Secret Service agents outside. In addition to Mar-a-Lago and the bunkers that come with the job of president, Trump has bragged about having bunkers under his property in Westchester, New York, and under his International Golf Club in suburban West Palm Beach.[19] He isn't the first president to have built his own personal bolthole: John F. Kennedy also had a bunker near his Florida vacation home, not far from Mar-a-Lago on Peanut Island, a tiny plot made of spoils from a dredging project. His bunker was a more modest affair, however: built over seven days in 1961, it was lined with lead and buried under twelve feet of dirt.[20] Unlike Trump, however, Kennedy built the bunker for one reason: to survive a nuclear attack.

Today's bunkers are built not so much in response to one single imminent catastrophe, but out of a more general sense of disquiet, in response to a greater variety of threats. These range from temporary civil unrest to "grid-down" scenarios to an extinction-level event (or ELE, in prepper lingo). This gamut of anxieties also reflects how widespread the idea of prepping has become. It has recently been estimated that 3.7 million Americans are prepping on some scale. It's now a multibillion-dollar-a-year industry and a practice that's quickly being exported around the world as the burden of personal protection shifts to the private sector in many places.[21] Prepping isn't just a result of contemporary conditions of social life, but a lens through which to perceive and understand those conditions.[22]

As an ethnographer, a cultural storyteller, preppers and their practices fascinate me because they make the time to look beyond the present, and then act on their imaginations of what the future might be. I wanted to meet preppers, to spend time with them, and to figure out what the motivating forces were behind the construction of spaces built (or adapted) to weather the end times. I wanted to know whether it was paranoia or practicality that was driving them. I was also acting on my own impulses to burrow, to disappear, to feel sheltered from the modern world's invasive din.

I left the United States, and my previous career as an archaeologist, more than a decade ago. Since that time, I've traveled to more than forty countries, and worked in four. My previous ethnographic research in social geography, which involved trespassing with fellow urban explorers into off-limits locations like abandoned buildings, tunnel systems, and skyscrapers (as well as government bunkers), took me to some of the most awe-inspiring places humans have created. That project also led to my doing research and journalism for some of the world's most venerable institutions. My adult life has been a blur of international flights, research projects, conferences, public lectures, and long days in libraries. And the longer I spend thinking about the *geo*, and our place in it, the more I end up realizing that my work as a geographer has been about exploring human limits as much as new places. I find myself circling around one conclusion: the way we have been living cannot continue. This was made painfully obvious during the 2020 COVID-19 pandemic that originated in Wuhan, the capital of Hubei province in Central China, and quickly spread around the globe. As the virus spread, supply lines, international travel and trade routes, economic systems, and social norms collapsed over a matter of weeks. The pandemic was precisely the kind of breakdown preppers had prepared for. While most people went panic-shopping for toilet paper, preppers closed their blast doors and watched the chaos unfold from a safe distance with wry amusement.

For this project—which involved hanging out with preppers in the spaces they were constructing in half a dozen countries over three years—I was determined to saturate myself in disaster, roaming our damaged planet to collect stories from those who felt that humans have reached the end of a terminal phase. Many people I met are convinced something disastrous is coming down the line, and they are determined to protect themselves from it and to survive it—whatever "it" may be. Wherever I traveled, I found prepping communities filled with dread about nuclear war and waste, a collapsing ecosystem, runaway technology, pandemics, natural disasters, economic meltdown, and violence. Most of all, people decried the deterioration of political discourse, cooperation, and civility, the very things needed to address these problems.

Their fears are hardly surprising. Let's consider the nuclear threat. Today, nine countries on Earth—France, China, the USA, the UK, India, Pakistan, Israel, North Korea, and Russia—wield almost fourteen thousand nuclear weapons. North Korea's missile tests are ongoing, while Iran's nuclear program has restarted following Trump's reimposition of economic sanctions on the country. With America's power waning under the influence of isolationist policies, in 2019 Australia began seriously debating whether to start its own nuclear "deterrence" program. Meanwhile, some Scandinavian countries have begun reactivating their Cold War bunkers. The window in the late twentieth century when denuclearization seemed possible now seems to have closed shut.

In 2018, a year into writing this book, the Doomsday Clock was advanced to two minutes to midnight. The clock, created by a team of atomic scientists in 1947, represents the likelihood of a human-induced global catastrophe. It had not been at two minutes to midnight since 1953, after Russia and the United States tested their first four-hundred-kiloton and five-hundred-kiloton hydrogen bombs, respectively. In 2019, the board of atomic scientists kept the clock hands where they were, signifying what they called the "new abnormal." Early in 2020, prior even to the COVID-19 outbreak, the scientists set the hands at one hundred seconds to midnight, the closest the clock has ever been to symbolic doom.

But the scientists' decision wasn't solely based on the threat of nuclear war. Another, overwhelming, factor they cited was the fast-developing climate crisis. The 2018 report observed that the world is in "a state as worrisome as the most dangerous times of the Cold War, a state that features an unpredictable and shifting landscape of simmering disputes that multiply the chances for major military conflict to erupt [, and] to halt the worst effects of climate change, the countries of the world must cut net worldwide carbon dioxide emissions to zero by well before the end of the century."[23] These grim tidings have been reasserted, and elevated, by scientists ad nauseam. Despite this, little action has been taken by countries to roll back emissions. In fact, worldwide carbon dioxide emissions reached record highs in 2019, just as they did in 2018.

A 2012 UN Intergovernmental Panel on Climate Change (IPCC) report suggested that in the next twenty years the temperature increase will almost certainly cause widespread global flooding, wildfires, infrastructural collapse, crop failure, species extinction, and mass migration. Former vice president Al Gore has described the future we are swerving into as "a nature hike through the Book of Revelation," the apocalyptic final section of the Christian New Testament. We are already seeing many of these effects: sea levels are submerging Pacific Islands, wildfires rage in drought-stricken Southern California and Australia for months on end, and species of plant, insect, bird, and mammal are going extinct at one thousand times "normal" rates.[24] In Norway, the Svalbard Global Seed Vault facility colloquially known as the "doomsday vault," which contains almost a million packets of seeds from all over the world, was flooded when the permafrost that was supposed to protect them for eternity rapidly melted.[25] As a response to all the damage we have inflicted on the world, the world, it seems, is now trying to eject us from it.

According to James Lovelock, the English scientist who invented the "Gaia theory"—the idea that the Earth is one giant living organism—by 2040 Florida will be seafloor, much of Europe will be Saharan, and large parts of London will be underwater. By 2100, he suggests, 80 percent of the world's population will be wiped out. His advice in the meantime: enjoy life while you can.[26] A number of scientists have agreed with Lovelock, coming to the conclusion that we're too late to stop this disaster from unfolding. The philosopher Glenn Albrecht, an honorary fellow of the School of Geosciences at the University of Sydney, where I was based as I wrote this book, coined the term "solastalgia" to describe the sense of grief and existential dread caused by rapid environmental change. It's like nostalgia without geographic distance, mourning for a place we still call home.[27]

Many preppers believe—not unlike many of the geoscientists who work across the corridor from me—that we're already acting too late to avert widespread catastrophe and that because of the interconnectivity and interdependence created by globalization, incremental breakdown will eventually lead to chaos that could domino us back to the technological middle ages.

And then there are the not-so-incremental natural disaster wild cards that loom large in the mental landscape and everyday chatter of the prepping community: pandemics, volcanic eruptions, a rogue asteroid slamming into Earth, or even the possibility of artificial intelligence achieving escape velocity and outflanking us. None of these disasters is mutually exclusive. Of the five great extinctions in the history of the Earth (generally defined as the loss of more than 70 percent of species), though they had different triggers, all, eventually, were caused by climate change. For instance, the Chicxulub asteroid that slammed into Earth 65 million years ago near the Yucatan Peninsula in Mexico sent the heavy metal iridium into the atmosphere and essentially choked out Earth, killing the dinosaurs that had existed for 180 million years. Even further back, during the End-Permian mass extinction 252 million years ago, colloquially known as the "Great Dying," 97 percent of life on Earth was wiped out by the planet's warming five degrees Fahrenheit over roughly one hundred thousand years. The cause? Mega-volcanoes erupting in Siberia, which slowly poisoned the atmosphere.[28] The temperature of the planet is now rising at a much faster rate, having spiked 1.8°F (1°C) above preindustrial levels of only a few hundred years ago. A single catastrophe, like a large-scale volcanic eruption, could accelerate this situation exponentially.

One of the creatures that survived the Great Dying was the *Lystrosaurus*, a pig-sized mammal-like reptile that burrowed into the underground and possessed lungs capable of filtering oxygen out of contaminated air.[29] For humans now facing disaster who wish to similarly escape underground, the construction of such spaces can only be achieved with extensive resources. Yet what I found in my journeys is that there is a surplus of such places, mostly remainders of the Cold War, around which there now flourishes a vigorous private market, enriched by the public spending of the past.

At the same time, the state's role in subterranean expansion continues apace. In 2019, I attended a lecture in Singapore by Zhiye Zhao, the director of the Nanyang Centre for Underground Space. With a growing population, and limited land at its disposal, Singapore is being forced to find innovative ways to expand. Terraforming—building new land—is taking place, but rising sea levels may reclaim whatever is built. The other option is to dig. Zhao, who is working on a "subterranean masterplan" for the city-state, told the audience that his team thinks the future of Singapore lies in only one direction: down.

Singapore is now burying infrastructure, retail shops, pedestrian walkways, highways, storage, homes, and offices deep belowground. The underground city that Zhao imagines is one that will be planned, rational, calculable, and subject to constant surveillance: a new kind of underground space.[30] Just as the skyscraper might be considered the architectural form that defined the twentieth century, its foil, the geoscraper, a resilient structure built for density and control, might come to define the coming age of turmoil.

In contrast to Zhao's bracingly optimistic vision, I met many people who were unnerved by the speed of culture and technology, and who saw the underground instead as an effective space for severing connection and facilitating concealment. Some suggested to me that building a bunker was an act of civil disobedience in an age of mass surveillance. It can also be a place to hide from out-of-control innovation. Suspicion among preppers is leveled at experiments taking place in the Large Hadron Collider at CERN in Switzerland, which smashes together high-energy particle beams traveling at close to the speed of light; or CRISPR gene editing technology, which is making many wary about the potential for creating "designer babies" that taint our gene pool or render our own reproductive functions irrelevant. Perhaps because of our nuclear legacies, many preppers feel the scientists working at the new edges of research are unsympathetic to the consequences of their choices, or indeed that a single scientist might have the potential to become a rogue agent who decides, on behalf of all of us, to hit the "reset button" on their own. The underground is seen as a place to hide from the relentless march of science.

Many of the preppers I've met exhibit a clear sense of dread with respect to our collective trajectory as a species. Dread differs from fear: both because it is about the future rather than the present and also because it stems from a danger not immediately present or even discernible. In other words, fear has an object. Dread does not. Whereas we fear people, objects, events, and things, dread is an ontological orientation we find ourselves in that cannot be attached to something specific. And it is, I believe, the dominant affect of our era.

In "The Call of Cthulhu," H. P. Lovecraft's immensely influential 1920s tale about the subterranean terror that might be unleashed by human curiosity, the narrator considers: "The most merciful thing in the world, I think, is the inability of the human mind to correlate all its contents. We live on a placid island of ignorance in the midst of black seas of infinity, and it was not meant that we should voyage far. The sciences, each straining in its own direction, have hitherto harmed us little; but some day the piecing together of dissociated knowledge will open up such terrifying vistas of reality, and of our frightful position therein, that we shall either go mad from the revelation or flee from the deadly light into the peace and safety of a new dark age."[31]

This new dark age may be just over the horizon.[32] In order to support an unsustainable and voracious human population, we have constructed intricate systems that demand an increasing amount of energy, attention, and care. Failure to tend to them leads to disaster. We are left weary, staring into those "terrifying vistas" of "deadly light." All it takes is for one person among billions to hit the wrong switch, drop a vial, or neglect some routine maintenance, and suddenly disaster is at the door. It's not something we can control.

The problem of comprehending issues that seem to exceed our grasp is not a new one: humans have always been tortured by speculation.[33] As early as the seventeenth century, advances in medicine and science caused the English polymath Sir Thomas Browne to declare that "the world itself seems in the wane . . . since a greater part of Time is spun than is to come."[34] In 1704, Sir Isaac Newton used the Book of Daniel from the Old Testament to calculate 2060 as the date for the apocalypse. "It may end later, but I see no reason for its ending sooner," Newton optimistically wrote.[35] More recently, in one of his last interviews, the University of Cambridge theoretical physicist Stephen Hawking said that it was "almost inevitable that either a nuclear confrontation or environmental catastrophe will cripple the Earth at some point in the next 1,000 years."[36]

Grappling with what is unknowable through cognition may not be unique to humans, but our capacity to dread the unknowable almost certainly is. Whether the ability to know what we can't know is a blessing or a curse often seems to depend on whether we feel capable of responding to it. In order to do so, we must first try and render boundaries around the incomprehensible. That's why preppers do what they do, whether it be stockpiling food or building a bunker: action provides solace.

Most of the preppers I met would consider themselves realists, not doomsayers. Their dread stems from the knowledge that we are a Janus-faced species, constantly working for and against our own interests, but few are fatalistic. Often, I came away from my encounters with survivalists, scholars, bunker builders, and the devoutly religious with a sense of latent hope—hope of rebirth from disaster. All prepping is about hope for a better future, even if that hope casts a dark shadow.

It's in this context that prepping can be considered a "millenarian movement." According to John R. Hall, a sociologist of culture and religion at UC Davis, these movements always posit a "(typically traumatic) end of one era, promising relief from the sufferings of this world and its present age, and purporting to give rise to salvation in a new 'golden age,' 'heaven on earth,' or realized utopian social order."[37] But who is to say that this new order need necessarily be about preserving life as we know it?

It's in the interest of the dread merchants to raise the specter of Lovecraft's "black seas of infinity," so that people are more likely to buy the "life assurance solution" they offer. It's the same business model used to keep eyes glued to screens in the United States. It came as little surprise to me when I found that right-wing US media darlings—including Glenn Beck, Sean Hannity, and Alex Jones—all advocate doomsday prepping to their audience—and market products to meet those needs.[38] Networks like Fox News are bolstered by the fearmongering; the grimmer the news gets, the more people can't stop watching it. The narratives these networks spin effectively work to undermine public institutions until they falter, vindicating the "foresight" of doomsday shock jocks.

The televangelist Jim Bakker has built an empire selling "survival food" for the apocalypse. Bakker, who was once married to the Christian singer Tammy Faye Messner, came out of a prison stint for fraud and conspiracy dirt poor and obsessed with prepping for the rapture. He rebuilt some of his lost fortune selling five-gallon buckets of sodium-saturated dehydrated food on his TV show, a weekly outpouring of apocalyptic rhetoric.[39] In his provocative sermons full of pregnant pauses, Bakker touts the flexibility of these buckets, reimagining them as table supports, Bible storage, and "port-a-johns."

The place where the show itself is filmed, Morningside, is itself a budding apocalyptic commune tucked into the Ozark Mountains, where—I discovered—one can rent a reasonably priced cabin and run into other doomsdayers while shopping at the general store. The wares here are generally not as reasonably priced as the accommodations: six twenty-eight-ounce "Extreme Survival Water Bottles" that they claim can filter radiological and biological contamination sell for $150.

Rating-boosting hyperbole doesn't solely flow from conservative outlets. On both sides of the political spectrum, the media propagates constant dread-saturated assessments of uncontrolled migration, fraught foreign relations, economic instability, endless natural disasters, and security risks to a wide and receptive audience.[40] This isn't to say, however, that it is solely the media that is driving the desire to prep. Even the Department of Homeland Security advises citizens to store "at least a three-day supply of non-perishable food" in every household, continuing a process that began in the Cold War of putting the burden of disaster preparation on private citizens.

In step with this news cycle, and with such government encouragement, is a political elite that increasingly sees crisis as an opportunity to solidify its own wealth and power, rather than a challenge to be confronted. There's a certain amount of hubris involved in imagining that we're living on the edge of a great disaster, that this age in which we happen to be alive will be that significant. An even greater degree of hubris is required to see the possibility as an opportunity, to imagine that we will ride out that disaster into a new phase of history, profiting handsomely in the meantime. Yet, many in positions of power—including presidents, prime ministers, cabinet members, CEOs, oligarchs, and plutocrats—seem to be willing to take that bet.

One of the unhappy ironies of prepping is that it becomes a

self-fulfilling prophecy: the more bunkers that are built, the more convinced people become that the end is truly nigh. This, as we'll see, was the dangerous logic of the Cold War. The more secure government officials felt in their bunkers, the more likely they were to push the nuclear genocide button. With a plan in place to save themselves, they calculated casualties of everybody else as "megabodies": a totally inhumane term that denoted one million dead citizens.[41]

Aware of government's willingness to abandon them to such a calamity, and mindful that threats have multiplied exponentially since the Cold War, people now want their own bunkers, a desire that has generated this surreal real estate market. What the dread merchants sell is shelter from the cascade of existential horror we all seem to be waiting for.

The founder of philosophical pessimism, Arthur Schopenhauer, once described insurance as "a public sacrifice made on the altar of anxiety."[42] Today, preppers regard the construction of bunkers to ride out calamity as a spatial insurance policy, a hedge against the self-destructive tendencies of our species. For those who can afford it, a bunker might provide safe passage through the turmoil to come. Crisis offers an opportunity for hope, change, renewal—and profit.

Taken together, these ways of thinking and behaving comprise a disaster ideology unique to our age. It's an ideology that accepts the calamity—almost as necessity—but also seeks to convert it into a political will for rebirth, where we not only survive but re-emerge into a greatly enhanced personal and social milieu (or, as evangelical Christians—who make up a significant proportion of the prepping community—might put it, paradise). The underground is seen as a safe harbor, from which to rehearse perpetual reincarnations; the bunker is a chrysalis, not just for survival but for transformation.

In building these spaces there's an implicit assumption that we've given up on fixing the world we broke. You might imagine (as I did, often) that the time, resources, and sheer energy invested in building these underground redoubts, stocking them, and tweaking them for various "events," might be better spent trying to address and mitigate, together as a society, the catalysts for disaster. Although prepping is an extreme manifestation of dread, it is symptomatic of a wider sense that we have lost the ability to constrain or control those catalysts, we've lost agency. Preppers build to regain it. This, more than any reason, is why we should pay attention to private bunkers: they are a reflection of how deeply our dread has saturated us.

Just as the preppers I met imagined multiple forms of threat, so, too, their ways of combatting those threats were equally diverse. I found forms of corporate prepping, state prepping, religious prepping, lone-wolf prepping, "naturalist" prepping, technological prepping, and prepping fueled by class insecurities. All preppers, though, were driven by one common idea: an overwhelming dread about the future, and a desire to create secretive, defensive, and resilient spaces that are ultimately dread-resistant.

While writing this book, a decade after our explorations in Burlington, I found myself in Australia, benefiting from the reassurance of a stable political system, a generous research fellowship, good public health care, and a quiver of astonishing technology that assisted my research. I also found myself unable to stop thinking about social, environmental, and political breakdown. By the time I left Sydney, the country was in the midst of catastrophic wildfires. Tens of millions of acres had burned in every Australian state, along with thousands of people's homes. Dozens of people died and many more had to flee. A billion animals burned to death. In January 2020, the suburb of Penrith in Western Sydney reached 48.9°C (120°F), making it the hottest place on Earth. The burning only ceased when severe floods caused by heavy rains put the fires out. In other words, humanity once again served at the pleasure of Mother Nature.

When I landed back home in California, the plane descended into a haze of smoke emanating from wildfires surrounding Los Angeles, blurring the distance across the Pacific. I'd returned with my partner, Amanda, to care for my mother, who needed spinal surgery, en route to Ireland, where a faculty position at University College Dublin awaited. My mother was discharged from surgery just as the COVID-19 pandemic began to tendril into the United States. As we lifted her from the wheelchair to the car, tents were being erected in the parking garage of Torrance Memorial Medical Center for the expected patient overflow. The three of us ended up holed up in our own bunker of sorts in South Los Angeles for months, where I worked on the end of this book in lockdown. It was a tantalizing horror, feeling my words take on a different weight as I reread them in the midst of a global crisis caused by an invisible and alien power.

I fear this is only the beginning. As I wrote this book, I was drawn into a new awareness of disaster, one which calls for constantly assessing, moving, planning, and preparing. And, too, an unexpected hunger for the bunker. The only place I don't see shadows is underground, where I found those notebooks. I often think of the bunkers I have been in, of the silence and solace they offered me. I also think about how unlikely it is that I'd be able to get to them in time after the Fall. When disaster strikes, place matters.

1

The Dread Merchants: Selling Safe Space

> "The disaster takes care of everything."
> —Maurice Blanchot, *The Writing of the Disaster*, 1986[1]

I made my way from Salt Lake City to South Dakota in 2017 at the tail end of one the coldest winters in a decade. In Wyoming, a snowstorm shut down Interstate 80, forcing me onto backroads where I vied with 18 wheelers for space on the ice-crusted asphalt. I almost turned back more than once, but the snow eventually receded, and rime gave way to pasture. I made it to Edgemont, a sleepy town of just under eight hundred people, only half a day behind schedule.

I was finally within reach of what promised to be the largest community of doomsday preppers on Earth: the xPoint.

I drove on from Edgemont toward the abandoned United States Army Black Hills Ordnance Depot in Fall River County, a stone's throw from both Nebraska and Wyoming. Ahead, an expansive horizon slowly shifted into a warm gradient of light sliding under a flat seam of cloud. Squinting under the sun visor, I veered onto Fort Igloo Road, a remote track leading to the base. The pavement rapidly broke down as it cut in between crumbling brick chimneys, their long shadows stretching over the landscape. I crept between hillsides over a dilapidated railway bridge and past half-buried monster truck tires pinioned with "No Trespassing" signs flanking a small guard shack with rock-shattered windows.

I pulled off the road near a row of derelict houses and walked through a field of broken glass to squeeze past a door hanging off its hinges. Inside, mushrooms grew from rotting floorboards covered in a thick layer of shit. The roof was a sagging mess. There were racks of something slumped in the back of the room, but to investigate might have meant falling through the floor. Instead, I tightrope-walked across the structural support beams and peeked into the next room. It was more of the same. I wondered if I'd taken the wrong road, and made my way back to the car.

As the lane sloped into a valley, the span of the property came into breathtaking view. An expanse of eighteen square miles, or nearly three-quarters the size of Manhattan, was dotted with regularly spaced bunkers set out along an orderly road grid; it was easy to imagine a city blooming here. Robert Vicino, the California developer who was interested in Burlington, and the CEO of the Vivos Group, was behind the xPoint. He claimed there was space for ten thousand families. Yet as I scoped the site, no movement could be seen for miles. The emptiness relieved a tension that had accumulated in my shoulders on the drive up: after all, I was about to go off-grid with hundreds of heavily armed doomsday preppers for the better part of a week.

Construction had begun on the Black Hills Ordnance Depot in 1942. By the summer of that year there were six thousand people employed there, completely transforming the nearby towns of Edge-mont and Hot Springs.[2] The depot's original function was to store munitions for the war effort. Arms and ammunition were packed into 575 semisubterranean reinforced concrete bunkers that the military personnel stationed there and called "Igloos"—hence, Fort Igloo Road. The depot served its function during and after World War II, but by 1967 the base had begun a slow slide into dereliction. The site's remoteness and the architectural resilience of the abandoned bunkers are what made it a perfect site for the xPoint, the place, in Vicino's mind's eye, where our species would crawl out of the postapocalyptic ashes to start again.

I'd met with Robert Vicino at a Starbucks near his house in Del Mar, California, a few months earlier. The shopping center that included the coffee shop was the antithesis of a survival community: a row of clean eggshell-colored stucco buildings with outdoor vapor misters and a glossy asphalt parking lot. Yet as I pulled in for our meeting, I was greeted by two incinerated vehicle shells next to a bank cash machine. It's the kind of thing you see often in Southern California: traces of inexplicable violence intruding onto the movie set wealthy people live in. Vicino was staring at the scene from his Lexus sport utility vehicle (SUV). Catching sight of me, he waved me over and said, "Give me your camera, I'll take a photo of the future for you."

As we walked in from the car park, Vicino implored me to make the trip to South Dakota to see "the point from which humanity will arise after the great calamity." He was hosting the first annual xFest, a weeklong festival designed to pull doomsday preppers from all over the world together onto this sprawling treeless prai-rie, which he claimed was one of the safest places on Earth, being "high, dry, and far away from all known targets and metro areas." Vicino had chosen the site well. A map produced by the Federal Emergency Management Agency (FEMA), compiling data from all federally declared disasters between 1964 and 2003, made it clear that southwest South Dakota is one of the least disaster-prone places in the United States. Nestled among half a dozen federally protected wilderness areas that have checked population growth in the area, it's also not far from geothermal hot springs, Mount Rushmore, and the Old West tourist town of Deadwood: recreational opportunities before the fall of civilization.

This wasn't the only development by the Vivos Group. He explained that he was building underground shelters all over the world. He had a fully occupied bunker in Indiana and was negotiating deals for bunkers in Germany and Seoul, in addition to the Burlington Bunker in England.

At Starbucks, Vicino put on a big personality to match his six-foot-eight stature. He picked up other people's babies, joshed the teenager bagging bagels with tongs, and ogled every woman who passed by, rating them "a seven," "a two," "a nine." He bought me lunch, and as we settled into some chairs outside, he wasted no time in getting down to brass tacks.

"What do you know about Planet X, Brad? Nibiru?" Vicino said, leaning back with expansive authority.

"Can't say I've heard of it."

He slammed forward in his chair. "Wowee, you're a researcher and you don't know about Nibiru? Looks like you need to go back to school."

Planet X, Vicino told me, was discovered by the NASA Interface Region Imaging Spectrograph (IRIS) telescope in 1983. Nibiru, he continued, passed the Earth every thirty-six hundred years, and when it did it caused a pole shift—meaning that the magnetic poles of Earth would physically move, creating a three-thousand-mile-high tidal wave that would "reset" the planet.

He arched his eyebrows. "So. Noah's Flood. Obviously. That's why my bunkers can be submerged in two hundred feet of water."

Deluged in Vicino's apocalyptic sales patter, I hesitated. He used the opportunity to pick up my voice recorder and move it nearer to his chair. "You're not really recording this right, you need to get closer."

He took a deep breath and carried on. "People can sense the end coming, so the world is in social meltdown. Did you know a third of Swedish women have been raped by Muslims? It's a mess out there. . . . For all we know there's a comet coming our way and the government is ready but they're not going to protect us. You look at the dinosaurs, they got hit by a comet and what life survived that event? The life that went underground, Brad. The bunkers I'm building are an epic humanitarian project."

The conversation—or, rather, monologue—continued in this stream-of-consciousness vein for nearly three hours, during which time I had trouble figuring out what the story was there. It was hard to know what to ask Vicino that would clarify the parts of his narrative that seemed off-kilter.

One thing, though, was clear. In building bunkers, stocking them with food and supplies, and filling them with people, Vicino was acting on his beliefs. Evocatively portraying the bunkers at xPoint, the other, more polished, site in Indiana, as ships and arks, he made clear that escaping into the Earth would buy humanity the time we needed to start again. If we couldn't stall the collapse of the world, or leave it, burrowing into it might be the next-best thing.

"We can't build a celestial ark like Elon Musk," Vicino told me. "We can't leave Earth, so we're going to go into the Earth. I'm building a spaceship in the Earth. Whether or not people want to board that ship is a choice they're going to have to make."

I asked him about his selection process for xPoint, and whether economic considerations overrode everything else, if only those who could afford to survive should survive. Vicino's response was blunt. "Do you mean will the survivors survive because they were successful? Sure they will. Who do you think the government is putting in their bunkers? The homeless? The criminals? The bad apples? No, Brad, they're putting their most intelligent, successful, necessary, and reliable people in there. In the private sector, those people are wealthy."

Vicino was hardly alone in his attitude. It was, after all, one held by many Americans, one that had been forged in an age of wealth and excess, where hard work was rewarded. Now speculators like Vicino were using this narrative to justify their own profit-making activities. If the government could do it, he reasoned, so could he; as far as his bunkers were concerned, it was the survival of the richest.

Vicino himself was doing well from it. I managed to gather that the bunkers at xPoint were owned by a ranching company who bought them from the US government as part of a plan to graze cattle on the land. Vicino negotiated with the ranchers to be able to offer ninety-nine-year leases on the bunkers, profits from which he would share with them, without affecting their ability to use the land. Essentially, he was leasing the land and then subleasing it to preppers. I quickly calculated that even at the introductory price of $25,000, if he leased all the bunkers in xPoint, Vicino could rake in more than $14 million. Since bunker owners are meant, and indeed desire, to be self-sufficient, operating costs are low. The crucial factor in getting that self-sufficient community up and running, Vicino explained, wasn't technical or logistical; rather, it was about engineering the right kind of community.

"Tolerance is the key to survival, Brad. We have to fill the bunker with tolerant people. Anyone intolerant will not have a place in the community," he said, without a hint of irony.

In preparation for our meeting, I'd scrolled through the promotional material for xPoint on the Vivos website. Vicino suggested there that once you bought one of his bunkers, "built to withstand the forces and effects of virtually all threats," you could fill it with an "ample supply of food, water, fuel, medicines, clothing, air filtration, and security to ride out an event." Thus equipped, and surrounded by "a community of like-minded individuals," you could survive for weeks, months, and even years in the facility, until the time came to re-emerge.

The Vivos website provides a handy—and remarkably specific—timeline of what will be happening aboveground or outside the blast door in the "days following the event": on day three you can expect anarchy, and by day ten vigilante gangs; by day twenty-one people are resorting to cannibalism. Things have calmed down a bit by day 365, which is labeled the "Restart," when the lucky residents of xPoint emerge into the postapocalyptic world—or PAW, in doomsday prepper parlance.

The website looked pretty slick, but there was no guarantee of success at xPoint, and I knew Vicino had a couple of false starts under his belt. Back in 2010, he announced he was building a thirteen-thousand-square-foot bunker in the Mojave Desert, inside a Cold War–era hardened-concrete telephone routing station. It was meant to accommodate 132 people. The buy-in was $50,000 each. Vicino had signed up a number of potential residents, including two Californians—Steve Kramer, a fifty-five-year-old respiratory therapist from San Pedro, and Jason Hodge, a labor union organizer in Barstow.[3] Vicino told me he scrapped the project when the location was revealed by the *LA Times*, rendering it a potential target during the end times.

In 2013, Vicino then announced he was building a sixty-thousand-square-foot, five-thousand-person bunker in Atchison, Kansas, in an old salt quarry that he would fill with RVs around a public space that would include an indoor golf course and skateboard park. Some would-be residents signed up before Vicino canceled the plan because he said the bunker didn't feel safe, an idea that was laughed off by Jacque Pregont, president of Atchison's Chamber of Commerce, in an interview with CNBC, where she said that there are several businesses operating in other parts of the mines, all of which were "very safe," and that the Vivos project simply had difficulty attracting interest.[4]

At another proposed Vivos development in Seoul, called Vivos Asiana, Vicino intended to store the blood of every person in South Korea. In what seemed to me a strange mixture of get-up-and-go and complete fantasy that can be characteristic of a certain strand of prepping, he proposed that the project would be funded by Samsung and Asiana Airlines. The idea, as he explained it to me, would be to "collect three drops of blood from every person in the country, which we can store in the bunker. What we will have then is essentially the entire genome of all of South Korea. People who can't afford space in the bunker will be able to be reincarnated through cloning later." I suppose those corporations might see holding that data as a fine investment opportunity, though in the context of the Chinese surveillance state collecting biometric data, including DNA and blood, from the minority Muslim Uyghur population, to track and control them, it takes on a more ominous tone. I couldn't imagine South Koreans consenting to this en masse.

Vicino's bunker in Germany—Vivos Europa One—was on hold while they scoped out a new business model, after failing to attract much interest from individual preppers. "We're looking at a corporate model, renting it out to BMW or Mercedes so they can shelter the entire executive staff in there," Vicino said. "We got some bad press out there with people saying the fire marshal wasn't going to let us build it, but we're just talking about installing some sprinklers—this is nothing on a one-hundred-million-dollar project."

Like the blood vials he was going to store in Vivos Asiana, this seemed less than likely. Not that the media seemed to care; they kept running stories as long as Vicino-supplied pithy acerbic quotes and convincing photographlike CGI renderings of the facility.

Following my chat with Vicino, I was sitting in the Starbucks parking lot scrolling through the Vivos website, trying to separate the present from the projected, when I remembered that my brother Pip, a contractor, was in the middle of building a walk-in closet that doubled as a panic room for a client about an hour from Del Mar. When I called him to chat about it, Pip wasn't at all surprised by the popularity of the xPoint bunkers and told me that his clients were increasingly asking for "hardened" elements in the homes he was building. He was drawing up plans for air filtration systems or secret compartments in the same way that he installed fireplaces and granite countertops. Some clients even wanted rooms that could shield possessions from an electromagnetic pulse, or EMP—a burst of gamma rays from a solar flare or nuclear explosion that could disrupt or destroy electronic equipment. Pip invited me to come and see the panic room he was working on and meet the owner, a guy called Rogan.

The house was in a dusty future suburb being scraped out among the granite boulders and baking desert sagebrush of San Diego County. The panic room, square in the middle of the house, measured twenty-six by sixteen feet and was ringed by fire-resistant cinder blocks filled with poured concrete. Entry to the room was through a one-foot-thick fireproof door with two locks: one with an electronic keypad and one with a mechanical tumbler in case an EMP fried the keypad. The room also had a safe in the floor, fire sprinklers, a buried landline, closed-circuit television (CCTV) that streamed from every room in the house, and—most important—a dedicated ventilation system.

Rogan, a muscular guy with a straight-billed baseball cap and a soul patch, who'd hired Pip to build the house, told me that "the entire thing could burn down, but this room, with everything we need to get back on our feet, would stand. The rest is for the insurance company to deal with." I asked Rogan how long he might stay in the room during an emergency. He assured me that weathering a low-level event like a blackout for three days in the panic room was feasible, but after that "who the fuck knows, dude, people will eat their babies. People are nuts." A common saying among preppers, "seventy-two hours to animal," suggests that even the most mild-mannered of people might turn wild within days.

My encounter with Rogan seemed as good an illustration as any of the prevailing social climate in the United States. A survey conducted by National Geographic in 2012 found that 62 percent of Americans thought the world would experience a major catastrophe in less than twenty years; 40 percent believed that stocking up on supplies or building a bomb shelter was a wiser investment than saving for retirement.[5] A 2015 article in an academic special issue about future catastrophic threats to humanity surveyed people from the USA, the UK, Canada, and Australia and found that 54 percent of them rated the risk of our way of life ending within the next one hundred years at 50 percent or greater. A quarter of respondents believed humanity had a 50 percent chance of being wiped out altogether during that time.[6]

Rogan didn't expect to ride out the end of the world in his panic room; he just wanted to buy himself a few hours or days. Because the house was on a relatively isolated lot, the three things he worried about were home invasion, robbery, and wildfire, all of which, ensconced in his panic room, he could wait out.

"When you're building a house worth millions," he told me, "what's another twenty-five or thirty grand to make sure the closet space you're already going to have is multifunctional?"

By the year 2000, a third of all new homes in the United States were being built in gated communities: a kind of social contract–failure architecture in which every community must fend for itself.[7] In these private communities, private roads connect hardened houses patrolled by private security services. In the years since 9/11, as media narratives have become increasingly frightening regarding threats both foreign and domestic, Americans' desire to hunker down has only become more prevalent. I imagined satellite images from America's future showing fragmented archipelagos of fortified semisubterranean residences, where open expanses were traversed by armored SUVs. I imagined South Africa on steroids, *Blade Runner* without cities, a permanent state of civil war running on the fumes of empire. xPoint, as I first saw it in the glare of that low winter sun, seemed to exceed these imaginings. It was a monstrous escalation of disaster architecture.

As I pulled up to the central meeting point for xFest, where I was supposed to link up with Vicino again, a banner flapped in a crisp plains breeze over a derelict loading dock. Rows of sterile, spotless port-o-potties stood lined up like sentries across from a food truck staffed by two bored workers. I asked them where everybody was, and they said they didn't know. Driving around the site, the only people I encountered were three film crews (one from Japan), and members of the xFest "security detail"—a bunch of local teenagers drunk-driving hoopties up and down the dirt roads. I parked in front of the banner, fuming. I'd come here, at great expense, to see the largest gathering of preppers in the world and had the distinct sense I would, instead, be spending days photographing empty concrete Igloos. As a grazing cow rubbed itself gratefully against a port-o-potty, I recalled Vicino's boast that he was building subterranean time ships and welled up with disappointment.

Determined to find something happening, I followed a car with a "Vivos Security" magnet stuck to the door, to an abandoned house where a few people were squatting for the duration of xFest. Outside, leaning on a post and nursing a bottle of Crown Royal whiskey, was Wyatt, a bushy-blond-bearded twenty-eight-year-old in tasseled rawhide leather chaps. In a distinct regional drawl, Wyatt told me he didn't know what the plan for xFest was, or if there was a plan.

Out of nowhere a mud-splattered red pickup roared up. In the passenger seat was Vicino himself, his son Dante at the wheel. Vicino curtly advised me that there was "nothing here" and told me to follow him, speeding off in a filthy haze at fifty-five miles an hour up the blown-out road I'd come in on. After driving for days through snow to attend this overhyped event, I followed behind the red pickup with a sinking feeling.

We drove back into Edgemont, to the Hat Creek Bar and Grill. The entire security detail had also followed us, in a caravan of three or four cars, looking to get a free dinner out of Vicino. Local patrons eyed us up. Tables were quickly pushed together; the owner scrambled from behind the bar to welcome the twelve men who commandeered them. The teenage waitress was the owner's daughter, and Vicino immediately fixated on her, telling her, as she spread menus over the tables, that when he incorporated Edgemont into xPoint in a few years she could be a "permanent fixture." He then whispered to a gray-goateed man next to him, "Is it wrong to say I want to chain her up in my bunker?"

"Robert, shut the fuck up," the guy said with a smile. Shaking his head, he introduced himself as Jerry, an old friend of Vicino.

"He's got a big mouth but he's totally harmless, don't worry," Jerry said. He asked me what I was doing there. I mumbled that I was working on a book, not wanting the whole table to overhear. Many people who prep place a premium on secrecy and might, I thought, take offense at having a writer in their midst.

"Well now, that's something," he said, smiling. "It'll be nice to talk to someone who has half a brain out here." Jerry, as it turned out, had a good working knowledge of Hegel's dialectic philosophy, which we happily butchered over dinner. As we did so, I had a chance to quiz him about what it was that brought people to xPoint; what they were preparing for. He explained that I'd get as many answers to that question as there were people at the table. People were worried about civil war, contagion, inflation, martial law, asteroid strikes, climate change, crop failures, artificial intelligence, and a host of other issues.

"More than anything, people are worried about the unknown," Jerry told me. "There seems to just be a lot of crazy stuff going on in the world that people have no control over. Making the decision to be here is something they can control, would be my guess."

"I'm no hard-core prepper," Jerry continued, "but I've known Robert for twenty-two years, we go way back, so we've talked about these things." Jerry owned a graphic design business, and Vicino had come to him to get some work done for a previous business he had making inflatable objects. (Vicino's previous claim to fame came from mounting a giant inflatable King Kong onto the Empire State Building as a marketing gimmick for the film's fiftieth anniversary.)

Jerry seemed dubious about whether xPoint would be a financial success, but like me, he saw the gathering as a sociological curiosity and had come along for the ride. He did admit, when I pressed him, that Vicino's anxiety had rubbed off on him a bit over the years, and that he was involved in some low-level prepping.

When I asked him if survival was a natural instinct, Jerry got confessional. "You know, man, a couple of years back I had a heart attack," he said. "I was forty-seven years old. I've always been super healthy; I've never had a broken bone. I wasn't a candidate for this. I asked the cardiologist what the hell happened, and he said one word: 'stress.'" Jerry had lots of bills, a mortgage, and lots of "big boy toys": RVs, boats, and motorcycles. Expensive holidays, meant to alleviate the stress, just added to it.

"I just ran myself into the ground," he said. "After that I got really depressed, I mean down in the dumps, drinking every morning and waking up worried that every day was the day my heart was going to give out and I was going to die."

Jerry paused as the young waitress delivered a plate of tacos with a smile of thanks, causing him to chuckle in response.

"I've got another friend that thinks if there's a disaster there's no point in being alive," he said, turning back to me. "Let me tell you, after what I went through, it's not in our DNA to die. Your survival instinct will kick in and you're going to find a way to live."

"Do you think xPoint is a good model for survival?" I asked Jerry.

"Well," he said, spooning some salsa onto his tacos, "if I'm sitting here and that guy over there, without knowing it"—he pointed vaguely with the spoon—"is having the same survival thoughts, it multiplies exponentially. That's how you get these three or four dozen people here. None of us joined a club, man, no one forced us to be here. Robert put his thoughts out there, and everybody came together. That's the idea and I think it's a great idea."

We careened home past midnight, sometimes taking the old ordnance depot roads, sometimes weaving our own. Vicino directed me to the "B-Block," where some preppers—prospective tenants of xPoint here for xFest—were camped out. On the way there, I drove past a boxy pickup truck perched on a hill. The dome light was on inside the truck. Against the all-consuming dark, it illuminated a brief tableau: a gun on the dash and a lanky man in camouflage in the passenger seat, drinking from a tall can.

B-Block was also dark when I drove down it. There were no running lights, water, or any infrastructure to speak of, let alone amenities, just rows of empty concrete shells. I popped my tent inside an empty bunker—number B-207—and closed the blast door with an unsettling sucking thud. Once I was inside, with my lights turned off, every sound I made, even just shifting on my sleeping mat to get comfortable, echoed back at me in eerie receding waves of reverberation that bounced off the bare walls.

As I lay in my tent, eyes open but seeing nothing, my mind replayed the rambling conversation with Jerry earlier that evening that had taken in philosophy and the dread of the unknown. It then flicked onto the gloomy figure of Søren Kierkegaard, the Danish progenitor of existentialism, a school of thought with an emphasis on individuality, freedom, and choice. The phrase that looped in my head was his description of dread, or angst: a "sweet feeling of apprehension" about the future, an anticipation of "freedom's reality as possibility for possibility."[8] This, it struck me, resonated with the preppers' tantalizing apprehensions about the unknown.

As Kierkegaard suggests, something about dread is strangely alluring. His words again: dread doesn't "tempt as a definite choice, but alarms and fascinates with its sweet anxiety. Thus, dread is the dizziness of freedom which occurs when . . . freedom then gazes down into its own possibility, grasping at finiteness to sustain itself." Dread stems from the knowledge of the cost of our choices, but also from the freedom to be able to choose. Hence that repeated, uncanny adjective: "sweet."

Contemporary life, it occurred to me in my mausoleum-like bunker, was dominated by a feeling of being overwhelmed by a multitude of choices, all of which seem inconsequential on a personal level and collectively irresponsible. This—if you believe Kierkegaard—only works to increase our dread. As a Christian,

Kierkegaard suggested that "it is only at the instant when salvation is actually posited that this dread is overcome." My last thought as I drifted off, dimly aware of my breathing reverberating off the bunker's naked concrete shell, was that maybe, for the preppers who made their pilgrimage to xPoint, buying the bunker was the moment when salvation seemed tangible.

Steeped in the most thorough darkness I'd ever experienced, I slept well. Very well.

I awoke to a piercing birdcall coming through the bunker's ventilation shaft, where larks had nested. Their call was the only hint that the sun was up: inside, it was still pitch black. Opening the blast door with a full body shove, I was reborn into searing morning light. Walking up the dirt road, shivering, past clumps of cows staring at me, I ran into Tom Soulsby, Milton Torres, and Mark Bowman, three preppers who'd camped in another B-Block bunker. They were lying on the ground in mud-caked shoes, trying to get a flat tire off of a truck axle with a rubber mallet. A glance at their well-stocked trailer made it clear that they were no weekend warriors. This was a committed crew.

Tom had the air of a hunter. Bald, bespectacled, and dressed in a camouflage jacket and well-worn hiking boots, he greeted me with a firm two-handed clasp. As I pulled out my notebook, he explained that he'd bought land in Kansas that was strategically located but not well fortified, and that he was looking to upgrade to a bunker. Milton, a burly, twitchy information technology (IT) manager for the Department of Veterans Affairs (VA), in Chicago, told me, in between tokes of THC from a vape pen, that he'd become a prepper because "people forced me to think I was crazy," and he was going to show them he was right. Mark found this hysterically funny: he'd had his fair share of similar comments. He was a towering, jovial man in his fifties, with a diamond earring and a prosperous belly tucked into a many-pocketed vest stuffed full of pencils, measuring tapes, and spirit levels. The crew warmly invited me into their shared space.

The contrast between my lonely tent in the empty concrete shell and the home they'd put together from material unloaded from Mark's hand-built trailer was stark. The accommodation included camping chairs, tents, personal protective equipment (PPE), multiple stoves, large plastic buckets of dried food, and two different battery banks. One was for solar, the other for a wind turbine Mark was going to "mount on top of the bunker." He'd even rolled out a carpet in the makeshift living room, which worked to separate it from the back, since the bunker was a single cavernous, open space—virtually identical to the one I'd slept in and 573 others. These three had been the first preppers at xPoint to take a bunker for a test run.

Mark affirmed emphatically that he was going to sign a contract with Vicino and lay down the $25,000 required to buy into xPoint. For this, he would receive an empty concrete shell that he'd build out himself. An expert machinist from northern Minnesota, he assured me that his skills weren't limited to metalwork. He proceeded to show me a "washing machine" that he'd made from a five-gallon bucket and a toilet plunger. Sensing that I wasn't much of a craftsman myself, he ripped a page out of a mail-order catalogue and handed it to me dismissively, saying, "You don't have to build all this stuff, you can just have it delivered."

While we drank coffee boiled on a propane camp stove and sweetened with freeze-dried honey (the tin confidently advertising its twenty-five-year shelf life), I told them I thought it was interesting that they all camped in the bunker together, rather than each claiming one. I wondered aloud if they wanted to build a community. Milton jumped up energetically, using his vape as a pointer. "We've already got one! We've got Mark, Mr. 'I'll build a toilet out of a two-by-four and a tube' over there, which is neat. I do IT, so I can keep us connected after things go downhill, and I'm into sports. You're going to need to play, too, while you're waiting stuff out."

Tom laughed, "Yeah, it's already 'home sweet bunker' around here."

Having been abandoned for more than fifty years, many of the bunkers had been left open at some point. They were cool places for the cows to hang out on hot days, and the ungulates were the ones running the place. The bunker the guys were staying in had had to have a foot of poop shoveled out of it just a few weeks prior. The man doing the shoveling was Ojay, an Edgemont local with a pointy red beard, a missing front tooth, and a consolatory phrase that he repeated like a mantra: "It's all good, man; it has to be; it's the only way it can be," which seemed strangely to equip him for casual work on a doomsday commune. I mentioned to the guys that I'd be interested in seeing what the bunkers looked like before they were cleaned up for sale, and it was agreed we should go and find one.

As an aproned Mark got breakfast started, Tom, Milton, and I ventured out of B-Block past a herd of white-masked cows with grass hanging out of their motionless mouths. They looked lost in thought. Dew on the tall grass soaked our jeans as we walked. Underneath the pasture, the bunker field was a wet, sticky clay that formed a corona around our boot soles, and had to be continually scraped off on the sharp edges of blast doors.

It took a good fifteen minutes to reach the next row in B-Block. Exploring the whole place by foot seemed beyond hopeless—the site was massive. Blocks A–F each consisted of ninety-some bunkers laid out in rows of eight. Nonetheless, we scrambled over a rubble pile into a bunker whose interior was decorated in one corner with pencil drawings of naked women, signed and dated by a soldier stationed there in 1942. The discovery felt archaeological. Externally, each bunker was a clone stamp of the last, offering no hint as to its contents. Milton mused that you could hide anything out here in a random bunker: food, gold bars, a body.

"Just don't put a lock on it," Tom mused. "Because if I'm a thief, I'm looking for a bunker with a lock on it and I'm going to get it open."

"Shiiiiit," Milton responded, "that's sneaky, Tom!"

Tom and his wife, Mary (whom I'd not met, but who'd initiated the family search for a bolthole), were semiretired, but I got the sense that they enjoyed keeping themselves busy with travel and projects. I asked if his move into the bunker field was an attempt to escape society.

"Oh, no, no, that's not it, Brad," he explained. "This is just an insurance policy. I'm going to fix it up and pass it down to my family. I hope no one ever has to use it. The way I see it, being prepared puts me in a better position to help others. It's like when you fly, and they tell you to put the oxygen mask on yourself first. If you're dead you're not helping anyone."

He made one exception to helping others, however: a pandemic. "If there's a pandemic, nobody can come in, period," he said. If a pandemic were to break out, Tom said he'd hightail it to the bunker with Mary and "pray there's not somebody already there who's infected." It would be a race against an unseen enemy.

"Some of the pandemic scenarios have wiped out 100 million people on a planet that's not nearly as populated or as mobile as what we have today," he said lamentingly. "Now, you could have something spread across the planet in a week."

Nevertheless, Tom seemed to think most disasters would actually bring out the best in people at a time when many of us have come to see our fellow citizens as suspect; that, strangely enough, disasters might be a way of enabling us to recover a lost social solidarity—among survivors, that is. This view, which I'd often hear repeated among preppers, was at odds with media depictions that promised your neighbor would just be another body in the horde coming to take your "preps" when they realized their bank cards were about as much use as drink coasters. The idea was that the dread we now feel would be punctuated by the disaster, bringing with it clarity of choice and meaning.

Footage of Hurricane Katrina, for instance, which ripped through New Orleans in 2005, drastically misrepresented the scale of chaos, looting, and ill will. Though the Category 5 storm killed twelve hundred people, those people didn't kill each other. In fact, the post-storm evidence collected indicated that the only murders that took place were perpetrated by police officers.[9] In her book *A Paradise Built in Hell*, the California-based author Rebecca Solnit found that when disaster strikes, it often brings about the best in people as they "fall together." Communities arise in the wake of disaster, even in places where there doesn't seem to be a strong sense of community before the event; catastrophe becomes an opportunity to exhibit camaraderie, what Solnit calls "disaster solidarity."[10] Records from recent disasters back this up: immediately following 2012's Hurricane Sandy, New York City saw a record eight-day run without a single homicide.[11]

Tom had a similar instinct, and was keen to tell me about examples of that instinct in others. He recounted a story about a seventy-four-year-old New Jersey prepper named Joseph Badame, who had spent decades preparing for an apocalyptic event and had fifteen thousand pounds of emergency food on hand. In the aftermath of Hurricane Maria, the Category 5 hurricane that wracked Puerto Rico in 2017, Badame shipped his entire stockpile to the island and fed a thousand people. Pictures of him happily doing so could be found in newspapers all over the world.

Tom said, "Sure, Badame wasn't in the midst of the emergency. He probably would have taken care of himself first in such a situation—but we can help each other out like that here."

"Yeah," Milton chipped in, "because FEMA ain't gonna save you, dude, people that think that are drinking the Kool-Aid." Mark later told me that many preppers say FEMA stands for "Foolishly Expecting Meaningful Aid." Both Mark and Milton demonstrated an unabashed skepticism toward what they saw as sclerotic government infrastructure and politicians who seemed to be either inept or corrupt. In contrast to the distant interests of elites that left them feeling listless and abandoned, the practical preparation they could undertake at xPoint, with no government in sight, gave them a clear sense of purpose.

Back at the base bunker, on the only block in the entire facility that had been cleaned up for xFest, a succession of film crews lined up to interview Mark while he used his five-gallon bucket washing machine. In the midst of that odd phenomenon, one of Vicino's workers arrived with maps, breaking the monotony. He was also clutching historical photographs, and diagrams of the facility. I viewed the images of bunkers filled with rows of bombs and reminded myself that the bunkers were originally built to protect weapons, not people. But if the weapons had never existed, bunkers wouldn't be needed to protect people—from the threat of weapons, at least.

Tom and Milton were debating the relative importance of access to well water in B-Block versus getting a spot on high ground in F-Block—so as to, as Vicino's worker put it, "keep control of ingress and egress." The worker also pointed out a building close to the entrance on the map and told us not to go in there because it used to be for mustard gas storage. This was the building I'd wandered through on the road in, with the slumped racks in it, and I felt my abdomen clench.

Suppressing my vague sense of unease, I joined an exploratory crew to go and survey F-Block, the bunkers with the best vantage point. Getting there would be challenging. F-Block was a good five miles away, and most of the roads had long disintegrated into the mud and tall grass. We formed a three-car caravan. On the way, we passed the boxy truck with the gun on the dash that I'd seen the previous evening. Its camouflaged occupant was in the exact same place, can in hand, scanning the skyline.

Halfway to F-Block we encountered Pat and Sue, a wizened retired couple—he slender and quiet, she stout and effusive—driving an ancient station wagon coated in prairie dust. Sue told us she knew the area and that we needed to be careful driving off-piste because there were small cacti that would needle through the sidewalls of our tires: this was what had happened to the truck with the flat the guys were hammering on earlier. She also directed our attention to moss on the ground, unusual for prairie: a sign that water wasn't draining properly. Squatting down, Sue pulled at it with her nails and told us that you had to dig a mile into the Earth to hit groundwater, at which point it spurted out in a scalding stream.

"Every foot deeper you go, the water gets one degree hotter, so I don't know how in hell they're going to build water infrastructure," she called up to us from her squatting position. I asked Sue if she was looking to buy a bunker.

"I'm just trying to find someone here who knows what the hell they're talking about," she said, shielding her eyes from the sun with a wrinkled hand.

Later, during a rambling sales pitch that Vicino made mostly to film crews in the empty bunker where I'd slept—one of the only clean ones—Sue threw up her arms in exasperation and walked out. I watched her speed off in the dusty station wagon, Pat radiating contented indifference from the passenger seat. Peering back in through the blast door, I felt uneasy. Like most people on camera,

Vicino appeared a caricature of himself. With shutters snapping, he was talking about how North Korea was going to wipe the West Coast off the map. The only thing missing from the meeting were buyers.

Not for the first time since arriving, I wondered if xPoint was a twisted vision. Or maybe I'd become enmeshed in some kind of *Truman Show* scenario, in which I was actually the quarry. People at home were sitting on their couches, popcorn bowls on their laps, watching me wander through this South Dakotan Potemkin village trying to figure out whether, and how, I was going to make sense of it. Vicino's sales pitch did little to dispel my sense of unease.

That night we gathered for a party under the xFest banner and a night sky unpolluted by city lights, speckled with a dizzying array of celestial bodies. The scruffy security detail had piled up under the banner a small mountain of pallets, broken chairs, and particleboard full of plastic resin glue, which they doused with gasoline and set alight, vanquishing the stars. Black smoked curled off the pyre.

Vicino was manspreading in a wrinkled camping chair, swigging a pale ale and shouting to everyone who walked by—"everyone" being Tom, Milton, a cameraman from Switzerland, and the security detail. The couple with the food truck was long gone. Altogether, there were twelve of us there—the sum total of xFest.

Vicino had been occupied all day with organizing the sales pitch, and finally asked how my night had been in the bunker. I told him, truthfully, that I'd slept extremely well, but that I wasn't sure I could handle more than a few weeks inside. I asked him what he would do in the bunker if he was locked in there for a year.

"Well, you could do anything, you could learn how to meditate, you could learn how to levitate, you could learn how to walk through walls," he said offhandedly. "When you get rid of all the distractions and crap around us keeping us from doing these things, who knows what you can accomplish?"

We all soon moved over to huddle into a tight ring around the fire, and I listened into a flood of opinions on everything from the secret reign of Illuminati lizard people to flat Earth theory. I threw in one of my favorite ideas, proposed by Swedish philosopher Nick

Bostrom, that it's entirely logical to believe we live in a computer simulation, *Matrix*-style. In Bostrom's view, technological advances will inevitably end up creating a computer with more processing power than all human cognition combined; humans, meanwhile, run "ancestor simulations" of their evolutionary history by creating virtual worlds inhabited by virtual people with fully developed virtual nervous systems.[12] If we were actually in one of those simulations, Bostrom argues, we wouldn't know, because we could never out-compute the simulation.

Later in the evening, the man from the boxy truck chimed in. Captain, as he introduced himself, was a precisely spoken Iraq and Afghanistan veteran, and a serial consumer of energy drinks: he cradled a very large can as he spoke. Captain had no interest in a bunker. He'd made his way to xFest to offer an unsolicited contribution, which had been to sit in his truck for two days on the ridge, "keeping an eye on things." Asked by another member of the group whether there were wars in space that we didn't know about— Captain was, after all, a military man—he nodded.

"Yeah, I say there are. Think about the Cold War," he said, words now tumbling out of him, "about how the government spent hundreds of millions of taxpayer dollars building deep underground military bases. Remember how they denied they existed—and then suddenly all this shit is declassified, and it turns out all the 'conspiracy theories' were true. That's all the proof you need that what's known is a tiny fraction of what's happening. We can't know the unknown unknowns, but coming to know the known unknowns is why we're all here."

"Hell yeah," Milton responded, leaning back in his camping chair. "When people at work find out I'm prepping, they tell me I'm crazy, and I think *they're* crazy, because they only live in the present. You look at history and what do you see? People getting caught by surprise over and over again because they don't think through these things." With this, Milton tapped his temple with his index finger.

Listening to them talk, I heard a curious mixture of conspiracy theory and good sense. It was clear the preppers were determined to reason through these scenarios rather than simply accept them— just as I'd treated the unprovable simulation argument earnestly.

They were energized by thinking they might pull back the curtain on something.[13] Standing around this bonfire were just a bunch of uncertain people who, in this age of constant crisis, refused to sit with their uncertainty. They demanded explanations for the inexplicable—and were happy to debate their theories. Not unlike academics, perhaps.

While Vicino's xFest seemed a bit of a belly flop, those present didn't seem to mind. Besides, camping around a bonfire in a military ruin, hours from a major population center, was just my speed, bringing to mind the countless hours I'd spent breaking into abandoned buildings and subterranean infrastructure as an urban explorer. As I gazed unfocused into the wood glue smoke, I felt a sense of common ground with my companions around the bonfire. I might reach for Michel Foucault, and they for InfoWars, but we understood each other: we were all getting screwed by technology, corporations, and the government.

The party lasted into the early morning. When we ran out of things to burn, Rex Bear, a minor YouTube celebrity among the preppers, set up a giant telescope to track moons around Jupiter. Then a woman arrived from nowhere. Swathed in a cape and carrying a small kerosene lantern, she started to grill Bear about Planet X, the celestial body Vicino had mentioned. At her side was a guy, shirtless and covered in soot, and a near-naked child, who was stirring melted glass in the embers with a piece of rebar. Vicino started yelling at the shirtless guy, I gathered, for starting a cooking fire inside one of the bunkers. I realized I was drunk, and had no idea where these new people had come from.

I got the sense that these preppers were operating on a variation of Pascal's wager: the precept that even if the existence of a higher power is unlikely, the potential upsides of believing in one are so vast that we might as well. If these preppers were right about some, or just one, of their theories, then they just might survive a cataclysm—it's a payoff for faith that costs little in the present.

As the group scattered, I took the long, drunken walk back to my bunker under the stars and thought about the different scales of prepping. Preparing for every unknown eventuality was an impossibility, the road to craziness. What I didn't understand was the total disjunction between the actual terrible things happening at any one time and the preparation for events that by any measurement were total outliers. Why, for instance, was North Korea testing long-range missiles not enough reason in and of itself to build a bunker? Why did we need space wars?

But why not prepare for it all? As Milton said, you look at history and what do you see? People endlessly being caught on the hop. The fourteenth-century Black Death that may have wiped out half of Europe's population; the 1815 eruption of the Tambora volcano that killed 100,000 people in Indonesia; the 1931 Yangtze, Yellow, and Huai River floods in China that killed 225,000 people, and millions more indirectly from crop, grain storage, and road destruction. Anyone prophesying these events would have sounded like a crank, but they happened, and they changed the world.

Nassim Nicholas Taleb, a professor of risk engineering at New York University (NYU), calls these Black Swan events. In his book *The Black Swan: The Impact of the Highly Improbable*, Taleb writes that they're outliers, that they have an extreme impact, and that people tend to explain them away after the fact, which deludes us into thinking they could have been predicted.[14]

With the majority of the world's population now clustered in cities that cannot sustain themselves, the likelihood of a Black Swan event increases. This view, that the world is becoming more fragile because of its increasing complexity, has strong roots in contemporary thought. Nobody expressed it better than the late Paul Virilio, a grouchy French Marxist who was obsessed with bunkers, war, and speed. Recalling the 1979 Three Mile Island nuclear disaster, Virilio wrote that it's realistic to think that "there is an accident brewing that would occur everywhere at the same time."[15] As space and distance are compressed by speed and connectivity, Virilio thought, they also become more vulnerable. Virilio's work begs consideration of the impacts that would be felt from a cessation of global trade networks due to, say, a volcanic eruption on the scale of Tambora. Even a two-month blip could wipe out millions of people dependent on international imports for survival.

Both Taleb and Virilio suggest that what we dread today—more than at any time in history—is the unknown; and they argue that the possibilities of the unknown are multiplying through our own actions. In other words, progress and disaster go hand in hand.[16]

In nineteenth-century America, those who warned of impending disaster were called calamity howlers, and they were often lambasted for their predictions.[17] People today tend to treat preppers in the same way, questioning their credulity, even though their views are often backed up by research and despite instances where their anxieties have become realities. Prepping often looks prudent in hindsight.

Whether we think of them as concrete Igloos or more metaphorically as a gated community, bunkers are not spaces built to increase systemic resilience. Rather, they are an architecture that concedes we humans have lost control of our trajectory. Those selling bunkers aren't investing in some kind of greater societal fix; basically their profits hinge on growing disquiet about what confronts us. Equally, most preppers buying bunkers have given up trying to mitigate the apocalypse; instead, they're seeking shelter from it, withdrawing into their underground boltholes in order to be reborn. As Vicino told me back in Del Mar: "No one wants to go into the bunker, they want to come out of the bunker."

Despite the weak turnout at xFest, and a serious argument with Vicino over the merits of developing F-Block rather than B-Block, Mark was seduced by Vicino's vision. He signed a ninety-nine-year lease on a bunker there and then; so, too, did the optimistic Tom. Milton went further. Not only did he buy a bunker, he quit his lucrative job at the Chicago Department of Veterans Affairs and moved into it full-time. Unlike Tom, who'd bought his bunker as insurance against the future, for Milton, the bunker became his present. He went on to appear in numerous documentaries. In this footage he could be seen doing martial arts in the snow outside his blast door, bobbing around in a virtual reality system he played while stoned, and reflecting on how his bunker offered him space for contemplation. So, while xFest failed to fulfill Vicino's grandiose vision of attracting preppers from all over the world, a community *was* formed. These pioneers were the first people to move into what would become, a few years later, a decent-sized, if not very bustling, doomsday commune.

On my last night of solitary confinement in bunker B-207, I had trouble falling asleep. Initially, it had felt good to be locked away somewhere where my phone didn't work, where I was safe, and where I could experience true solitude. After a decade of living in major cities surrounded by noise, lights, and people, the lack of stimuli felt luxurious. As I lay there on that final night, however, a sense of dread, the very concept I had been pondering, crept in.

My mind spiraled into an apocalyptic meditation. A cinematic drone shot of a flurry of human activity on a city street: packed buses bumper to bumper, gridlocked cars, horns blaring, cyclists weaving in between and hanging on like feeder fish, hawkers shouting to pedestrians who dodged each other as they talked and tapped on phones. My mind's eye ascended further, panning out to reveal the endless stream of products and materials that arrived to feed the gaping maw of the megalopolis: soot-belching trucks filled with under-ripe exotic fruit coming from a nearby seaport; planes stuck in holding patterns waiting for space on packed runways; lines of extraction stretching from some Saudi oil field, or Canadian tar sand, or Congolese mine to fuel it all.

I saw overflowing garbage cans tipped into trucks decanted into other trucks, all joining an endless queue to discard waste, the everyday disposable detritus of human existence, into a pit the size of a small city. All this activity, multiplied to infinity across the globe, interconnected by a ceaseless web of planes collecting and disgorging their human cargo like streams of ants, the motion constant, ceaseless. From somewhere my submerged mind dredged up factoids: 250 more resource-sucking humans born every minute; 10 percent of the humans who have ever been alive are alive today; eleven billion people on Earth by 2100; nine billion new people added to the planet in the 150 years from 1950 to 2100.[18]

I thought about cosmologist Carl Sagan encountering the first picture of the Earth from space: rather than borders, strife, or disasters, he simply saw home. Yet to look in the opposite direction, out into the boundless universe, was to see infinity: a view, moreover, that offered "no hint that help will come from elsewhere to save us from ourselves."[19]

Those preppers I spoke to at xPoint—Milton, Tom, and Mark— were all in vigorous agreement that as a species we're stepping onto a sacrificial altar of our own creation, and that we must take responsibility for saving ourselves. Their way of doing so was to hunker down. What drew me to these preppers, I thought, lying in my concrete shell, was the probability of their pessimism being justified. In a world this messy, they seemed rational actors, people who weren't taking anything for granted.

On my way out of xPoint the next morning, I stopped in front of the Hat Creek Bar and Grill to glom onto their WiFi and allowed my neglected emails to flood into my phone. Hundreds of messages pinged in, from friends, family, and work. I felt an overwhelming desire to retreat to the bunker. Then one last message pinged. It was from Robert Vicino, who said simply, "I hope you met some good people, drive safe." Under his signature block was his now familiar tagline: "Nobody believed Noah until it was too late."

2

Geological Deterrence: Prepping Like a State

"Nuclear destruction destroys the meaning of death by depriving it of its individuality. It destroys the meaning of immortality by making both society and history impossible. It destroys the meaning of life by throwing life back upon itself."
                    —Hans J. Morgenthau, "Death in
                    the Nuclear Age," 1961[1]

Lingering outside a U-Bahn station in Berlin, I noticed the sharp concrete angles of a nearby pillbox gradually being blurred by snowfall. The German city looked uncharacteristically soft. When Kate finally arrived, she seemed oblivious to the city's transformation, anxious to get underground, out of the cold. Kate is a British-born guide for *Berliner Unterwelten*, a group of tunnel and bunker enthusiasts who have, over time, become custodians of the city's subterranean heritage. Lying on the geographic fault line between the Cold War superpowers, Berlin seemed like the obvious place to get some context on the abandoned government bunkers that preppers were snapping up and retrofitting, so I'd signed up for a tour. I followed Kate into the station, where she unlatched a door and took our small group into an antechamber sixty-five feet under street level. The rumble of trains could be felt through the reinforced concrete walls.

This space had been created ninety years earlier from the remains of subway excavations: what architects call "space left over after planning" or SLOAP. It sat unused until World War II, when UK Royal Air Force planes suddenly appeared over the new National Socialist capital in August 1940 and started dropping bombs. With existing shelter available for only 4 percent of the population, Hitler tasked his architect Albert Speer to make space under the city to provide refuge from Allied aerial attacks. From 1940 to 1944, hundreds of bunkers were located or built under Berlin as part of a wartime civil defense plan. The bunker we were standing in was one of them. After the war, it lay disused until 1981, when it was reactivated during the Cold War.

The year 1981 was also the year I was born. As an elder millennial, I view the Cold War as more history than memory. When the Berlin Wall came down in 1989, I was still learning to read and write. Kate was eager to provide us with a visceral connection to history, letting us take turns operating the hand crank on the nuclear, biological, and/or chemical (NBC) sand filtration system. Even cranking it for ten seconds was exhausting. The bunker was built for about a thousand people—one person per three square feet—and the idea was that, once the city's power infrastructure had been incinerated, people would take turns at cranking the filter perpetually. But it was hard to imagine people being able to stay more than a day or two down here, cranking the thing in shifts.

Yet, if civil defense planners were to be believed, people were supposed to remain there for fourteen days—the magic number during nuclear fallout, at which point radiation from any nuclear strike, it was believed, would have subsided to a reasonably safe level.

Kate explained that there were four categories of bunkers in Berlin, and that this was a category one, the most rudimentary shelter. "The fact is that during the Cold War, this bunker wasn't likely to keep you alive," she told us bluntly. "But a population that believes the end of the world is coming loses their minds. This place at least gave them a way to respond, a place to go." In other words, the bunker was largely a confidence trick. Kate looked up at the air filter, the lifeline to the surface, and shook her head.

"Come on, I'll show you a category three bunker where people would've fared better," she said, heading back out onto the train platform.

We took the U-Bahn to the Pankstrasse station. It was sixty feet or so underground. There, at the bottom of the station stairs, Kate showed us a sixteen-inch lead-lined blast door that would slam shut, transforming the station itself into an NBC shelter that could sustain exactly 3,339 people for fourteen days. Train stations were similarly adapted to double as nuclear bunkers in parts of the former Soviet Union. I'd seen one such site in Kiev, Ukraine, in the deepest metro station in the world, Arsenalna, which at nearly 350 feet deep needs nothing more than the closure of a steel curtain to turn it into a blast shelter.

The category three bunker had all that you would expect to sustain people over fourteen days: bunk beds, a kitchen, an airlock, an infirmary, a decontamination room, and a filtration system—not hand-cranked, this time, but on an independent power system. This technology, new then, has now made its way into private bunkers around the world. And yet another aspect of this bunker was groundbreaking: state planners, aware that people would be expected to stay underground for fourteen days, had sponsored some of the first research into the psychological effects of extended subterranean dwelling. This bunker displayed some of the fruits of that research in that it was designed to boost the occupants' sense of well-being. For example, the walls were painted a pale green—the same color used in hospitals for instilling tranquility and obscuring bloodstains. Also, the mirrors were made of tin, and the bathrooms had no locks—both steps to prevent suicide attempts. Anything that could be readily turned into a self-harming weapon had been blunted or removed.

Most striking was the airlock leading into this "luxury" category three shelter. From the inside, the warden of the shelter could only see through a small pane of glass into a mirror (again, tin) that reflected the airlock threshold—but nothing beyond it, helping them to make the decision to shut the airlock, even if this meant separating families or severing limbs. The reasoning was simple: though 75 percent of West Berlin's U-Bahn stations had civil defense shelters concealed within their walls, there were only twenty-three working NBC shelters in West Berlin at the height of the Cold War, making available twenty-eight thousand spaces in a city of just over three million people. Less than 1 percent of the population would make it in—and those numbers had to be adhered to. If a shelter went over capacity, its predefined lockdown time frame of fourteen days would be jeopardized. After that time, and not before, an emergency hatch would be released capable of throwing off five tons of rubble, or even a car, and citizens would emerge into the blast-stricken landscape.

Material remains become archaeological with the passage of time, and enough time has now passed that the remains of the Cold War at places like Pankstrasse have also become sites of tourism and scholarship, visited by people like me. Recent geopolitical events make clear they are not follies, but harbingers: today, governments across the world are still building bunkers.

Today, the magnitude of state-level bunker excavation around the world is staggering—without even taking into account what remains beyond the ken of the public. According to Department of Defense (DOD) estimates, there were approximately ten thousand major underground military installations in the world just over a decade ago, many not visible from Earth's surface.[2] Russia's Mount Yamantau bunker in the Ural Mountains, for instance, purportedly contains an underground facility called Ramenki-43 that can house fifteen thousand people for thirty years in the event of a nuclear attack on Moscow.

In 1994, an urban exploration group in Russia called Diggers of the Underground Planet gained entry to Metro-2, a secret subway system built under Stalin. Metro-2 connects the Kremlin with various "exurban" command posts, including Ramenki-43, the Russian Federal Security Service (FSB) headquarters, and a government airport.[3] It's said to have four lines of track and be 650 feet deep in some places.

Elsewhere, satellite images have revealed that the Chinese People's Liberation Army (PLA) recently completed a fourteen-square-mile underground military complex in Djibouti in the Horn of Africa.[4] Meanwhile, India has built fourteen thousand new bunkers for families in Chachwal Village to protect citizens from shelling along the border with Pakistan in Jammu and Kashmir.[5]

Equally, the seventeen known deep underground military bases (DUMBS) built by the United States from the 1950s on would sound totally implausible if we didn't know they existed, and they're surely a fraction of the total built. Three of these sites are of crucial importance to continuity of government (COG), the government's ability to function after a catastrophic event.

One subterranean lair is known as Raven Rock or Site R, which in a 1954 edition of *Life* magazine was called out as the "alternative pentagon."[6] It was originally imagined as a five- to six-square-mile facility in which fourteen hundred inhabitants kept the space humming underneath a quarter mile of Pennsylvanian granite.[7] Five parallel caverns housed three-storey buildings mounted on massive springs that would flex during blast shock. The first version of the facility was completed in 1953 at a cost of $47 million. Billions of dollars have since been dumped into it, expanding the site to a flabbergasting thirty-seven square miles; today, the bunker has people working in it 24/7, 365 days a year. It's a fully functioning underground city, replete with a well-stocked bar.

In 1954 the government also broke ground on Mount Weather, a thirty-five-square-mile facility located in the Blue Ridge Mountains, some fifty miles from Washington, DC. In the early 1980s, the National Gallery of Art developed a program to transport the valuable paintings in its collection to Mount Weather in the event of a nuclear launch. It's also the bunker where the government "B Team"—the people who would run the country if all the top officials were dead—would assemble during a national crisis. On 9/11, after the first plane hit the twin towers, congressional leaders, including then Senate majority leader Tom Daschle were whisked there by helicopter. FEMA currently runs operations in the above-ground areas, fueling conspiracy theories about what they're *actually* training for.[8] One theory is that they're setting up concentration camps to house political dissidents after an event.[9] FEMA, like its predecessor, the Federal Civil Defense Administration (FCDA), is in charge of coordinating the nation's postapocalypse efforts, and their budget for this is classified, known to only twenty members of Congress.[10] This, surely, has fueled many of these conspiracy theories.

Finally, in 1956, after President Dwight D. Eisenhower hosted a conference at the Greenbrier Resort in White Sulphur Springs, West Virginia, construction began on another US government bunker. Project Greek Island, as the twenty-one-square-mile facility was code-named, was designed to house more than 1,000 government elites in times of crises, including the 535 members of Congress, and one aide for each politician, underneath a new wing of the hotel. About the size of a Walmart, it featured eighteen dormitories, industrial kitchen facilities, a hospital, a document vault, power systems, a hardened television studio, and a periodically refreshed six-month supply of food. Spoils from the excavation were used to expand the hotel golf course to hide digging operations from the public. In 1992, the *Washington Post* exposed the existence of the facility, rendering it all but useless.[11] Like Pankstrasse, it's now a tourist destination.

All three of these sites are a small part of a "federal relocation arc": an archipelago of dozens of facilities in which the government could take sanctuary, all about a hundred miles from the Capitol and organized in three increasingly fortified layers linked by an internal communication system. According to a declassified document from 1958, it was recommended that at least four sites be "hardened against blast, thermal and radiation effects."[12] Raven Rock, Mount Weather, and Greenbrier were part of that recommendation as the most secure layer in the arc. Unlike the European public shelters, North American DUMBS of the same period were constructed not for citizens but for the government elites. Citizens had to make their own preparations.

On the other side of the country, in the middle of Colorado, tucked under almost twenty-five hundred feet of granite, is the Cheyenne Mountain Complex, which is not so much a place as a negative space. Here is the alternate command center for the North American Aerospace Defense Command (NORAD), which has served as a fictional backdrop in films like *Dr. Strangelove*, *War Games*, and *Terminator*. This is where the military monitors missile launches, activity in outer space, nuclear tests, and cyberthreats. The bunker called off its "nuclear watch" in 1992 after the Soviet Union disintegrated, but in 2015—the same year that Russia reinstated its own civil defense training in the Metro—the Pentagon dumped a fresh $700 million into it. They'd found it was a natural Faraday cage—a grounded shield preventing electrostatic and electromagnetic interruption. Today, a thousand workers roam the mountain's innards. Six million gallons of fresh water are stored in pools carved out of the rock and 510,000 gallons of diesel are sealed behind a closed wall ready to run the facility off-grid for as long as necessary. You can even order a Subway sandwich there from workers who, during a nuclear attack on the country, might just be the luckiest "sandwich artists" in the USA.

Though these bunkers have never been used during a nuclear attack, there were times when humans edged close to such a disaster. During the thirteen-day standoff that was the 1962 Cuban Missile Crisis, when the Soviets attempted to deploy a ballistic missile program in Cuba within striking distance of the United States, the world came closer than at any time in history to a nuclear war between superpowers.

The Russians have had their own scares. During the Cuban Missile Crisis an American destroyer near the island, the USS *Randolph*, dropped depth charges on a B-59, a Soviet submarine armed with a ten-kiloton nuclear torpedo. The intention was to force it to the surface. The charges were nonlethal practice rounds, but the Russians had no way of knowing this, or indeed if all-out war had broken out on the surface. The launch of the B-59's nuclear torpedo required the consent of all three senior officers aboard. Only one, Vasili Alexandrovich Arkhipov, dissented. His sole refusal very likely prevented a nuclear war. Every year, on October 27, people celebrate "Arkhipov Day," toasting the man who saved the world.

Equally harrowing was an early November morning seventeen years later in 1979, when National Security Advisor Zbigniew Brzezinski was woken at 3 a.m. and told that two hundred fifty Soviet nuclear missiles had been launched at the United States. It was all-out nuclear Armageddon. Brzezinski knew that the president—Jimmy Carter at the time—had an extremely limited window in which to launch a counterattack, triggering the fabled mutually assured destruction (MAD) scenario. Sixty seconds before Brzezinski intended to call the president to advise him of the attack, he was told that it had been a false alarm. Someone had mistakenly put military exercise tapes into the computer system.[13] According to National Security Archive documents declassified in 2012, there were three more false alerts the following year, despite stern admonitions from the Soviet Communist Party command that such errors were "fraught with a tremendous danger" and must be avoided at all cost.

Even after the fall of the Berlin Wall and the easing of tensions between East and West superpowers, there were close calls. In 1995, Russian radar mistook the launch of a Norwegian scientific rocket, being sent to study the Northern Lights, for a surprise attack by the United States, potentially an EMP meant to wipe out electronic communications in the Russian capital. The benign rocket was heading on the exact trajectory of a Minuteman III nuclear intercontinental ballistic missile (ICBM) from North Dakota. President Boris Yeltsin was actually handed the Russian nuclear briefcase, the Cheget, to launch a retaliatory strike. He held off, but it remains the only known incident in which a head of state activated such a briefcase and prepared to launch an attack.[14]

Elsewhere, civil defense programs went beyond the creation of bunker space for the elite few and made attempts to build shelters for every citizen. These programs are still maintained today—at least, by some countries. Sweden maintains space in nuclear-, biological-, and/or chemical-filtered bunkers for 70 percent of its residents, though the structures have never been used in war. In 2018, the Swedish government triggered minor nationwide hysteria when they sent pamphlets to each of the country's 4.8 million households, reminding them where shelters were and telling them how to prepare for an enemy attack.[15] Next door in Finland, for decades the country has been hoarding medical supplies, oil, food, tools, and raw materials to make ammunition. When COVID-19 struck, the Finnish government tapped the stockpile for the first time since World War II and found it to be in superabundance, earning Finland the title of "prepper nation."[16]

Meanwhile in Switzerland, a 1963 law still in place dictates that every citizen has access to a nuclear bunker. As of 2016 there was bunker space for 8.6 million individuals—five thousand public shelters and more than three hundred thousand private bunkers—in a country of less than 8.4 million.[17] Just in case tourists are in town, I suppose. One of the public shelters is in Lucerne, inside a road tunnel that can be sealed by four three hundred twenty ton gates, and can house twenty thousand people over seven floors.

Perhaps unsurprisingly, bunkers are also ubiquitous in much of Israel, a country in conflict since its founding in 1948. *Merhav mugan dirati* or "apartment protected space," commonly known as *mamads*, can be found in almost half of Israeli houses. Ofer Gal, an Israeli professor of History and Philosophy of Science at the University of Sydney, and a good friend, explained to me that public shelters had always been part of blocks of houses, and people knew how to get to the community shelter during an attack. His own family did so, especially during the 1967 and 1973 wars.

But, he went on, "the Gulf War in 1991 changed everything." With the Israeli government worried about chemical weapon attacks, underground community shelters "were the last place you wanted to send people to. We were told to seal off a room with plastic sheeting and enclose ourselves there during attacks. Like everybody, I did. Then one day I was sitting in my living room and I felt a breeze—it was coming right through the sheet fortifications. It was futile; I ripped it all down. The next time we heard the air-raid sirens, I went up to the roof with two friends and we watched a Scud missile launch from Iraq and then a Patriot missile launch from Israel in an attempt to intercept. It was beautiful in a way; they totally missed each other and made two great arcs in the sky." When the group descended from the roof and turned on the TV, the official government line was that the Scud had been "successfully intercepted by a Patriot missile."

"Though I wasn't particularly young or naïve," Gal mused, "the unmitigated lie was quite an eye-opener," causing him to forevermore question government narratives. After the Gulf War, all new apartments had to include *mamads* with NBC air filters. As they became part of the home, and a private responsibility, people learned to turn them into studies or children's rooms. Their very existence created a constant sense of self-perpetuating emergency that residents tried to domesticate.[18]

The most bunkered part of the world is of course the Korean Peninsula. In North Korea, between eleven and fourteen thousand underground facilities have been dug out since the 1950s. Subterranean weapons factories are believed to employ as many as twenty thousand workers.[19] The North Korean People's Liberation Army Air Force is believed to have three different underground air bases, one of which reportedly includes a six-thousand-foot-long runway inside a mountain. They also have up to five hundred missile-launching hardened artillery sites, HARTS, carved into the sides of mountains.[20]

The California-based Nautilus Institute for Security and Sustainability is a leading authority on the Korean Peninsula. I spoke to Peter Hayes, the institute's director, over the phone while I was plotting my tour of bunker architecture. Hayes assured me that in South Korea I'd have trouble getting access to bunkered space and that if I went to North Korea I wouldn't see much but that "the country's surface architecture is epi-phenomenal; the essential North Korea is underground."

After the Korean War ended in 1953, the uneasy truce persisted. In this state of perpetual potential conflict, the South Korean government built nineteen thousand fallout and bomb shelters around the country, with thirty-two hundred public shelters in Seoul alone. It's hardly surprising, given the place nuclear war holds in the Korean psyche.

More than forty thousand Koreans—those working as forced laborers in Japanese industry—died in the bombing of Hiroshima and Nagasaki.[21] For Koreans, in other words, nuclear war was a lived experience with real and horrifying effects, not a speculative matter, as it exists in the imagination of most Westerners today. Korean nuclear survivors, Hayes told me, have drawn three simple lessons from their terrible experience: "Nuclear wars cannot be won; conflicts must be solved by peaceful dialogue; and nuclear strategy makes nuclear war possible."

"North of the DMZ [demilitarized zone]," Hayes added, "is another story." He explained to me that during the first six months of the Korean War, most surface buildings in North Korea were more or less destroyed. Unsurprisingly, North Koreans began investing heavily in burrowing.

"Every hill is honeycombed," Hayes continued. "Artillery, food, even an entire MiG airfield are buried underground. Multiple weapons factories, including the entire nuclear program, are in bunkers. Make no mistake, North Korea is the most bunkered society in the history of Earth."

South Korea is taking the re-emerging threat seriously. As in other parts of the world, bunkers there are being "reactivated," particularly in metro stations. John Delury, an expert in Korean Peninsula affairs, at Yonsei University in Seoul, met me in the midst of my travels and painted a vivid picture of the escalating sense of emergency in the Korean Republic around this time. He had friends in Seoul who had received "bug-out bags"—bags with enough supplies to survive for seventy-two hours—as Christmas gifts when tensions were ramping up in 2017. He also showed me a new government app called Emergency Ready. The app was complex and confusing. There was one tab for "natural emergencies," one for "social emergencies," one to call emergency services, and one for "lifestyle safety." Under the "natural emergencies" tab, one icon looked like it was to be used to report a giant squid attack. Delury said the app was supposed to direct you to a shelter if something did happen, but he worried how it would work if there was no mobile reception.

If open conflict did break out, Delury said, "It would be a mess. The reason people won't practice disaster planning or use the shelters in Seoul is because . . . it's a young democracy with a strong sense of social welfare and a deep distrust of authority." He explained that many young South Koreans feel that North Korea is used by politicians to keep them living in a state of fear, and therefore obedience. "These are the last people that are going to huddle in a bunker waiting to be saved," he said.

During the Cold War, then, most state bunkers seemed to fall into one of two categories. In the North American and English model, bunkers were kept secret and reserved only for those in power. Meanwhile, the public civil defense models adopted in places like the Soviet Union, Scandinavia, Korea, and Switzerland became normalized in people's minds: something to groan or joke about—or simply forget.

Before leaving Europe, I made an extra stop in the UK to go visit the University of Oxford, where I'd worked from 2012 to 2014. One of my colleagues at the time was Ian Klinke. During those years Ian and I could be found at the wooden picnic tables outside of the Kings Arms, catty-corner to the Bodleian Library, sipping pints and talking shop. A striking German-born political geographer with a penchant for trench coats and a habit of constantly adjusting his gold wire-rimmed spectacles, Klinke is one of the most exacting scholars I know—and a fellow bunker nerd.

I timed my arrival in Oxford so that I could tag along with him to a dinner at St. Johns College, Ian's base. I'd missed the familiar pomp of these affairs, the air that demands implicit secrecy. We stashed our laptops, collected our black robes, and gathered in the dining room. The head of house banged a gavel and words were spoken in Latin. As dinner progressed, wineglasses were discreetly refilled by white-gloved staff.

During dinner, Ian explained that scholars assume World War I to be the catalyst for widespread bunker construction: the introduction of bombing aircraft obviously rendered walls pointless. But, he went on, this was only part of the story. He suggested that the building of concrete bunkers, particularly from World War II on, was also a way of holding territory both horizontally and vertically. "In other words," Ian said, in military terms "territory went three-dimensional around this time."[22]

The next major leap forward in bunker building came with the Cold War and the nuclear threat that accompanied it, presenting state planners with another, greater challenge. If people couldn't be evacuated from cities, they had to be *invacuated* into bunkers—because a state without its people couldn't rebuild itself. Ian pointed me to a passage in the supremely depressing 1960 book *On Thermonuclear War* by the famous RAND Corporation nuclear strategist Herman Kahn, a man once described as "the heavyweight of the Megadeath Intellectuals." In it, Kahn intoned that "any power that can evacuate a high percentage of its urban population to protection is in a much better position to bargain than one which cannot do this."[23]

Playing out these and other horrific thought experiments on paper, Kahn imagined a nuclear-resistant bunker world on an epic scale. This included a $200 billion civil defense program for the USA, which would shelter 200 million Americans underground long enough to allow them to emerge into survivable postwar conditions, even if everything aboveground had been destroyed. As we made our way through several courses of an increasingly bibulous dinner, Ian explained that, with the final decision of who lives and who dies on a global scale in the hands of a few elites, US citizens responded in a variety of ways. Some grew fatalistic, seeing nuclear war as unavoidable and in some cases even foreordained by religious beliefs in the end of days.[24] Others responded by fleeing major cities that would undoubtedly be targeted in a nuclear strike, and whose populations had developed what Kahn called "prime-target-fixation syndrome." Once ensconced in their suburban homes outside the envisaged blast radius, these fleeing citizens then dug in, burying bunkers in their backyards. In the event of disaster, they pinned their hopes on resurrection.

"The hope was that enough people would emerge from the bunker to rebuild," Ian told me. "Yet in a worst-case Cold War scenario, there is nothing to emerge into, the surface of the Earth would be toxic and barren." This has been described as "the problem of the fifteenth day." As in: You may survive in a Cold War bunker for two weeks, but what do you find when you emerge on day fifteen? This is perhaps why Kahn imagined staying underground for months.

As Ian and I wended our way home from dinner, on wet cobble-stone streets past the Bridge of Sighs, I reflected on our conversation. Since the Cold War, bunkers had never really disappeared: the subsurface of the Earth continues to be a geological-geopolitical space.[25] What's really different now is that, globally, bunkers are being built by a wide range of government, corporate, and private actors all over the world. Ranging from new government DUMBS to tiny walk-in-closet panic rooms, contemporary bunkers are as ubiquitous as they are diverse. In order to understand how we got to this point in history, it's worth looking back in time.

3

Living with the Bomb:
A Cultural History of Prepping

"Disaster laughs at every attempt to write its epitaph."

—Garret Keizer, "Solidarity and Survival," 2016[1]

Illustration by Elmer Wexler: *Life* magazine, September 1961, *Fallout Shelters*.

Early in 1990, on the edge of Yellowstone National Park in Paradise Valley, Montana, construction was afoot on a state-of-the-art $25 million nuclear bunker facility under the thirty-two-thousand-acre Royal Teton Ranch owned by the Church Universal and Triumphant (aka CUT). The church's leader, the charismatic Elizabeth Clare Prophet or "Guru Ma," believed that nuclear Armageddon was imminent—and therefore that the construction of bunkers in her community was not only prudent, but necessary and urgent.

According to Guru Ma's son Sean, who managed its construction, the CUT bunker network comprised six distinct clusters made from stitched-together corrugated iron oil tanks salvaged from service. These tanks were buried in massive open pits, then covered in topsoil by heavy equipment. In each tank a kitchen, an infirmary, and laundry facilities were built. The largest tanks, a pair of 40-foot-wide, 325-foot-long arches, were connected by a central passageway to form a large H shape. Supposedly, there was space in the bunkers for 750 church staff members and leaders. For congregants, though, a place in them came at a cost. One devotee, who had withdrawn her life savings, paid $6,000 for space in a bunker with 125 other people and seven months' worth of food.[2] Others, for the bargain price of $200,000, had bought into specially designed survival condominiums in the underground community.

In the words of Cold War historian David Monteyne, a bunker "is both designed to protect its occupants and to command a field of fire; that is, the bunker's function is to control space, both interior and exterior."[3] It was hardly surprising, therefore, that the money being collected by CUT wasn't only being used to build defensive structures—it was also financing the arming of Elizabeth Prophet's followers. This militarizing had aroused the interest of federal authorities. In 1989, Prophet's husband, Edward Francis, had been arrested and convicted of purchasing $100,000 worth of weapons under a false name, for the "Rocky Mountain Sportsmen's Survival Club." The haul included ten Barrett M82 .50-caliber rifles capable of shooting down planes, Uzi machine guns, a rocket launcher with armor-piercing six-inch shells, and two Saracen armored personnel carriers (APCs) procured from a company in New Jersey called Tanks A Lot.[4] What Prophet and Francis planned to do with this matériel was unclear, but the feds were clearly nervous about their intentions.

On March 15, 1990, a day pegged by Guru Ma as the beginning

of Armageddon, outlined in the Book of Revelation as the gathering of armies for a battle during the end times, more than two thousand congregants locked themselves inside the bunker complex, waiting to cross to the other side. International news crews gathered outside the compound, also waiting for something to happen—if not *the* apocalypse, perhaps a mini one like the Jonestown massacre of 1978, which ended with more than nine hundred dead. Alas, on this day in 1990, the end didn't unfold as promised and the news crews packed their equipment back into their vans and sped off. Weirdly, the failure of Armageddon to arrive on the stated date didn't slow construction, or, for that matter, unit sales.

In an interview with KULR-TV in Billings, Montana, Sean Prophet suggested that the bad press over the prosecution, the media frenzy surrounding the failed end-times predictions, and a thirty-one-thousand-gallon diesel fuel spill on the property had made "relations between the church and the townspeople [in Paradise Valley] frosty," which prompted his mom to do a bit of PR work after the lock-in.[5] In an address to the Great Falls Rotary Club on April 7, 1991, more than a year after the critical date, Guru Ma explained that they'd built the bunkers because "our government has not provided civil defense for us. Whether it's the Soviets, a Hussein, a Kaddafi, or a Chernobyl, the threat is there and it's real." Plus, she hastened to point out, she'd never *actually* predicted the end of the world.

"Our fallout shelters have confused and frightened some Montanans, and this is understandable, since to many Americans shelters connote paranoia and extremism," Prophet said. But, she asserted, her bunkers were based on science. She had seen astrological parallels between the fourteenth century and the twentieth. In the fourteenth century the world was wracked by war, famine, economic hardship, and a plague that killed a third of Europe's population. In 1991, she suggested, AIDS, cancer, the hole in the ozone layer, and the proxy war with the Soviet Union unfolding in Iraq were cracking the seven seals described in the Book of Revelation.

Evangelical Christian beliefs in the apocalypse are often refracted through the prism of the Book of Revelation, the final chapter of the New Testament. In it, Armageddon is triggered by the breaking of seven seals that secure a scroll that John of Patmos—the author of the Book of Revelation—saw in an apocalyptic vision. The four horsemen of the apocalypse—conquest, war, famine, and plague—correspond to the first four seals. According to some theological interpretations these horsemen have already been loosed on the world.

Guru Ma suggested that the fifth seal, defined in the Book of Revelation as the martyrdom of the saints, where even the devout are slain, was embodied by nuclear weaponry, a creation that did not exist on Earth until humans channeled it through dark arts. Her preparations, she informed the Great Falls Rotarians, were simply a practical way of surviving the inevitable unfolding of events long enough to enter the new era, which would come about after the breaking of the fifth seal was unleashed and the wrath of God delivered. Salvation, she preached, lay on the other side.

Prophet had already written about these theories in her 1990 book *The Astrology of the Four Horsemen*, a geopolitical field manual steeped in a very West Coast brand of astrological eschatology.[6] In the year the book was penned, the US military moved into Baghdad during the first Gulf War as then-president George H. W. Bush spoke of creating a "New World Order." For many Americans, the phrase was resonant: people were quick to point out that the archaeological ruins of Babylon were just over fifty miles south of Baghdad, and saw the invasion as resonating with a passage from Revelation. "Release the four angels who are bound at the great river Euphrates," it's written in Revelation 9:14. To doomsayers like Guru Ma, this was clear evidence for the inevitable forthcoming apocalypse that would result in the formation of Bush's New World Order.[7]

Measured though she might have thought she was in her beliefs, a clear sense of disorientation bleeds through Guru Ma's speech, one that all too recognizably stems from nuclear dread. This phenomenon had become embedded in the American psyche over the previous three decades and more. It was the subject of a powerful piece of writing by that colossus of international politics Hans J. Morgenthau, who in his 1961 essay "Death in the Nuclear Age" meditated on what such a nuclear war might mean, at a time when most people were still getting their heads around it.

"The significance of the possibility of nuclear death is that it radically affects the meaning of death, of immortality, of life itself," Morgenthau wrote. "It affects that meaning by destroying most of it. Nuclear destruction is mass destruction, both of persons and of things. It signifies the simultaneous destruction of tens of millions of people, of whole families, generations, and societies, of all the things that they have inherited and created."[8] The concept of nuclear war has long since embedded itself deep in our collective psyche as the possibility of the erasure of everything: our bodies, attachments, objects, and memories. Indeed, Morgenthau insisted that our desire to hold on to life is more than biological or individual; it is also about a desire to hold on to these social attachments. Many of us find the idea of isolation more terrifying than death. Guru Ma was among them. Faced with the obliterating prospect of nuclear Armageddon, she sought to preserve her connection to the world through her community of survivors. They would survive the breaking of the fifth seal because they were prepared.

That desire lives on. A few years after the turn of the millennium, two cultural geographers traveled to Paradise Valley to see what had happened to the Church Universal and Triumphant. Locals had reported hearing extended bursts of weapons fire on church land at night. One resident told the researchers bluntly that "if those people don't still have an underground warehouse of weapons, I'll kiss a cow."[9]

In the intervening years, the Church Universal and Triumphant has continued to flourish, with local congregations in more than twenty countries. CUT, and other similar "survivalist" movements—subterranean communities meant to arise, thrive, and survive, with or without the state—help us to understand how the modern prepper movement evolved into the multibillion-dollar-a-year industry that it is today, putting flesh on its ideological and eschatological roots.

I recall clearly the time I first experienced sublime nuclear terror. I was in my late twenties, on one of my road trips around the American Southwest, and had stopped at the National Atomic Testing Museum in Las Vegas. There, an oversized photograph of the 1946 nuclear tests on Bikini Atoll is mounted on one of the walls. At first, I could barely take it in. But when I moved to study the details, I could just make out the five-hundred-sixty-foot United States Navy battleship *Arkansas* being sucked into the six-thousand-foot stem of the mushroom cloud, frozen in time, just before almost two million tons of radioactive seawater came crashing back to Earth. Transfixed by the image, I thought, as have many others, that these tests constituted a moment in which humanity transcended itself.

Geologists have proposed that if there's one key event marking the transition from the Holocene Age to the Anthropocene—a geological age defined by the impact of human activity on the Earth and its atmosphere—it's the detonation of the Trinity atomic device in the Jornada del Muerto ("Journey of the Dead Man") desert in New Mexico at 5:29 a.m. on July 16, 1945. This precursor to the Bikini Atoll tests may not have seemed as iconic, but it was more significant. The Anthropocene is an age marked visibly from this moment in the Earth's subsurface stratigraphy as a slice of radioisotopes; it's a marker of anthropogenic geology symbolic of our ability to destroy not just ourselves but the entire planet.[10]

In Christian thought, the "Trinity" represents three elements: God, the Son, and the Holy Spirit. This name was given to the implosion-design plutonium device by J. Robert Oppenheimer, lead physicist on the Trinity atomic project. Oppenheimer had read John Donne's seventeenth-century poem "Holy Sonnet XIV: Batter my heart, three-person'd God," and saw in it a reflection of his own monstrous creation. The poem opens with these four searing lines:

> *Batter my heart, three-person'd God, for you*
> *As yet but knock, breathe, shine, and seek to mend;*
> *That I may rise and stand, o'erthrow me, and bend*
> *Your force to break, blow, burn, and make me new.*

Upon detonation of the device, Oppenheimer, ever the poet, recalled a line from the Hindu holy book the *Bhagavad-Gita*: "Now

I am become Death, the destroyer of worlds." It's in this context that survivalists like Guru Ma and her followers were attempting to come up with solutions to a frightening problem they didn't create and could scarcely comprehend.

Despite being the only nation to drop atomic weapons on an enemy—at Hiroshima and Nagasaki—and possessing the fullest awareness of their devastating destructive potential, the US government has never attempted to build nuclear shelters for all, or even a significant fraction, of its citizens. After the Soviets developed their own atom bomb in 1949, President Harry S. Truman oversaw the establishment of a Federal Civil Defense Administration. Early research by the FCDA found that 30 percent of those who died immediately in the US atomic attack on Nagasaki would've been saved by fallout shelters. However, estimates provided to Eisenhower when he took the presidential reins from Truman suggested that creating underground community shelters for the entire US population would cost somewhere in the realm of $300 billion. A decision was made to eventually spend $2.5 million (one-ten-thousandth of this) on a National Shelter Policy, mostly focused on galvanizing private citizens to build shelters on their own properties. This policy left many Americans feeling frustrated, betrayed, and abandoned. In a 1956 Gallup Poll, only 29 percent of Americans thought their families were likely to survive atomic war.[11]

As tensions with the Soviet Union escalated over the next few years, the US government doubled down on efforts to get citizens to take responsibility for their own preparations. In a nationally televised speech in July 1961, John F. Kennedy told the American people that in the US conflict with the Soviet Union, "our primary purpose is neither propaganda nor provocation—but preparation," and that Americans had the "sobering responsibility to recognize the possibilities of nuclear war."[12] Kennedy's speech, and the underwhelming government protection mandate, triggered what social scientists now call the first doom boom. Americans built millions of fallout shelters in their backyards, many following plans provided by government pamphlets as well as a 1961 edition of *Life* magazine. This shelter boom created a new segment of the economy: the phenomenon that we now call prepping. According to University of California sociologist Andrew Szasz, "Local contractors reinvented themselves and miraculously became, overnight, fallout shelter specialists. Sears rushed out a prefab shelter kit that had been featured in the article in *Life*. Companies rushed to market shelter supplies."[13]

Even Amway, a company that would eventually become one of the largest marketers of health, beauty, and home care products in the United States, got in on the act. The company sold egg-shaped, fourteen-foot bunkers, kitted out with four bunk beds for eight people, air and water purifying systems, and a portable toilet. The bunkers were installed fifteen feet underground for $1,750—about $15,000 today. For an extra $160 Amway would even dig a connecting tunnel through the home's foundation to create an alternate escape route to the bunker.[14]

In 1962, *Life* magazine ran another cover story, which renewed the call for the construction of public shelters and gave instructions on how best to survive a nuclear attack if caught out away from one's backyard bunker. I got hold of an old copy on eBay and, flipping through it, was taken aback by the magazine's language, which makes today's hysterical media sound like Dr. Seuss. One lurid passage described how "11 miles from the burst, the clothing of people exposed would be set aflame," and how, if someone were on Long Island facing a twenty-megaton burst in Manhattan, "the image of the fireball would burn holes right through the retinas of his eyes."[15] As someone admittedly addicted to a daily drip-feed of awful news, I can only imagine that such imagery instilled a terrible sense of nihilism and despondency, contrary to the author's purpose—getting people to prep.

Nevertheless, *Life* assured readers that proper shelter construction and preparation by both individuals and the government would make rebirth possible. The magazine asserted optimistically that "with trousers tucked into sock tops and sleeves tied around wrists, with hats, mufflers, gloves and boots, the shelter dweller could venture forth to start ensuring his today and building for his tomorrow."[16]

This period in the early 1960s is of crucial cultural significance in the United States, Canada, and the United Kingdom, because it marks the moment when the state abandoned its duty to protect citizens from perceived enemies. After the declassification of sites like Burlington and the Greenbrier Bunker in Virginia, exposed by investigative journalism from the 1990s on, we now realize that while Cold War administrations were rejecting budgets to shelter the population, government insiders were busy building bunkers— to save themselves, not their citizens. Though we might see sense in declining to provide public shelters on a scale that amounted to a country's yearly gross domestic product, these decisions had social and policy repercussions. In the United States, the government's call for citizens to build their own bunkers was an effort to preserve the state by encouraging people to save themselves, but it also fostered a sense of self-preservation that made the state seem superfluous. A deep sense of alienation was fostered among citizens during this period. This was particularly the case in the American West, where self-sufficiency has long been a component of frontier imaginaries.

In the same year that Kennedy gave the speech that triggered the first doom boom—1961—the Minuteman Militia was formed by Robert DePugh. (The modern-day border-patrolling vigilante movement called the Minuteman Project, started in 2004, isn't associated.) Taking their name from the American Revolutionary militia, DePugh's Minutemen were anti-Communist vigilantes who promoted preparation for guerrilla war inside America. DePugh advocated for his members to learn wilderness survival skills and marksmanship in preparation for crisis. Started in Missouri, the militia cells were quickly established in many other states, leading DePugh early on to claim a national membership of twenty-five thousand. In addition to being a militia leader, DePugh was, according to James Coates, an investigative reporter for the *Chicago Tribune*, the "godfather" of American survivalism, prepping's cultural progenitor.[17]

After discovering a Minuteman plot to bomb government buildings and a power station in Seattle, police quickly infiltrated the group. In police raids, agents seized ten Molotov cocktails, nine sticks of dynamite, blasting caps, face masks, and three pistols.

Militia members, including DePugh, were also charged with conspiracy to commit bank robbery to fund their activities. Militia members saw this as a compound betrayal. First the government had abandoned American citizens to their own devices in a nuclear war the citizens had no control over; then they persecuted them for taking self-reliance seriously. DePugh used his survivalist skills to go on the lam for two years before his eventual capture and imprisonment—which only added to the growing mythology surrounding him. In the eyes of future survivalists and militia members, DePugh was being persecuted by the government. This is a line of reasoning that can be traced to the present. Survivalist militias like the Three Percenters, who during the presidency of Barack Obama claimed to have up to ten thousand enrolled and heavily armed members, use resentment about persecution by "big government" as a recruiting mechanism.

In the 1990s, a day's drive away from Elizabeth Clare Prophet's bunker complex, close to the Nez Perce Indian reservation in Idaho, Bo Gritz was also building a community. Gritz is a decorated Vietnam veteran who's said to be the inspiration for both Rambo and Hannibal from the television series *The A-Team*. Around the time that show was airing in the mid-1980s, he purchased a thousand acres of land and soon after founded a "constitutional covenant community" called Almost Heaven.

Gritz was a charismatic dread merchant. He assured would-be buyers that society was on the verge of breakdown and would re-form as a "New World Order"—echoing George H. W. Bush's words before the 1990 invasion of Iraq. When the Fall came, Gritz stated, community members were expected to continue to defend the Constitution in a world Without Rule of Law (WROL). He picked the site of Almost Heaven after careful study of fault line locations, extreme weather patterns, access to water, proximity to nuclear strike targets, and defensibility, and billed it as "the safest place in America" in which to build a redoubt—rather like xPoint, some three decades later. For just under $14,000, you could buy a quarter acre with sewer, water, electric, and phone hookups.

The community sold out almost immediately. It was demographically diverse, attracting everybody from right-wing paramilitary white nationalists to off-grid back-to-the-land hippies who built houses out of hay bales and old tires. One family of six built an "Earth ship" buried in a hill, with a large south-facing window acting as cockpit. People from across the political spectrum appreciated living in a place without building codes, inspectors, and oppressive rules. These groups overlapped in their interest in survivalism. There was a shared feeling among residents that the government was actively undermining their rights. In turn, the government, seeing that people were becoming "paranoid," ratcheted up surveillance, which only made residents more anxious.[18] Many of them were dodging taxes and the law. But this was of no concern to Gritz, so long as they upheld a single principle: to defend the Constitution and fight for each other, should any resident's constitutional rights be threatened.

It was my visit to xPoint that got me thinking about Gritz. A few days after I left South Dakota, I made contact with Andrea Luka Zimmerman, an old friend and director who made a controversial film about Gritz called *Erase and Forget*. When I called her, Zimmerman was keen to talk, though her energetic voice was made soggy by the Skype connection. She told me that Gritz's life had been full of paradoxes, foremost among them "the paradox of survivalism," which required breaking away from American society and government in order to protect the United States. In Zimmerman's film, Gritz said that he felt a "desire to defend the Constitution amidst government betrayal."[19] Indeed, in the late eighties and early nineties, Gritz built a public profile that stretched way beyond Almost Heaven. He appealed to the political right, as a pro-life, pro-gun, small-government champion; and to the left as a whistleblower who called out the CIA when he learned the Reagan administration had hypocritically worked with cocaine traffickers in Latin America while declaring a "war on drugs" domestically. In 1988, just before founding Almost Heaven, Gritz even ran for vice president on a Populist Party ticket, but dropped out of the race when he discovered the party had nominated Ku Klux Klan grand wizard David Duke as his running mate. In 1992, he ran for president. One of his campaign slogans was "If ballots can't do it in '92, bullets may have to in '96." Gritz's campaign didn't last long.

At the time, there were suggestions that Gritz's public persona was all about marketing: he was preaching fear and then selling the product—Almost Heaven—to cope with that fear. Other antigovernment populists suggested that he was "a publicity hound and survivalist huckster."[20] As at xPoint, residents were offered leases rather than title to the land, meaning, of course, that ultimate ownership and control remained with Gritz. A few residents eventually banded together to sue, alleging Gritz had misled them. Contractors also sued for nonpayment for infrastructure construction, and Gritz's business partner Jerry Gillespie, a former Arizona senator, left Almost Heaven in disgrace in 1997 after squandering $1 million of the land sale revenues. The next year, Gritz found himself $85,000 in debt when his wife left him. Having hit rock bottom, he shot himself in the chest with a .45-caliber semiautomatic pistol. But Rambo didn't die.

In an interview with the Wyoming newspaper the *Casper Star-Tribune*, Gritz said he eventually abandoned the idea of a community, out of frustration because "there were about six individuals who were looking for Armageddon, and if it didn't come, they were going to cause it."[21] This bunch had split off into a paramilitary outfit called the Idaho Mountain Boys, had planted land mines in the Almost Heaven compound, and were accused of plotting to kill a US district court judge. Their conviction on federal bomb-making charges was the final nail in Almost Heaven's coffin.

The dissolution of Almost Heaven echoed a famous standoff between survivalists and federal authorities in Idaho colloquially remembered as Ruby Ridge. In 1992 Randy Weaver, an avowed survivalist, was caught in a sting when he sold sawed-off shotguns to US Bureau of Alcohol, Tobacco, Firearms, and Explosives (ATF) officials posing as survivalists. When Weaver declined to become an ATF informant, and then failed to appear in court, having been given the wrong court date, federal officials descended on his property. Weaver, his wife, his two children, and a family friend barricaded themselves inside and an eleven-day siege ensued.

On the first day of the siege, six heavily armed US marshals hiding in the bushes were discovered by the Weavers' dog. Authorities shot the dog, leading to a firefight in which US Marshal William Degan was killed and Weaver's fourteen-year-old son, Sammy, was also shot in the back and killed. As the family retreated back into their cabin, the FBI dispatched a hostage rescue team to the property. Before they had much of a chance of negotiating, a shot by Lon Horiuchi, an FBI sniper from Hawaii, struck Weaver's unarmed wife, Vicky, in the head while she was holding their baby Elisheba.

As more and more police flooded to the property, survivalists from around the country also flocked to the siege. Their de facto spokesperson, none other than Bo Gritz, was brought in to talk Randy Weaver down, which he did successfully. A few years later, in 1996, Gritz less successfully negotiated with the Montana Freeman, who declared political sovereignty from the US government, resulting in another eighty-one-day standoff—again with the FBI.

Less than eight months after Ruby Ridge, the FBI sniper Lon Horiuchi was again in action: this time during the Branch Davidian standoff at Waco where David Koresh, the leader of the apocalyptic religious sect, had hunkered down with his seventy-five followers. According to Malcolm Gladwell, reporting on the siege for the *New Yorker*, the FBI had assembled "the largest military force ever gathered against a civilian suspect in American history."[22] Almost nine hundred officers came to remove Koresh and his disciples from the property. They'd even brought twelve tanks. Fifty-one days into the siege, three simultaneous fires broke out in the house, possibly caused by police tear gas canisters fired into the compound. Seventy-six people, including twenty-five children and two pregnant women, died in the ensuing conflagration. Under the charred remains of Waco, the FBI found a school bus buried in the ground and stocked with food.

The US government was clearly concerned about the extreme right-wing views of Weaver, Koresh, and their like. But the FBI, in its handling of both cases, had hardly covered itself in glory: the episodes only served to entrench further the survivalists' opposition to government. Timothy McVeigh, another survivalist, could be found at gun shows soon after, handing out free cards printed with

Horiuchi's name and address, encouraging people to hunt him in the same way he hunted survivalists. McVeigh would later retreat home to draw up plans for the 1995 Oklahoma City bombing.

These have become seminal moments in survivalist mythology, and similar events today continue to resonate with them. During the 2014 standoff between cattle rancher Cliven Bundy and federal authorities at the Malheur National Wildlife Refuge in Oregon, survivalists and militia showed up in full force to defend the Bundy family's right not to pay to graze their cattle on federal lands. LaVoy Finicum, a skinny Mormon cowboy in frameless glasses and a tan Stetson—and a media firebrand during the standoff—became the newest martyr to antigovernment sentiment when police shot him in the back in the snow at a roadblock after Finicum reached for his gun when they tried to arrest him.[23] Rallies by survivalist militia, including the Three Percenters, now the largest militia in the US, followed in the wake of his death.

Since the founding of the Minutemen in the 1960s, membership in militias has ebbed and flowed with politics, usually hitting high tides when Democrats are in office. Many of these groups suggest that their rights—particularly gun rights under the Second Amendment—will be threatened when "liberals" are in power. According to the Southern Poverty Law Center, in the three years after Obama took office, the number of active militias in the United States increased eightfold.[24] By 2012, there were 1,360 radical militias and antigovernment groups, in forty-one states, with a total membership that soared into the tens of thousands.

Making a clear distinction between survivalists and those who self-identify as militia members can be tricky. Survivalist groups interested in self-sufficiency often overlap with militias concerned primarily with self-defense. Both are often rabidly antigovernment. Kurt Saxon, the man who coined the term "survivalism" in 1980, also advocated for armed revolution and wrote primers on how to create improvised weapons and munitions. Today, however, most preppers distance themselves from survivalists and militias, taking a distinctly pro-community rather than antigovernment stance.

Vicino's xPoint, then, can claim a wider variety of progenitors. Besides Almost Heaven and CUT, there was Ponderosa Village:

built by Peg and Larry Letterman in 1982, this was a one-hundred-acre "intentional community" with bomb shelters in Washington State. Two years earlier, in La Verkin, Utah, Terrene Ark I, a two-hundred-forty-unit subterranean condominium complex founded by Ron Boutwell and Lane Blackmore, quickly racked up sales, leading to discussions of franchising the model.[25] "Only group survival allows for pooling of resources and a continuing cohesive society unit," read the Terrene Ark I development prospectus. It was a false dawn: the development was abandoned in 1986. "We never got it off the ground, or in the ground, so to speak," Blackmore said at the time.[26] Finally, just outside of Topeka, Kansas, new-ager spiritualists Ed and Dianna Peden converted a seventy-eight-foot-long Atlas E missile silo into a redoubt after buying it from the US government for $40,000. Such developments could be found springing up across the country until the end of the Cold War.

The survivalists and militias of the first doom boom were the right's counterculture. They pushed conservative sentiment in the direction of libertarian populism, evincing the same sort of apocalyptic antigovernment isolationist desires we see today, and they were roundly suppressed by the state, further fueling their paranoia. Both backyard bunkers and more ideological survivalist and militia communities arose in the shadow of dread—and they never disappeared; they just went deeper underground. The backyard bunker industry, as I would soon find, is still thriving around the world.

4

Pipes in the Ground:
Burying Secret Spaces

"There are eyes everywhere. No blind spot left.
What shall we dream of when everything becomes
visible? We'll dream of being blind."
—Paul Virilio, interview with
Louis Wilson, 1994[1]

When I was about twelve years old, I had a friend named Miles
whose dad used to put us to work reloading bullet shell casings
in his garage in Riverside, California. Periodically, and spontane-
ously, he loaded the car with guns and supplies, and we all headed
for the Mojave Desert. I know now he was bugging out: retreating

to a location outside of an anticipated disaster zone. One evening during dinner he saw some kids tagging a fence by their house with spray cans. He grabbed his loaded Uzi submachine gun and went out to confront them. He returned badly beaten, and without the Uzi. My friend's dad, I realize now, was a prepper, dealing with his anxieties about the state of society by practicing escape and—not always wisely—confrontation.

I grew up in the Inland Empire of Southern California, a dry suburban outpost east of Los Angeles with marmalade sunsets, good spots for skateboarding, and a lot of methamphetamine labs. In the 1990s, gentrification in LA had pushed people inland, and houses for those transplanted rapidly replaced orange groves as the dominant feature from a car window. Some of the new arrivals were from LA gangs. The parties were always good, but my childhood was also scarred by turf wars. I was once jumped by a car full of people simply for looking at them as they passed. A couple of teenagers I knew were murdered, one of whom was bludgeoned to death with wood from a construction site. I had no idea my childhood was abnormal until I moved to England to start my PhD and casually dropped these stories into conversations at the pub. I quickly learned to stop mentioning them.

In hindsight, my drift toward prepper culture in my late thirties wasn't surprising. In my youth, I felt capable of weathering any hardship, whereas age triggered caution, resignation to casualty, and an acknowledgment of my limits. I was drawn to prepping at the point in my life when my conviction in my own invincibility was faltering, but it also reinforced my expectations of the world as a dangerous, chaotic mess. The more I thought about it, the more I was curious to know if buying a bunker brought people peace of mind. I was keen to see how the backyard shelters of the Cold War had transformed through time, to know if they were effective as a bulwark against today's threats. Luckily, since the firms building these shelters have public-facing storefronts, they weren't hard to track down. Two of the largest companies, Atlas Survival Shelters and Rising S, have assembly facilities just outside Dallas.

I headed there from Los Angeles by road and went out of my way to drive through Arizona and New Mexico via the Diné (Navajo)

Indian reservation. I pitched my tent in the dark at the edge of a mesa and awoke to a searing sunrise climbing up the red umber sandstone buttes of Monument Valley. A pale dirt road cut across the vista. There were no cars, no traffic of any kind. In the cold morning air, I stared out at the emptiness, sipping coffee. As I did, I recalled from my undergraduate classes in archaeology that the indigenous cosmology of the region is based on dividing the world into four eras. The First World was made by the "creator," but it was destroyed by fire and the people took refuge underground. In the Second World, people re-emerged from the underworld, but other animals no longer trusted them, and the world was frozen. The Third World was destroyed by floods. The people then emerged into the Fourth World, which is ours. The moral of the creation story is that just as the worlds before it were destroyed, so, too, the Fourth World will be destroyed, whether by cosmic decree or human hubris.[2]

Late in the evening I arrived in Dallas, where I checked myself into an Airstream trailer I'd booked on Airbnb, in some hipster's back garden. The Airstream, originally built in the 1960s, was old enough to be retro cool. Strung with Christmas lights, it had a couple of fold-out chairs with a firepit next to it. If you buried it, I thought, it would also make a decent bunker. It was home for the next week.

The next morning, I drove to Atlas Survival Shelters in Sulphur Springs, northeast of the city. It was easy to spot. In the front parking lot, under a giant American flag, a bright yellow truck with a vinyl wraparound sticker of a nuclear explosion on it was parked catawampus, taking up two spaces. The side of the truck had another sticker stretching across, depicting a vertical cross-section of a bunker and a phone number: 1-855-4-BUNKER. The timing of my arrival was fortuitous: workers were loading the company's signature BombNado shelter onto a flatbed truck with a forklift. They told me it would be driven to Florida and dumped into a hole in somebody's backyard. The shelter was square, about the size of a walk-in closet, made of thick metal painted matte black, and had a flange on top leading to an emergency escape hatch. It looked like an oversized woodburning stove.

The owner, a man named Ron Hubbard, wasn't there. He'd taken off to deal with an issue at a second facility he had in California and had probably been flying over me as I drove in the opposite direction. His on-site manager, Pedro, however, said he'd be happy to answer all my questions, and took me into the workshop, where a dozen massive corrugated pipe bunkers were in various stages of completion.

"These are ten-foot-diameter, galvanized corrugated steel conduits welded together that we bury twenty feet underground," Pedro told me as we walked through the factory. "We make them from thirteen-foot to fifty-one long and you can see all the sizes here," he said, nodding at the neat row of shelters.

The only shelter prepared for delivery already had the end cap welded onto it, and the ladder wouldn't be installed until it was in the ground. The only way in was to slide down the ladder chute. Pedro held my camera while I took the plunge. Inside, there was a greenish hue filtering onto the corrugated walls from some sort of weather sealant they'd been painted with. It was sweltering without the air filter running. I could see the filter in the corner: it looked like an electricity meter or built-in vacuum system. Next to it was a deep stainless-steel sink and a brown leather couch. In the adjoining room were two bunk beds. The bunker was austere, reminiscent of the fallout shelters pictured in the September 1961 issue of *Life* magazine, or a British Anderson Shelter: constructed from fourteen sheets of corrugated iron, Anderson Shelters were ubiquitous during World War II. Though there were 3.5 million of them built, they're hard to find today—many were pulled apart and had their materials repurposed after the war.[3] These bunkers, similarly, wouldn't have the lasting power of those at xPoint. It was easy to imagine them abandoned, in a state of decay, food buckets floating in a flood caused by someone's lawn sprinklers.

Pedro explained that he'd just shipped a fifty-one-footer to Canada, with an escape hatch that would be buried under just a thin layer of sod. It could be pushed through the turf with little force if the main entrance got sealed or the bunker was under attack.

"That one was rare, cool to work on," he said.

My friend Robert Macfarlane suggests that despite our best

efforts, the Earth's "underland" remains resistant to our usual forms of seeing. "It still hides much from us, even in our age of hypervisibility and ultra-scrutiny. Just a few inches of soil is enough to keep startling secrets."[4] It was bizarre to imagine these living spaces vanishing under people's lawns, visible only by their breathing tubes to the surface, so easily obscured by some shrubbery.

On my way out, I ducked into the main office. A row of fake guns was lined up next to a five-foot-high safe ostensibly full of real ones. I assumed the fake guns must have been used as props for a photo shoot or something. On the desk were stacks of structural plans and contracts and a couple of books, including *Surviving Doomsday* and the undoubtedly riveting six-hundred-plus-page *Corrugated Steel Pipe Design Manual*.

As I walked to the car, I called Robert Vicino to get his opinion on backyard shelters. When I told him where I was, he howled with laughter.

"Those shelters can't have viable air filtration for twenty thousand or whatever Ron Hubbard is asking," he told me. "And anyway, some of those things are fifteen feet long—even Japanese people would feel cramped in them!" I waited for Vicino's laughter to tail off. Then he continued: "The more serious problem with what they're doing is that those bunkers are made of corrugated pipe; they're not going to survive, Brad. They're only making them like that so that they're shippable. These guys are selling widgets, not serious bunkers." He promised to email over an academic journal article about how the 6.7-magnitude Northridge earthquake in 1994 collapsed a large-diameter flexible corrugated metal pipe at the Lower San Fernando Dam.

"When people ask me about those shelters," he said by way of signing off, "I always tell them 'I wouldn't be caught dead in one of those. . . .' Get it?" Within minutes, the article had dropped into my phone's inbox.

As I sat in my car reading through it, I thought that comparing the structural integrity of a reinforced concrete bunker to a pipe welded together in a shop didn't really make sense.[5] Architecturally, they were a world apart. But getting a backyard shelter also didn't require complicated community planning with a property developer at the helm. More to the point, while xPoint appeared to be having trouble attracting a full community through the gates, the Atlas warehouse was packed with bunkers and churning with activity. There was so much business to be had, in fact, that there was enough market share for Rising S Bunker to also be doing steady business across town. I spun back onto the highway to go see.

I drove south through Texas for an hour to Murchison, past prime grazing country and sprawling ranch houses. When I arrived at Rising S, the massive shop floor had teams of people swarming around dozens of angular multiroom quarter-inch-steel-plate bunkers, their stairwell escape shafts reaching up to the ceiling. The whole scene struck me as a bit, well, Freudian.[6] Certainly my Oxford colleague Ian Klinke would have seen it that way; he always said the desire to get into a bunker was a subconscious desire to crawl back into the safety of the womb.

While I waited for Gary Lynch, the CEO, to appear, I chatted with Ned, a gangly shelter engineer in an oil-smeared blue jumpsuit and frameless glasses so dirty they were almost opaque. Ned took me through a bunker and showed me the kitchen and the standard NBC filtration setup, but refused to tell me where any of the bunkers were being shipped.

"You got one of these in your backyard?" I asked.

He stopped and looked at me, considering. "If there was going to be a nuclear war, I'd just want to die." Elaborating, he said he thought people were terrified of death because they didn't have religion: in his eyes, the bunker was just a stalling mechanism for not making peace with God.

"If these bunkers give people peace, fine, who am I to judge, but what is it in life that people are clinging to so desperately?" he said. "But hey, maybe these are just somebody's man cave and it's all the time they get to themselves, fixing it up. It may have nothing to do with the end of the world."

Gary Lynch emerged from his office in a tidy plaid button-up shirt tucked into a large belt buckle. He smiled at me through a gray goatee, shook my hand firmly, and then gestured sweepingly across the shop floor.

"There you have it; we can't build these things fast enough," he said. His phone rang and he held up a finger, then answered it and walked away. Ned shrugged as if to say, "Yeah, good luck with that," and bustled over to a shower of sparks coming from one of the teams.

"Sorry about that," Lynch said when he returned. "But this is a perfect example of what's wrong with society. I've got this woman calling me to ask for directions to a property they want to survey that doesn't come up on Google Maps. How are they going to survey what they can't find?" Lynch's accent was lush: he sounded like an actor playing a Texan.

"People aren't taught to be free thinkers and to use their own common sense," he said, shaking his head. "When her computer or phone screen doesn't tell her what to do, she freezes. They're like sheep looking for a shepherd."

I asked when business kicked off here. "One word: 9/11," Lynch responded. "The United States took a major turn during the World Trade Center ordeal." Lynch put forward a widespread conspiracy theory: that the airplanes that had crashed into the Twin Towers weren't commercial airliners; that it was a planned act necessary to get the Patriot Act passed, thereby facilitating a massive expansion of US government surveillance over its citizens. He described it as "the biggest single loss of freedom in American history." Lynch's phone rang and he walked away again briefly, clearly exasperated to see it was the same number before picking up. As he walked off, I mulled over the conspiracy theory. It wasn't so surprising to me that people who didn't trust government and media latched on to such ideas. After all, the 9/11 attacks *were* used as a justification for expanding government surveillance of citizens. Neither was it so surprising that dread merchants like Lynch would take it a step further. After all, the events of 9/11 had been good for business on two fronts, bringing in customers worried about terrorism and customers who wanted to hide from state surveillance.

"Anyway." Lynch was back. "Yeah, politics plays a role. Sales increased seven hundred percent from 2015 to 2016. Many of our new clients were liberals buying in because of the uncertainty introduced by Trump's election."[7] This was a novel demographic for

Lynch, different from the post-9/11 crowd. "So," he said, "I'll walk you through and you can ask whatever you want."

I waded in. "I was just thinking: these bunkers are like wombs, and I saw that you have crosses in your logo," I said. "Is there a religious message here in the idea of being reborn from the bunker?"

"That's exactly correct. Clyde, the owner of the company, made that sunburst of the three crosses of Calvary for the logo," Lynch said, inspecting a weld. Clyde Scott was out of town, but Lynch was happy to let me in on the fact that Rising S was short for Rising Son: an allusion to the resurrection. "It's Clyde's belief that Jesus Christ died for our sins, and so sure, the bunker is like the cave Jesus came out of. But there are many parallels in life. . . . The company wasn't started for that reason. We were already manufacturing, and we had a prepper mentality, and things just happened in society that caused product evolution. When something big happens in the news, which is basically every day now, we get more orders."

"What's the difference between the bunkers you build and shelters from the Cold War?"

"Comfort. I mean, if you can afford it why be stuck underground in a cage? Everybody cracks differently. When one of my clients asks me, 'How long can we stay down there?' I tell them: if you've got food and water and don't need medical attention, you don't need to come out."

"What's the longest someone has stayed in one that you know of?"

"We did one in Venezuela for this guy that travels between there and Panama. When civil unrest came to a head last year, he went into the bunker. I sent him an email to see if he was all right, and I didn't hear anything back home for five or six weeks. When he emerged from the bunker, he replied, saying everything was fine and he was headed to Panama. He had to abandon the bunker, but he's alive and that's all that matters."

The bunkers Lynch was leading me through felt like more robust versions of a shipping container. You could piece them together to make larger bunkers, a bit like Lego. This made for easy transportation, since they could be assembled at the other end before they were put in the ground. Lynch said the largest he ever assembled, outside Salt Lake City, could house a hundred people. He also described some of Rising S's methods of covert excavation and installation, meant to keep the existence of the safe space secret from those who might seek it out in a disaster. It made sense that if you had a bunker you'd want to maintain operations security (OPSEC) during its construction so that you didn't end up with your neighbors pounding on the blast door begging to get in after an event. (In fact, there's a famous episode of Rod Serling's *The Twilight Zone*, called "The Shelter," about this very idea.) One client, Lynch said, paid for his neighbors to go on holiday so that they wouldn't see him digging. When they came back, he told them he'd decided to resod the lawn.

"We made a fake sign for a landscaping company and everything," Lynch said, laughing.

I recalled that Burlington, the underground city I broke into with the urban explorers in 2010, was supposed to be secret. Its existence wasn't made public until the inimitable British investigative journalist Duncan Campbell revealed its whereabouts in his book *War Plan UK*—a reveal that eventually led to the declassification and abandonment of the facility. Secrecy, after all, is paramount to the function of a bunker, whether in the hands of a private individual or a state. Governments around the world continue to protect their underland secrets, and deny their citizens a right to do the same. You might say that building a secret bunker is an act of civil disobedience in an age when almost everything is meant to be seen, known, tracked, and traced by the corporate state.

Lynch took another call, leaving me to wander the shop floor and ponder the trade-off between security and privacy. The Cold War satellites that once took spy photos have given way to newer ones that have provided us with the Global Positioning System (GPS) and can guide nuke-tipped ICBMs, but they also created a volumetric network of control and surveillance.[8] This is the same surveillance network being wielded by our governments to spy on us. These networks surround us: they are not just in the air but also in the ground—in the form of fiber-optic cables and data servers—

and in our pockets and bags, embedded in our everyday technologies, which are near impossible to opt out of.

One of my early mentors, the American cultural anthropologist Adam Fish, has delved into these issues more than most. He argues that we have entered a new stage of capitalism called technoliberalism, a form of governance in which politicians across the spectrum are willing to erode civil liberties, the environment, and the social safety net in exchange for campaign financing and cozy relationships with the wealthy libertarian technology companies that are turning all our movements, purchases, and relationships into usable (and sellable) data.[9] Athens-based artist James Bridle, who uses technology as a medium, suggests that this widespread acceptance of surveillance culture is the catalyst for a "new dark age," a paranoid feedback loop in which "the failure to comprehend a complex world leads to the demand for more and more information, which only further clouds our understanding." More information, Bridle writes, doesn't provide more clarity, but rather more confusion.[10]

All of this has created a permanent pathology of "autoscopy"— where, in the words of another keen student of our changing cultural habits, Texas-born cultural theorist Ryan Bishop, each of us is seeing ourselves "as a self viewing itself: both viewing subject and viewed object" all the time.[11] That's to say, we will forevermore live without knowing whether we're being ourselves or a version of ourselves that we know is being watched. Alienation from the self only intensifies dread.

With advancements in imaging and with the advent of drone technology, government surveillance has become increasingly granular. A decade ago, the United States Air Force (USAF) deployed over Afghanistan a technology it calls the Gorgon Stare: a spherical array of nine cameras attached to a drone that can transmit live video images of physical movement across an entire town.[12] The USAF also used a similar system in Iraq: a 192-megapixel twelve-camera array, attached to a small plane, which was capable of tracking every vehicle and person across an area the size of a small city, for several hours at a time.

Within a few years, this technology moved from the battlefield to US city streets. A company with the ominous name Persistent Surveillance Systems, run by tech entrepreneur and Air Force Academy graduate Ross McNutt, worked with Baltimore police to secretly monitor all human movement across the city in 2016, field tests that were conducted for up to ten hours a day with small Cessna airplanes.[13] In 2020, despite numerous objections from civil rights groups, Baltimore approved use of the system, citing the need for the technology's effectiveness in gathering evidence of criminal activity. Having these planes in the air means that anyone living in Baltimore who steps out of their front door may have their every movement traced without their knowledge—and that includes the police. The 2016 field tests recorded images that contradicted officers' reports of shooting a suspect through his windshield while stopping him for not wearing a seat belt.[14] The officers had no idea the incident was being recorded from the air.

"Gorgon Stare" was an apt name for the program that spawned these technologies. "Gorgon" derives from the Greek word for dread: *gorgós*. In Hesiod's *Theogony*, a Greek poem from 700 BCE, three cave-dwelling Gorgons with venomous snakes for hair would literally petrify anyone who looked at them.[15] Our idea of the Gorgon, though, comes from Homer. In the *Iliad*, he wrote of the Gorgon Medusa, who was beheaded by Perseus in her cave after he used his mirrored shield to see her without looking at her. Her head, retaining its power to petrify, was given as a gift to Athena, the goddess of wisdom and war, to be placed on her shield, so that the terrible petrifying glare could paralyze mortals with dread during battle.[16] According to historian Caroline Alexander, "this conjecture conjures the dread object's power to petrify—to turn to stone—all who gaze upon it. . . . The most terrifying conceivable object, the Greeks well knew, was not a snake-haired monster of imagination, but the concrete work of human hands."[17] There is no doubt that surveillance systems are the result of such work. At present, the underground is the last place human beings, free of the Gorgon's stare, can exist without dread of being traced and tracked.

However, this may not last for long. In 2017, the US Defense Advanced Research Projects Agency (DARPA) held a "subterranean challenge," in which it solicited bids for techniques to enhance "situational awareness" of global underground areas, with a $2 million–

prize purse. The challenge was to create machines that could make their way through tunnel systems, urban undergrounds, and natural caves. Robots had to be able to climb, crawl, squeeze, and sense their way through these environments, with an eye toward future deployment in underground environments that human bodies can't access—like the air intake system of a bunker. Though the competition won't be complete until 2021, a team from Carnegie Mellon University and Oregon State University took home first prize in the inaugural round. The robots they built may well become autonomous subterranean avatars, capable of seeking, finding, and destroying underground redoubts. Their deployment will mean that there really is nowhere left to hide.

Gary Lynch returned from his phone call with apologies. Having thought about the steps his company took to conceal the location of the bunkers they installed, I had a question ready: "Is it Christian to hide your salvation from your neighbors?"

"No," Gary acknowledged. "But in the aftermath there will be a new community of people: they just might not know each other at first. The social contract will be rewritten. I've buried five or six bunkers within forty miles of here. Eventually, those people would find each other. I've got areas in the US where we have a really high concentration of bunkers. Within central Texas I have an area that is probably a ten-square-mile radius with twenty-five bunkers. Vegas is a hot spot, too."

"What do people in those places tell you they fear?" I asked.

"People worry about four major things: nuclear war, government collapse, financial collapse, and social unrest. Any one triggers the other, but I think the economy goes down first. The country is twenty-something trillion dollars in debt. How do you recover from that? And that's happened in twenty to twenty-five years." Gary had a point. On top of the astounding national debt, by 2020, 45 million Americans owed $1.6 trillion in student loans alone. According to the Brookings Institution, a centrist American think tank in Washington, DC, 40 percent of these borrowers are likely to default on those loans by 2023.[18] I am one of those 45 million, and like other Millennials I work long hours, pay exorbitant rent, own no property or assets, and have no intention of paying off those loans. Student loans are now second only to mortgage debt in the country, and unless drastic relief is offered—of the sort the US government offered to the banking, airline, and automobile sectors after the 2007–08 financial crisis, or the trillions shoveled into the economy during the COVID-19 pandemic—the situation is bound to implode. What that looks like, no one knows. It's an unprecedented situation, like so much of what we've experienced of late.

"So, if people don't know what's coming, are you building for the unknown?"

"That is not correct," Gary replied in his sprawling Texas register. "There are not more unknowns these days, there's just a lot more awareness created by media, our phones, technology, communication. When you were a child, I was a child. There weren't cell phones. There really wasn't email. Things went a lot slower. There could have been a disaster somewhere, but you might not know about it for a couple days because you had to wait for a newswire with all the information—probably factual information back then—to make it to the *Dallas Morning News* or the *Boston Globe*. By the time you got that information, often the situation had been resolved. Information is moving faster, society is going in debt faster, everything's happening faster." It was jarring, but not surprising, to hear Lynch talk about factual information and media distortion when he had, just thirty minutes earlier, pitched an unproven conspiracy theory to me.

Gary's phone rang again, followed by the now familiar ritual: finger held up to halt our conversation, he retreated into one of his nearly complete bunkers. I could see him through the open door: phone pressed to his ear with one hand, running the other lovingly along a freshly installed kitchen countertop. I was left standing in an aisle bordered by a few dozen steel bunkers. One of the other doorways was lit up by flickering blue light: sparks from a welder—the only color in the building other than a yellow crane hanging overhead, used to load the bunkers onto flatbeds.

As much as anything, the second backyard shelter doom boom seemed fueled by an overwhelming desire to hide. Gary's diagnosis—that everything was now happening faster—was right in line with some of the most significant thinking on our rapidly changing world. Paul Virilio, one of the most influential explorers of our accelerating society, developed a philosophy of speed, which he called dromology: the logic that demonstrates how connectivity is introducing complexity and shrinking room for error.[19] Back at xPoint, Milton had told me that his bunker was the only place he felt alone, and I'd experienced much the same sensation for myself. For me, this sense of being constantly watched and monitored, my life reduced to a series of algorithms sitting on some massive corporate-owned server, always feels more overwhelming than the idea of nuclear war or the climate crisis. I feel like a fish in a trawler net, pointlessly flopping around, trying to get back to the ocean.

Lynch emerged from his bunker phone call. "What do you think of the bunker communities people are building?" I asked him. "Is a community a good model for survival?"

"It's not," he replied, pinging off a text message. "Places like xPoint, where the location is known—people will converge on those locations. And," he added, "who are you going to be stuck in there with? It's like living in a high-rise building. Just because someone can afford to be there doesn't mean that they're not a child molester, psychopath, or rapist. Our clients are responsible individuals who see a bunker as an insurance policy. They don't like to be called preppers. Look at Weaver at Ruby Ridge, David Koresh, they were all survivalists. It took a few big hits like that for the idea of preppers to emerge—no one wanted to be a survivalist anymore. Now with preppers the media have made a lot of them out to be complete lunatics, and those people will be attracted to those communities, you know they'll attract each other."

Having spent hours upon hours watching National Geographic's 2012 series *Doomsday Preppers*, I knew what Lynch meant. The show used foreboding music and a throaty "voice of God" narration to introduce preppers as paranoid and obsessive antiheroes motivated by extreme ideologies—in other words, the same as the survivalists who preceded them.[20]

"And just like survivalists," Lynch continued, "you're going to have the government there on day one to round those people up and disarm them. The people paying to get into those communities are doing exactly what that woman on the phone was doing, relying on somebody else to take care of your problems. A hundred and fifty years ago, everybody had a garden, they were self-sufficient, now I can't even fix this thing," he said, holding up his phone. Technology, he was suggesting, was causing us to lose agency over our lives. "It's gonna take some kind of traumatic event to hit reset," he concluded. I had to admit that Lynch made the bunker seem like a totally rational addition to the house, a place of safety from future disaster, yes, but also a hidey-hole from overbearing state and corporate technologies.

On the way out, I saw Ned and went over to press him on where these bunkers were going. He told me that Rising S was in the General Services Administration (GSA) catalogue now, and some of the bunkers were being purchased by the government. "Does that concern you?" I asked. "That the government wants bunkers from private contractors?"

Ned was tight-lipped. "I can't tell you about it," he said, shrugging. "Some of them are simple storm shelters. But otherwise I can't talk about it." It was obvious that business was good for the backyard bunker builders, but that the US government was clearly one of Rising S's main customers came as something of a surprise.

Back in the Airstream trailer, I started reading up on my final destination in Texas. North of Dallas, a new community called Trident Lakes was forming that looked like it might rival xPoint in scale and sounded almost sumptuous in comparison. The website for the development described lagoons, a helipad, a spa, and a golf course inside the bunker complex. As I scrolled through the images of the blue lagoons on my phone, warming myself next to the firepit outside the trailer, it started snowing.

5

Texas Redoubt:
Tribulation in Style

"Anyone who either cannot lead the common life or is so self-sufficient as not to need to, and therefore does not partake of society, is either a beast or a god."
>   —Aristotle, *Politics: A Treatise on Government*, fourth century BCE[1]

I waited for Jim O'Connor, CEO of Trident Lakes, at a McDonald's in North Dallas. Between sips of burned coffee, I put a fresh battery in my camera; on a wall-mounted plasma screen, Donald Trump was emphatically denying that Russia interfered in the

United States presidential election. At the table next to me, a Bible study group was in full swing. I overheard one of the group members tell the others through a mouthful of Sausage McMuffin: "Six months after 9/11 happened my brother tells me he's just glad he wasn't there. I tell him he'll get his chance."

The group leader responded, raising a Bible over the table, "Amen, you tell your brother that Satan will take the form of the beast!" There were murmurs of approval. Across the restaurant, in a corner booth, a man was holding his knees and rocking, yelling "motherfucker!" repeatedly at the top of his lungs. No one but me seemed to notice.

Since I was in Dallas to see an under-construction doomsday community, I took these as auspicious omens: the end times were all around me. In its promotional materials, Trident Lakes touted itself as "a five-star playground with DEFCON 1 preparedness."[2] The development—a one-square-mile plot incorporating six hundred semisubterranean condominiums ranging in price from $500,000 to $1.5 million, will boast resort-style amenities, including a one-hundred-square-foot equestrian center, a golf course, a spa, restaurants, and retail outlets. An eight-foot security wall made of shipping containers will enclose eight hundred fifty reinforced, subterranean luxury condominiums, a navigable tunnel system, a shooting range, a school, a DNA vault, and helipads. The phases of the construction are named after Italian medieval towns—Lucca, Perugia, Montagnana, Verona—to add a splash of upmarket Euro chic.

The Epcot Center aesthetics of the property were due to the influence of the founder, John Eckerd, a millionaire in his midfifties, long involved in a range of slightly off-color business ventures. On his website, Eckerd describes himself as a "serial entrepreneur." He made his first wad working with satellite and television hardware, then moved into producing exercise videos, including the *Dallas Cowboys Cheerleaders Country Western Workout*—still available on Amazon for twenty bucks—and a NASCAR-themed porno called *Track Girls Gone Nutz*, which NASCAR sued him over.[3] Just before the global financial crash in 2008, Eckerd began designing and building armored limousines to ferry around sports and film stars, including the basketball superstar Shaquille O'Neal (Shaq), who later became a backer of Trident Lakes (according to their director of celebrity relations, Paul Salfen).

I'd imagined Jim O'Connor to have bleached teeth and a fake tan, so I was surprised when he walked through the door with wispy brown hair wearing a cream-colored knitted sweater, and gold wire-frame glasses. He looked like an affable high school math teacher. We drove north through falling snow flurries that covered the ground in a soft carpet of white. From the passenger seat, he gave patient directions, moving me into the appropriate lanes long before I needed to make a turn. His speech and manner were precise, and his answers offered at a friendly distance. I got the sense that Christmas at his house would be perfect.

We drove through a small town called Ector, composed of one brick building and some clapboard houses: population 695. As we crawled down an empty highway, snow pellets swirled into tiny funnels on the verge. Then, O'Connor pointed to a fallow agricultural field, in which a sixty-foot fountain ringed by four stone horses suddenly emerged from the pale backdrop. It was wrapped in plastic like a new toy. As we pulled up to it, I asked him if the horses symbolized the four horsemen of the apocalypse; he shrugged. The fountain, purportedly one of the largest in the United States, was the gateway to Trident Lakes. It also seemed a Potemkin flourish, given that no condos had yet been built.

I pulled up near the fountain and we got out. As I took photos, Jim shivered alongside me in the cold and apologized. "There was a statue of Poseidon on the top, but a contractor knocked it off and it smashed," he said. "We'll fix it soon."

As I snapped away, I told O'Connor about the backyard bunker factories I'd visited earlier in the week, explaining the premium the owners placed on secrecy to maintain security, and queried the logic of calling out the location of Trident Lakes with the fountain. He didn't seem fretful about the possibility that the prominent feature, and the media attention surrounding the project, would pose a problem in keeping future residents safe. Even if people came looking for bounty, he insisted that the security architecture would make it a "high-risk target." He thought that most people would be huddled up during a disaster, not wandering the streets with a plague on the loose, or gassing around under radioactive fallout, looting the locality. Besides, if Dallas was nuked or swept by disease, Trident Lakes was eighty miles away.

"If we have families moving in, at an average of four per unit, that's twenty-four hundred people. If they've got the right skills shared between them, we have a totally internal community here capable of sustaining itself." I told him he made it sound like a commune.

O'Connor stared at me and blinked. "This isn't political," he said. "I have an interest in politics, but I've been frustrated that politicians aren't coming up with solutions. . . . What we're trying to build is a total solution matrix." He paused, looking up at the broken fountain. "This is John's vision," he said, referring to Eckerd, Trident Lakes' entrepreneur owner. "He's always had an interest in building a prepper community." He tailed off uncomfortably.

I soon found out why. It turned out O'Connor's vision was rather different from Eckerd's. O'Connor focused on the environment, and on ecological sustainability, and saw Trident Lakes as a test bed for renewable technology. Creating a village that could produce its own water, food, energy, education, and entertainment would draw on innovations such as superefficient solar panels that followed the sun, large-scale compost systems, and machines that could distill water from the air via condensation. O'Connor wanted Trident Lakes to function totally off-grid in the present; he seemed to care less about the end-of-days scenarios.

Leaving the fountain, we drove for another ten minutes, down a dirt lane past clusters of grazing horses, their manes powder-coated with snowfall. As we drove, it struck me that even though Eckerd's concerns were global ones, the "solution matrix," as O'Connor described it, was local. O'Connor wasn't interested in America-as-world-police geopolitics, he was concerned about himself and his family, and in finding "like-minded" people with whom he could build something new. But even more important, in striving toward self-sufficiency, O'Connor almost saw prepping as a challenge to governance that needs people to be afraid, dependent, living hand to mouth, and reliant on government infrastructure.[4] Unlike the backyard bunkers that are often never utilized after burial, Trident Lakes would be an island village for the present where people could prepare for a self-sufficient future.

The landscape further in was a pastoral roll of fields divvied up by birch stands, weeping willows, and old oaks. Small lagoons had been created in depressions—by previous landowners, I guessed, as water holes for cattle. Now they would play a new role, O'Connor explained, as the eponymous lakes of Trident Lakes. He explained that as the site was developed, the depressions would be cleaned out and backfilled with clean, white beach sand. The water itself would be dyed azure (using nontoxic chemicals, he assured me), and the "lakes" would serve as hubs around which the condominium complex would be built. Each block of condos would be crafted from a specially prepared plastic resin called Ellox, produced by the security firm Chubb. This resin could be poured like concrete and mixed with synthetic material harder than diamond. The finished structures would be bulletproof and able to withstand heat up to 1,000°C (1,832°F). In his book *A Burglar's Guide to the City*, Geoff Manaugh, of the renowned speculative architecture website BLDGBLOG, says that the use of materials like this makes it easy to imagine that such structures would be the "last architectural structures standing after the collapse of civilization."[5] If the monuments we leave behind as we move from one age to another are material rebellions against finitude, these plastic bunkers could be the last remaining artifacts, outlasting even concrete.[6] As a former archaeologist, I secretly enjoyed imagining that Trident Lakes would become the Mesa Verde or Çatalhöyük of the twenty-second century. I envisaged some future researcher spending a lifetime trying to decode the "secrets" of the bunker ruins.

We arrived at the base camp and staging area for the project, a two-story, three-bedroom residence that must have been the ranch house for the property before Eckerd bought it. The dining room next to the kitchen had been transformed into a meeting area, with a large ebony table surrounded by bar stools.

O'Connor had contacted Eckerd to let him know I'd arrived, and that I wanted to interview him. While we waited to hear back, O'Connor showed me site plans at the table. It wasn't a blueprint, though; it was a slick 3D CGI model. We zoomed through a virtual world with wide, clean roads leading to the condos, each of which had an outdoor patio with a pool and BBQ and easy access to the beckoning soft white beaches of the lagoon. The rendering looked like the online video game *Second Life*, with methodically plotted flowering trees, beach chairs, and little avatars mingling around the BBQ, swimming in the lake, and punching a beach ball back and forth. This was phase one, called Verona: it had space for 104 units and maybe three times as many people.

The units themselves were half buried in a semicircle. Large round support columns and steel walls bolted together and covered with the Ellox pour would be packed with a layer of structural foam and rammed earth to shield each residence. Double-clicking on the condos took us behind ballistic-resistant sliding glass patio doors. Rotating the view in the living room revealed in the ceiling blast panels that could be slammed down to isolate this condo from the others, buttoning up the bunker. Once they were closed, light would be supplied through CoeLux artificial windows, O'Connor explained.

CoeLux is an Italian company making simulated windows that use nanotechnology to artificially produce "natural" light by emulating the temporal rhythm of the sun's movement through the sky. This provides, according to CoeLux's website, a "sensation of infinite space."[7] The website product page offers both "Tropical" and "Mediterranean" packages. O'Connor assured me that, psychologically, there was no difference between real windows and CoeLux: important, given that the shutters that rolled down over the front windows of the condos would blot out all natural light. In addition, of course, to blocking out pathogens, radiation fallout, and conventional weaponry.

"Once the blast shield is in place, this should also effectively make the condo a Faraday cage," O'Connor said. This would block magnetic fields, allowing for preservation of electronics in the event of an EMP.

With EMP-hardened solar panels on the roof, ventless clothes dryers, a water recycling system by EcoloBlue that would pull twenty-six gallons of water out of the air per day, and another device by the Swedish company Orbital Systems that recycled

90 percent of water used and reduced the energy to heat it by 80 percent, these condos—so O'Connor assured me—would be completely self-sufficient. He'd done extensive research into these technologies, even touring the Orbital Systems factory in Malmö.

"This is technology developed for a NASA Mars mission that we're putting into the Earth shelter," O'Connor said, before asking me not to photograph the CGI models.

This all sounded expensive. I asked him where the seed money was coming from, and O'Connor replied, "John's mind is firing at all times with different ideas." He explained that in addition to his armored limousines and exercise videos, Eckerd also had an ice sculpture business and made a great deal of money facilitating tire transport for autonomous mining vehicles in Western Australia. And they were chasing a new opportunity, looking at purchasing coal impoundments, or "ponds," in Appalachia, where they'd found lithium in the mine tailings that might be salvaged and sold to make electric car batteries.

"The future of renewable energy," O'Connor told me, "might just be inside coal."

"This all sounds great," I said, "but isn't there a disjunction here between raising money through mining and implementing 'green' technologies in the condos?"

"No," O'Connor responded flatly. "The technological and sustainable elements at Trident Lakes are not driven by ideology. Lower energy consumption is not about climate change—and, by the way, no evidence has been produced that that's been induced by humans—it's about making the structures more efficient. We're driven by what's possible today, not by politics."

Jim's was an instrumental view of technology, one purely based on function. His was a view replicated more generally among the dread merchants. They weren't interested in using sustainable, clean technologies to mitigate disaster. Their deployment was a last-ditch effort at stalling our demise after our failure to achieve mastery of the Earth—which, as far as many of them were concerned, was now just a giant piece of failing technology.[8] Sustainable tech was simply a means by which to squeeze through the next jam, like hitting the ejector seat on a crashing fighter jet.

The problem with this plan, however, is similar to the problem with geo-engineering our way out of the climate crisis: technology is what created the disaster in the first place. Asking people to put faith in science to solve the problems science caused seems like perverted logic—it's an endless feedback loop.[9] The crisis we face as a species doesn't have to be cataclysmic: it might just be our continual failure to fix a slow leak. Perhaps O'Connor had a more realistic perspective than I did. People were never going to give up their cars, their technologies, or their plentiful options at the grocery store voluntarily, and governments were never going to make them do so. Trident Lakes was a test bed for solutions that might help in the long term, without forgoing those comforts in the meantime.

Though O'Connor was a bit of a technophile, he also recognized that cooperation was the crux of maintaining social stability after an event. It was vital that everyone contributed to the group.

"Every person who wants to move into Trident Lakes is required to fill out a form on the website, which clearly states their reasons for moving into the community," he told me. "The form also asks them to be explicit about what skills and contributions they can offer." He opened an Excel spreadsheet on his laptop and showed me hundreds of responses that he'd collected so far. Expecting it to be full of gruff language from hard-nosed ex-military types, I was surprised to find that the range of responses pointed to a diverse demographic and a wide variety of motivating factors.

A fifty-four-year-old Christian woman in Texas named Judy, with a net worth of more than $1 million, declared that she was a trained horseback rider and marksman, taught Sunday school music classes, and was firm in her belief that "community living with mutual goals is my utopia." After reading about it "in some prepper magazine," she thought Trident Lakes would be the ideal place to find this utopia.

If all went according to plan, Judy might end up living next to Jeb, a sixty-five-year-old "extreme conservative Christian with a massive biotech background" who enjoyed "bluegrass gospel music" and offered a skill set on "anti-aging, tissue and organ regeneration," hinting that he might volunteer to run the future DNA vault where they would store residents' genetic profiles. Was this vault, I asked O'Connor, built with the idea of potentially resurrecting people later in time?

He shrugged. "It's just another layer of security, Brad." I wasn't sure what that meant, but perhaps it gave people solace to know there was some part of them preserved even if the worst-case scenario—not surviving—were to happen.

There were some common themes among respondents. Many had military and law enforcement backgrounds: there was a senior officer with the Houston Police Department, and another respondent who claimed to be a former chief of police. Some of these individuals offered their "riot control" experience in maintaining order both outside and inside the gates: one had served on police "active shooter response" and "crowd control dispersal" teams. Other respondents offered less straightforward contributions. One, a sixty-two-year-old man from Oklahoma, indicated with the drop-down box that he had "below average physical fitness" and wrote, "I like being the gray man who blends in." His next sentence made me wonder exactly how well he *would* blend in: if he found people standing around, he wrote with vague menace, he would "compel them to contribute."

Every single person, without exception, had labeled their personality either as "calm" or "intellectual"; many proffered community classes in woodworking, oil painting, jujitsu, tennis, or language training. O'Connor's imagined utopia was beginning to take shape: a community of overachieving and wealthy but also overworked and lonely people coming together to cultivate and share skills in a cashless closed society; a carefully crafted community—including, I noticed, a hobbyist in "armadillo trapping."[10]

O'Connor had to take some calls in his office and left me to ponder. I stood at a large window in the living room, looking out through a white veil of snowfall. I could just about make out some horses grazing next to a deserted backhoe that looked poised to dredge one of the lagoons. Lacking the vision of a property developer, I had a hard time reimagining the murky pool surrounded by tired-looking willow trees and snow-sprinkled pastures as a thriving one-square-mile community of doomsday preppers, sunbathing before their archery lessons.

That night, the Airstream trailer I was staying in had no running water. The pipes snaking to it from the main house were frozen solid. I cocooned myself in a pile of blankets, and scrolled through James Wesley, Rawles's SurvivalBlog.com, the most widely read prepper blog on the planet.[11] I'd become familiar with posts on the website, and with the sentiment, frequently expressed in the blog's comments, that a crisis was due, inevitable, and even necessary, as well as Rawles's contention that what he called the American Redoubt—Idaho, Montana, Wyoming, eastern Oregon, and eastern Washington—was the place to be in such a scenario. According to the Southern Poverty Law Center, Rawles once called Islam a "religion of evil and death," and thinks a "war of world views" may come as early as 2021.[12] I was never quite able to find a foundation text behind the ideology. That night, however, as I read, I struck gold. According to Rawles, the 2021 date is not random: it was ordained in a 1997 book called *The Fourth Turning*, which I'd never heard of. I downloaded the book and started reading.

Written by pop sociologist William Strauss and California-based consultant Neil Howe, *The Fourth Turning* pitches a cyclical understanding of history called Generational Theory. The core idea is that major events take place within a one-hundred-year cycle. The cycle has four "seasons," each lasting roughly twenty-five years: growth (The High), maturation (The Awakening), entropy (The Unraveling), and destruction (The Crisis). This temporal structure bears remarkable similarities to the cosmology of the Diné and Hopi people of the American Southwest, who also break their world into four epochs. As I'd recalled on top of the mesa in Monument Valley on my way to Dallas, the Hopi call the world we're in the Fourth World.

"We cannot stop the seasons of history," Strauss and Howe write, "but we can prepare for them."[13] It's a philosophical outlook that argues that life's purpose is to learn to ride the cycles of rebirth—precisely the kind of rebirth that the bunker facilitates.

These ideas also mirror the meaning of the original Greek

word for apocalypse: *apokalyptein*, a crisis that brings about disclosure and renewal. Apocalyptic thinking disrupts our sense of things as immutable and timeless, and the Greeks thought it was healthy.[14] It kept a culture or society from becoming too deeply entrenched in a particular way of life. Throughout human history, when civilizations have reached what seems to be a stagnant phase, apocalyptic thinking surfaces. It's not—as commonly assumed—a termination, but an acknowledgment of the turning of the wheel of time, combined with a hope of seeing time through to its next revolution.

Within the one-hundred-year cycle of Strauss and Howe's Generational Theory, years eighty to one hundred are a crucial "fourth turning," marked by a crisis that upends the social order and creates a new one, after which a new cycle commences. According to the authors, the USA is now in a twenty-year period of entropy that will result in an opportunity for the prepared who make it through "winter" to shape the next age.

Generational Theory, I discovered as I continued my research, has spooked elites, who envision populist pitchforks. It has also intrigued them as a potential opportunity to create new structures that benefit them when we emerge from the Unraveling. Steve Bannon, the former executive chairman of Breitbart News and the populist strategist who gets much of the credit for propelling Trump into the White House, is a believer. Bannon directed a film called *Generation Zero* based on Strauss-Howe Generational Theory (and featuring Howe). In the chaotic early days of the Trump administration, Bannon could be seen carrying the book into meetings with the president. He felt that his insider knowledge of the Generational Theory gave him an edge—an edge he presumably tried to pass on to Trump, but the president sent him packing.

Undeterred, Bannon took his apocalyptic right-wing populism on tour to Europe, where it dovetailed nicely with the political ambitions of Jacob Rees-Mogg, one of the arch-engineers of Brexit, the UK's prolonged and painful exit from the European Union. Bannon and Rees-Mogg met privately in a London Mayfair hotel in 2017 to discuss the advancement of the conservative movement in the UK. It seems no small coincidence that both men were among the puppet masters behind what we might call "pro-collapse governments," in both the US and the UK. Leaders in these movements see chaos as an opportunity to seize wealth and power. Rather than geopolitics, it's a kind of chronopolitics, a way of leveraging power by propagating short-term chaos.[15]

It seemed to me, as I plugged in my phone and turned in for the night, that *The Fourth Turning* is a secular interpretation of the millennialism that provides fuel for devout doomsday preppers. It seems like a building block of the prepper ideology, in which bunkers—from Trident Lakes to xPoint—are imagined by their developers as spaces for transmutation during the turning.

For now, though, there wasn't much to see at Trident Lakes; construction on the condos hadn't yet begun, and the workers were all waiting out the bad weather. Nevertheless, I hung out with the team for three days, trying to extract more information on the project from O'Connor and Paul Salfen, a Dallas-based TV host.

On the drive back to Trident Lakes from my Airbnb on day two, we all carpooled together from Dallas. On the drive, Salfen told me from the backseat that investment by key individuals was crucial to the development's success.

"John Eckerd has known Shaq for a long time and of course he's going to be involved in this project—to what extent I don't know," he said, leaning into the area between the front seats of the car. Shaq, or Shaquille O'Neal, the former basketball player, once said on his own podcast that he believes the Earth is flat (and then later said he was "trolling" listeners).[16] "Also, Donnie Wahlberg and Jenny McCarthy will be out here for the opening, so you'll want to be here for that." I wasn't sure adding Wahlberg, a founding member of the 1990s boy band New Kids on the Block, and McCarthy, an ex–*Playboy* model and prominent critic of child vaccinations, to the mix was the best publicity for the development, but I guessed controversy would also sell condos.

More to the point, having millionaires involved seemed incongruous with O'Connor's vision of a bourgeois middle-class community of people looking out for each other. He assured me that this was part of the business model. "We're building for a wealthy client base, sports stars and actors, friends of John, and for more common people," O'Connor said.

When we got back to Trident Lakes, it was still snowing. We'd still heard nothing from Eckerd. I could tell that O'Connor was getting annoyed that he'd arranged the interview and was being snubbed. While we waited, O'Connor put me on a Skype call with Rob Kaneiss, a former Navy SEAL and the head of security at Trident Lakes, to discuss plans. Kaneiss told me that as a geographer I would understand that "if you can't control the geospace, then you're going to have a potential breach or security issue . . . so we'll use cameras, lights, dogs, roving patrols, [and] the physical perimeter is going to be a combination of chain-link, hard fence and walls."

"What we're planning to do is to buy a bunch of shipping containers," O'Connor chimed in, "which we'll use to build a perimeter, an eight-foot-high, eight-foot-wide wall . . . so it's not stone, but this is also a possible storage solution as there's a lot of space there inside the wall." I had still been watching a lot—too much—of the disgraced prepper televangelist Jim Bakker on YouTube and imagined the containers filled with Bakker's food and Bible long-term storage "survival buckets."

Kaneiss added excitedly that they were going even further than this. They had to "address risk through a different paradigm." I asked him what he meant. His response was depressingly predictable. The "paradigm" turned out to be difference.

"Look, I go about six to eight pages deep on Google . . . and I found two or three Muslim groups that are actually in Texas," he said, rambling. "They're not violent and they definitely haven't been tagged by the FBI, but there have been very negative interactions with the community . . . that could potentially translate into risk. That means civil disruption, that means hate groups, that means monitoring Black Lives Matter. You know there's even white hate groups out there that are creating a lot of problems. We don't like any of those extremist views."

With the weather finally clearing, I toured the site in a work truck with Will and Angela, two wiry metalworkers in greasy plaid flannel shirts, from the nearby town of Ector. They'd been employed at Trident Lakes since Eckerd bought the property in 2016. I asked them what they thought of the development and Angela beamed, "Oh we love it."

"Yeah, I've always been into prepping, so it's right up my alley," Will said, then hesitated. Prepping, he opined, had always been done by the lower middle classes—but lately, in his view, something had changed. The rich had started to become involved, too, which wasn't a good sign. "I'm sure the upper classes know what's going on," he grimaced, "and when people with knowledge start doing this, then you know something's going wrong." I recalled something Milton had said to me at xPoint: "When politicians and the rich start building bunkers, you know something is coming."

On my third day at Trident Lakes I'd all but given up on the elusive Eckerd and was about to leave for the airport, when the summons came: I'd been granted an audience in his multimillion-dollar mansion in McKinney, a suburb thirty miles north of Dallas. We drove down there at a stately speed, as per O'Connor's precise navigation.

O'Connor stiffened when he rang the doorbell. The hefty polished wood double doors of the house opened to reveal a plump, bald, tracksuited man wearing a thick gold chain—this was Eckerd. Waving a dismissive hello, he turned and waddled toward the living room in unlaced sneakers. We followed, past tawdry faux-Roman statuary on pedestals, draping crystal chandeliers, badly chosen oil portraits, and a large semicircular bar with hundreds of wineglasses hanging upside down: awaiting the next opulent house party, which, no doubt, Shaq, Donnie Wahlberg, and Jenny McCarthy would attend.

In the living room, the remains of a breakfast of eggs, waffles, bacon, fruit, coffee, and mimosas were spread over a coffee table roughly the size of my apartment. Eckerd shooed his family away, flopped onto the couch, put his sneaker-clad feet on the coffee table, turned to O'Connor, and said, "So, what's this about?"

O'Connor, who was clearly nervous, reminded him that I was a researcher interested in prepping. I asked Eckerd if it would be okay if I recorded our conversation. He ignored me, turned to O'Connor, and said, "What does he want?"

Communicating through O'Connor, I assured Eckerd that I wouldn't record the conversation and then appealed to his ego, explaining how important it was that Eckerd have someone "pen the story of Trident Lakes for posterity." After I suggested that I could play that role, he finally thawed and deigned to address me directly.

Why, I asked him, was he building Trident Lakes?

"I see this whole thing as a giant social experiment," he told me. "You see, I used to dream of building a bunker when I was a kid, now I have the resources to do it." There was another side to it, too, of course: Eckerd saw a clear business opportunity amid America's decline.

Were there really enough people interested to turn a profit on the $30 million that was being invested in Trident Lakes?

"In my mind, this will either work as a business venture or it'll be a really secure property for my family." He'd invested millions of dollars of his own money in phase one construction, but that didn't matter: one day, money would be worthless when "it all kicks off." Again, there was that strange but characteristic mix of capitalism and eschatology—and again underpinned, it turned out, by the xenophobic, zero-sum view of cultural and religious difference that saturated online prepper forums.

It was only a matter of time, Eckerd expanded, before Trump began to "round up all the Muslims." He said the squads were already being formed. He told me that "it would be done quietly," but that there was likely to be a public backlash. O'Connor became even more uncomfortable once the talk had veered in this direction.

"That's where Trident Lakes comes in," Eckerd said. "Everybody can come back here, we shut the gates and we wait it out." In his business model, there was no reason why waiting it out should necessitate a change in lifestyle. While the world burned on the other side of the concertina razor wire, the Texas elite would be watching movies in their underground cinema, swimming in the crystal-blue lagoons, getting massages in the spa, and preparing for any breach of the "geospace" at the shooting range.

If I'd hoped for anything more insightful from Eckerd, I was to be disappointed. As I sat, increasingly irritated, through more of his monologue, I couldn't help myself: I told Eckerd it reminded me of the story of Emperor Nero playing his fiddle while Rome burned. The frost descended. Eckerd turned to O'Connor. "What's this guy talking about?" My audience was over.

On the drive back to the airport, Salfen, the director of celebrity relations, was absorbed in posting to Twitter about our trip out to Trident Lakes, explaining as he did so that "with social media and things like that people are understanding each other more." He wanted people to know that they were welcoming all sorts of people into Trident Lakes—"even professors," he added expansively. Salfen saw the "community" he was building on social networks as mirroring the community they were building inside the gates.

In the front passenger seat O'Connor, not in the best of moods after our visit to Eckerd, scowled and craned his neck around the driver's seat headrest: "But Paul, media amplifies violence, so people perceive the world in a way that is contrary to the truth." This statement seemed startlingly insightful. O'Connor, I felt, was wrestling with a few contradictions. But didn't he think, I asked him, that these violent media narratives were good for business, driving people to places like Trident Lakes? O'Connor said nothing and stared at the road ahead. The silence was punctuated only by the persistent tapping of Salfen's thumbs on his phone screen.

As we drove on, I reflected that rather than the organic community O'Connor hoped for, Trident Lakes seemed to be evolving into a private real estate venture driven by celebrity, media exposure, and a conflicting set of motivations and ideologies. I recalled a passage from *The Fourth Turning*, which stated that the "final season" was meant to be brought on by wealth, frivolity, entertainment, materialism, and defensiveness. That was Trident Lakes in a nutshell.

6

Preps Down Under:
Bugging Out of Cities

"In the Castle Keep I assemble my stores; everything over and above my daily wants that I capture inside the burrow, and everything I bring
back with me from my hunting expeditions outside, I pile up here."
   —Franz Kafka, "The Burrow," 1931[1]

The Australian city of Sydney, where I moved to take up a research
fellowship in 2017, had neither the edge-honing jeopardy of Los
Angeles nor the allure of London's two-thousand-year-old urban

layers that had enticed me to exploration. Sydney felt like a fragile paradise; it was comfortable, but I didn't expect it to last. And so, at weekends, I found myself increasingly drawn into the world of practical, low-level prepping as a way of upskilling while I watched and waited. In doing so, I realized that prepping down under had a different character. In the US, economic precarity triggers a lot of people into stockpiling; in the UK, political turmoil seemed to drive the practice. Australians, though, have even more reason to prepare: the country has already felt the sharp edge of a rapidly escalating global climate disaster.

Australian preppers often point to a single event as their catalyst: Black Saturday. On February 7, 2009, after an extended heat wave, more than four hundred small bushfires in the state of Victoria converged in a conflagration. Temperatures in Melbourne hit 46.4°C (115.5°F), the hottest ever recorded in the city. Inland, fires released energy equivalent to fifteen hundred Hiroshima-sized atomic bombs. Dozens of people who tried to get out by road got stuck and were overtaken by the fast-moving flames, killed by radiant heat or smoke inhalation, or in road accidents, unable to see where they were driving. By the time the fire was brought under control, more than eight hundred thousand acres—an area larger than the state of Rhode Island—had been incinerated, thirty-five hundred buildings had been destroyed, and a hundred eighty people were dead. At that point, it was the worst natural disaster in the continent's recorded history. In the intervening decade, many Australians have buried "fire bunkers" in their backyards, oxygen-filled cocoons that look remarkably similar to the nuclear shelters that Americans built in a panic during the first doom boom in the early years of the Cold War.

From my office at the University of Sydney I called Anthony Tratt, the owner of Wildfire Safety Bunkers, a company founded in 2008. Tratt produces heat-resistant and sealed bunkers where you can hunker down and wait for the flames to pass. He told me that mandatory evacuation orders are a huge problem in Australia because roads get clogged up, people get stuck and panic, then die. Tratt had the solution: his bunkers, buried thirty feet below the Earth, could shelter twelve people for $34,000 AUD (about $20,000

US). I asked Anthony if he thought the people buying his bunkers would consider themselves preppers. He didn't seem to like the idea that people had to be part of some kind of clique to prepare.

"Look," he said, "people buy these things and turn them into nice game rooms or something, but anyone staying down there for more than an hour is committing suicide. These bunkers are gas-tight, meaning they have no ventilation, because if they did they wouldn't be fireproof." So not a doomsday bunker, but still a bunker. Each one Tratt installed was equipped with temperature gauges, a carbon dioxide meter, and compressed air to breathe. Ideally, Anthony thought, you would get yourself out of town in an event, but if this was not possible, you could buy yourself an hour in his bunker and survive, making the $34,000 seem like a steal when you crawled out of the bunker alive.[2]

At the end of 2019 and the beginning of 2020, bushfires raged around Australia, coating Sydney, and then Melbourne, followed by the capital of Canberra, and then almost the entire country, with a thick, toxic ocher haze that required people to mask up. Air pollution rose to twenty-two times the accepted safety level as millions of acres, this time an area the size of South Korea, burned hot and fast. Outside the city of Adelaide, the national park resort destination and ecological bastion Kangaroo Island was ravaged. The heat on the island was fierce enough to melt concrete at a luxury lodge, whose staff survived by taking shelter in a bunker. Another couple in Victoria hid in their fire bunker eating Vegemite sandwiches as their home burned to the ground above them. They watched it through a thick glass viewing port like tank commanders rolling through a war zone. Just as Black Saturday was a wake-up call for many to start prepping, the 2019/2020 bushfires were the first time many Australians understood the drought ravaging inland areas in visceral terms. It didn't take long for the rest of the world to understand what those bushfires portended.

Earlier in the year, I had become acquainted with these conditions firsthand, when I struck out with my partner, Amanda—a Sydney-based lawyer—for an eleven-hundred-mile journey through five of Australia's ten great deserts in a US-imported Jeep Wrangler stuffed with camping gear, food, supplies, and maps. We'd spent countless weekends in Sydney training hard at the gym, turning the Jeep into a competent bug-out rig, and trying unsuccessfully to start wet eucalyptus campfires with magnesium and spark blocks at campsites, in preparation for our trip. However, once we got out of the orbit of the city, our provisions seemed tragically deficient.

The interior of Australia looked like Mars—and, according to my colleagues in geology, is not dissimilar in terms of rock and soil composition. At times, the water we carried strapped to the roof rack had to last us a week as taps and waterways were bone dry in most of the campsites. The sides of roads were littered with dead fauna. The only animals thriving were feral camels that can survive for seven months without drinking. Not that there wasn't water to be had. In one Queensland town called Tamborine Mountain, the state school ran out of water after millions of liters were pumped out of their local boreholes and shipped to a Coca-Cola bottling plant.[3] The Queensland government then bought the water back from the corporation and delivered it as emergency supplies. In the course of our trip, we learned firsthand what everybody now realizes: Australia is teetering on the brink. The more people there understand this, the more prepping on some level seems sensible to them.

Climate scientists had predicted that by 2020, "extreme fire days" in Australia would increase in occurrence by up to 65 percent.[4] They were spot on. By the year 2050, they predict that the incidence of such days will be up 300 percent. Scientists also worry about an increase in aridity, given that the continent's ten great deserts constitute 70 percent of its landmass.[5] Increased aridity, spreading toward the coastlines, could cripple food production. Social planners have referred to these threats as "wicked problems," meaning that they're problems that are difficult or impossible to solve because of incomplete information, contradictory evidence, or changing requirements that are hard to recognize.[6] Often the best we can do, faced with these wicked problems, is control what's in front of us.

Back in Sydney it occurred to me that, since we lived on a peninsula with only one road in or out, we needed a backup plan. We bought two kayaks and practiced paddling out from the beach near our house to the Royal National Park, where we could vanish into the bush if an emergency caused a panicked traffic snarl that prevented use of the Jeep. As a recent transplant to the city, I was eager to test out my draft escape plan with someone who had a better lay of the land, so I shot off a message to Nick Sais, an electrician who runs the Australian Preppers internet forum.

Nick met me in the beachside Sydney suburb of Sans Souci ("without worry") not far from my house, and close to many coastal fortifications. These somber nineteenth-century structures—now graffiti-laden ruins crowning sea cliffs—were built during World War II. Nick, looking sleek yet energetic, wearing a faded *Star Wars* T-shirt and wraparound sunglasses that reflected my face inside a multicolored swirl, wasted no time reassuring me about my plans.

"The Australian model for prepping is more secretive than for our American counterparts, but there are a lot of people in the game," he told me over coffee. "We've probably got fifteen to twenty thousand people prepping in Oz, and as almost 90 percent of Australians live in cities, bugging out is really the only option. You know when you go camping and you see people unpack a house from their ute in the bush? Those people are going to be all right, unless their ute's stuffed. Almost everyone else is gonna be in trouble."

Nick thought it made even more sense to escape on foot. Most weekends, he headed out with close friends and family to perform a bug-out *à pied*. He'd traced a route out of Sydney, using only national parkland, all the way to the South Coast, over three hundred miles away. Along his planned escape route, he'd buried capped plastic pipes the diameter of an outstretched hand, holding food and supplies and capable of doubling as water collection containers. Getting away from people was his first priority; he would escape the conurbation and blend into the bush. In a part of the world where the wilds are both dense and dangerous, Nick's confidence in his ability to walk all the way to the South Coast was impressive.

"But that's in a serious situation, mate, like total economic and social collapse," he said. "If we're talking about just waiting out a few days, I've got a sledgehammer and a bug-out bag ready and we're going straight into the bunker at La Perouse." Here, he was talking about the coastal defenses down on the coast a short walk from his house. The abandoned subterranean ammunition storage rooms and gunpowder magazines at Henry Head Battery there, built with doubled-up walls and ceilings so as to be able to withstand a direct hit from artillery, could be accessed through a tunnel complex. It was an ideal one- to three-day bolthole, and the entire east coast of Australia was littered with such structures.

There's a saying in prepper culture: *three is two, two is one, one is none*. It's an axiom for redundancy, meaning that there should always be a backup of what you're relying on, from can openers to energy. It also applies to bug-out plans.

"For the short term you want to hunker down, but if the situation keeps deteriorating, then you're going to jump in your ute or boat and get clear," Nick told me. "If things are really bad, you walk out. We've got a plan for all scenarios." For the maritime escape route, he'd gone with an inflatable military raft powered by an electric battery. I imagined him whizzing out of Sans Souci balaclava-clad, a firm grip on the tiller, in the dead of night.

I hesitated, thinking about how to phrase my next question. "I've only been here a short time," I ventured, "but Sydneysiders don't seem particularly adaptable. Is there a lack of foresight here that's putting people in danger, in your opinion?"

"Mate," Nick retorted, "I am continually astounded by how complacent people in this city are." Most non-Aboriginal Australians, he explained, had never experienced adversity. A wealthy country with a strong consumer culture bolstered by tourism from Asia, Australia had largely been spared the ravages of the 2008 global financial crisis. Nick's rationale for starting the forum, and for talking to people generally about his prepping activities, stemmed from a genuine concern that his fellow citizens would not make it through an emergency. He took off his sunglasses and stared through me. "If the worst were to happen, mate, we're talking about 80 percent of the population being decimated."

I wanted to better understand how people were now working to counter this possibility by skilling up, so Nick suggested I get in touch with Rich Hungerford, a wilderness and survival expert who runs training workshops through his company Bush Lore Australia. I'd managed to catch Hungerford just before he went into the bush for five days with a class. "The thing no one wants to hear," he told me over the phone from Queensland, "is that in the event of a low-probability but high-consequence event, no one is coming for you." Rich was ex-military, and like Nick, he was particularly concerned about the Australian population's concentration in cities: a clustering that makes the country's urban societies more sustainable in non-emergency situations, but more vulnerable in a crisis. Unlike the US citizens who'd left their cities in the fifties and sixties, Australians hadn't ever exhibited Herman Kahn's "prime target fixation syndrome" by fleeing from nuclear targets. It had to be said that the collapse scenario triggered by a drawn-out environmental breakdown, which Rich proceeded to outline to me, lacked the dark allure of atomic annihilation or a global pandemic. It was, though, a lot easier to imagine.

"The supply lines are just going to go down," he told me bluntly. "Once you don't have trucks and trains bringing in the food, fuel, and everything else people in the city depend on, things are going to turn chaotic very fast. Some people will get out, but others are going to get stuck where they run out of fuel. The transportation infrastructure will clog and collapse, and then Sydney, Melbourne, Brisbane, Perth, and Adelaide, which could never sustain themselves internally, will become ungovernable." This was of course the plot for that classic Australian dystopian film *Mad Max*: a collapse of resource networks, leading to a world without rule of law, would leave a bunch of hardened people in the outback lugging around precious jerry cans, ammo, and water. As Amanda and I drove around the continent doing exactly that, it was all too easy to understand how that plot had been scripted.

Hungerford felt that the "island approach" of bunker building wouldn't do much to help weather the storm. Even if people had stockpiled resources, he reasoned, they didn't have the "emotional resolve" to last, inside or out. This was where people like him came in. The Australian military had hired Hungerford to coach new recruits because the eighteen-year-olds signing up for the army couldn't make it through basic training. Physical fitness wasn't the issue: many of the recruits were far fitter than previous generations. Rather, they couldn't cope with pressure. They were incapable of problem-solving their way through spontaneous situations, constantly looking to someone else for answers. In Hungerford's mind, this was symptomatic of a failing in the wider culture. He feared that when the inevitable crisis hit, it would only exacerbate the chaos when no one would step up to the challenge. I asked him point-blank when he would take action. His reply: "Mate, I've already bugged out."

A few months later, at the end of the Australian summer, I drove our Wrangler the five hundred forty–odd miles from Sydney to Melbourne, through parched towns with brown lawns—still a tinderbox, I thought—to the Australian Centre for Contemporary Art (ACCA). The Field Theory artists' collective had built a twenty-foot-high scaffolding of shelves inside the gallery packed with preps—food, tools, outdoor equipment, medical supplies, books, games, radios, and communications equipment—giving visitors a sense of being inside a bunker. I'd been invited by the collective to participate in a panel discussion, along with disaster psychologist Rob Gordon, philosopher Patrick Stokes, who's an expert on Kierkegaard, and a doomsday prepper named Bushy, a stocky, licensed firearms dealer who'd driven his armored Humvee to the gallery. The back of his camouflaged rig was filled with MRE (Meal, Ready-to-Eat) packets, toilet paper, emergency blankets, and a Russian NBC warfare suit he'd bought on eBay. The purchase of NBC suit, he explained to the audience, had prompted Australian Federal Police (AFP) to show up at his door, wondering what he needed it for.

After the panel, Bushy and I got to chatting; he gave me a swift education on Australian prepping. "Getting your vehicle right is crucial," Bushy told me. "Having a bug-in location like a bunker is great, but you don't want to become a supermarket for other people; it's better to be mobile. That's why you need a proper bug-out rig. I have everything I need in here and I'm always within minutes of this vehicle."

I asked Bushy why there weren't many prepper communities in Australia and why prepping down under felt more secretive and individualistic. He chalked it up to rural Australians (most often the ones prepping) already living a long way from grocery stores and infrastructure. They're used to monotonous drives on empty roads where extra fuel has to be carried. They deal with dramatic weather, bushfires, and lethal animals as a matter of course. In contrast to the dependency cultivated in Australian cities, Bushy said rural Australians are effectively prepping all the time; it's just part of the lifestyle. His words made sense. When Amanda and I drove around the continent, there was often a paucity of fresh food. Filling our fuel tank from the jerry cans on the roof to get to the next outback outpost became routine. Twice, in two months, we had to stop and help other people who'd run out of fuel.

Our road trip made me conscious of how having no reserves puts a lot of faith in the future; it leaves little room for error. Today in Australia, very few people in urban areas have the space or knowledge to grow their own food. In comparison, according to the US National Gardening Association, 35 percent of US households grow harvestable crops. The numbers are similar in Britain, where people grow mostly in community allotments. Many of these people couldn't survive on what they're growing, but they are infinitely more prepared by knowing *how* to grow food. Not knowing how to grow is a dangerous gamble in faltering environmental conditions. Preppers get accused of being "hoarders" all the time, but prepping is an essential part of a post-nomadic existence.[7] Bushy agreed with Nick and Rich that if port and truck deliveries stopped, Australians in cities—89 percent of the population—would just wither. Given that more than half the world's population is now urban, and the United Nations expects that 68 percent of us will live in cities by 2050, Australia may end up being the laboratory for what Vicino describes as the "ripple effect," where one event triggers another event, like dominoes falling, with an eventual descent into chaos.

In the "if you build it, they will come" tradition, Bushy told me he was planning on building the first prepper community in Australia: a series of "sheds on farms with complicated wine cellars," connected through a management structure. Each farm's location would be secret until an "event," at which point you'd make your way to an allotted location, where you'd be connected to a mutual assistance group, or MAG. Bushy imagined a subscription model with a tier of packages. In the "highest tier" package, you'd have someone in a nonelectronic vehicle come and pick you and your family up at your house when things kicked off. Your bug-out chauffeur would whisk you to the nearest farm, where safety, community, and the ability to grow food awaited—along with, one would hope, a few bottles in the "complicated wine cellar."

Expounding further on those "nonelectronic vehicles," Bushy gestured at his Humvee. "Got it at auction for cheap. They're perfect for this, because they're electrical but not electronic. So, if an EMP goes off, you can push-start 'em. That's what you want—mechanical, diesel rigs with no electronics. Your Jeep will be dead in the water if there's an EMP."

The auction Bushy mentioned was one of those being run by Australian Frontline Machinery, a company selling off ex-military hardware. When I got back from Melbourne, I headed to their warehouse in Minto, just outside of Sydney, to check out the lineup of used vehicles and equipment they'd bought from the Australian Defence Force. There, in a place the size of an aircraft hangar, they had 4×4 Land Rovers, 6×6 troop carriers, motorcycles, Zodiac shore combat raiders, kayaks, assault wagons, and even an ambulance on the block. A guy inspecting the undercarriage of a matte-green Land Rover told me he'd snagged one for his son for $15,000, even though finding parts for it could be a hassle.

"He's a fucking sissy if I'm honest, mate," he said from under the vehicle. "I hope it breaks down in the bush and he has to sort it out—it'll teach him something."

The auction manager, John Leask, had neatly trimmed gray hair and callused hands. He met me in the warehouse to talk me through the wares on display. Lined up on the floor's left-hand side, dozens of Land Rovers were parked in perfect alignment on a pristine concrete floor. The only way to tell them apart, I gathered, was to climb under them, pop the hoods, and start them up, like the guy I'd spoken to had been doing. Then you marked down the number of the vehicles that appeared to be in the best shape and went online to bid. I climbed into a Land Rover and asked Leask who was buying them and what they were doing with them.

"Oh, we make it a point not to ask, but mostly farmers, I suspect. And surfers looking for rack space. Every once in a while you get someone who looks like they might be a survivalist, but it's a pretty conspicuous vehicle." Perhaps in everyday life, I thought, but in the middle of a disaster, driving what looks like a military vehicle might be a great way to deter road warriors.

"Do you sell a lot of them?" I asked.

"Oh yeah, they pretty much all go, a few dozen every month."

"And what about those?" I asked, pointing across the warehouse to an equally impeccable lineup of camouflaged troop carriers. "I mean, seriously, John, does the Australian government not care that people are buying troop carriers?" I told him about Bushy's run-in with the AFP.

Leask shrugged and rubbed the back of his neck. "I don't know, mate, probably they know where they're ending up, I expect. Keeping tabs."

I later saw Leask auction off two 165-foot "mine hunter" coastal ships. Who the buyers were was similarly unclear. A year or so later, when the Australian navy retired a fleet of camouflaged Bell "Kiowa" 206B-1 helicopters, I saw them go up for auction on the AFM website. With enough money, you could equip a private army by sitting at your desk and clicking.

If you *really* want to bug out, you can't get much farther than the island state Tasmania, or Tassie, off the southern tip of the Australian mainland. Known for its isolated wilds, it's the last port of call for research vessels heading to Antarctica. By searching through planning documents online, Amanda came across one that vaguely described the location of a substantial bunker in the middle of the island built in the 1970s by a wealthy American lawyer named Martin Polin. News reports from the early 1990s indicated that Polin was a conservationist, survivalist, and late-life recluse who had bought twenty-three different properties and some forty-four thousand acres of Tasmanian land. On the acreage, he built a wilderness redoubt, with a bunker perched in the center like an ominous temple.

I tried to find out more about Polin, but information online was scarce. The law offices he operated out of San Luis Obispo, California, had long since been boarded up, but there was a room in the nearby Atascadero Library named after him, built on land he'd donated for that purpose. A group called the Friends of the Atascadero Library helped me get in touch with his relatives, who were clearly fond of him and his eccentricities. Polin's nephew Jim told me that Martin was the only practicing attorney he'd ever heard of who had an unlisted telephone number: his client base was entirely from word of mouth. Despite this, he'd done well for himself. Then he read the Cold War novel *On the Beach* by Neville Shute, which described the last months of human life in Melbourne, Australia, after a nuclear war between Northern Hemisphere powers that created a fallout cloud that slowly crept south.[8] A family friend of Polin's, Cullen, told me that he'd first met Polin back in 1981. During the encounter Polin expressed serious concerns about a disaster unfolding at the Diablo Canyon nuclear power plant in San Luis Obispo. He'd gotten the prepping bug.

That Polin was impelled to move into survivalist mode by a novel was odd but hardly unprecedented: fiction has often generated disquiet. Most famously, a fake newscast of an alien invasion was delivered over the radio by Orson Welles on Halloween 1938. It was adapted from H. G. Wells's novel *The War of the Worlds* and caused widespread panic throughout the United States. In the words of one young college student who packed up and bugged out after hearing the radio broadcast in 1938: "I didn't have any idea exactly what I was fleeing from, and that made me all the more afraid."[9] In Martin's case, a similar dread of terror from the air is what caused him to flee to Tasmania.

Polin chose the island as the farthest place from the impending disaster he feared. Selling half of his property in San Luis Obispo, he bought a one-hundred-acre sheep ranch, a motel near Mount Field National Park, an apartment in the capital, Hobart, near the University of Tasmania, which he outfitted with a bomb shelter, and, of course, his fortress in the hinterlands, which could accommodate a dozen people and was stuffed with food and necessities.

Polin's nephew Jim and his wife went to visit him after he'd moved into the Hobart apartment. Polin had apparently installed shielding on his windows because of his fears of radiation from the ozone hole over that part of the world. Clearly pleased that they'd come to visit, he offered Jim and his wife open-ended airline tickets that could be used to fly back in the event of calamity. Jim appreciated it, but he told Polin he'd rather face such an event at home with his family. Even so, Jim told me, he'd been impressed with the prescience of Polin's dread: the nuclear reactor at Chernobyl exploded not long afterward.

When Polin died in 2007, his central Tasmania property was put on the property market, valued at $10 million, and passed into Aboriginal hands after private donors pooled their resources to wrench the land away from prospective developers. The land was set to be preserved, highlighting the biological diversity and Aboriginal history there. What had happened to the bunker, a unique piece of Cold War Americana in the middle of Tassie, was unclear.

Amanda and I flew to Tasmania with nothing more to go on than a pin on a Google map, at a place called Circular Marsh, a two-hour drive from Hobart. On the way, scrolling around Circular Marsh on Google Earth, we could see angular lines running through the densely forested area, which we were pretty sure was the bunker. What we couldn't see were the road barriers that we encountered, which the new landowners had put up five miles from the map pin. Pulling our car into the bush, we ignored the "No Trespassing" signs, swinging around the barriers and beginning the hike in.

The first hour was an uphill climb. Every once in a while, its monotony was broken by a wallaby crashing through the foliage or by a lumbering, furry wombat scurrying across the dirt track in front of us. Since we were already unsettled by the possibility of being caught on the property, each startling animal encounter increased our unease. The encounters seemed apt: when they sense danger, wombats dive headfirst into their large burrows, offering a powerful kick to anything pursuing them. They are survivors: they outlasted the 2019/2020 bushfire disaster, just like the *Lystrosaurus*, the pig-sized reptile that burrowed into the underground during the Great Dying 252 million years ago that killed off more than 90 percent of Earth's species and prospered in the early Triassic.

About four miles in we crested a ridge and entered a verdant valley. On closer inspection we saw that it was filled with man-made detritus: abandoned shipping containers, pieces of pipe, and a detached trailer that looked like it could house on-site security. The land had only recently been handed over to the Aboriginal Land Council. It wasn't impossible, I thought, that the pipes were infrastructure for the nature reserve, and that a security guard was posted in the trailer to make sure they didn't get nicked.

We sidestepped the trailer and wrenched open the door of one of the shipping containers. Moldy books spilled out. Stepping over them into the container, we found hundreds of hardbacks in tiered piles on the floor, their warped covers seemingly disintegrating into dust motes in front of our eyes. The walls of the container were damp; fleshy black mold clung to metal and paper alike. The books—mostly from the 1970s—clearly constituted the bunker's library: an odd collection of pop psychology, religious tracts, and self-help books, including *Your Pre-Teenager's Body and Mind*, *The Wisdom of Christ*, *Better Bowling*, *The Home Freezer Handbook*, and *The Time Trap: How to Get More Done in Less Time*. From the decomposing pile of matter underneath the books, Amanda pulled out the remains of a cardboard box with a return address on it: "Martin Polin, 1445 Marsh St., San Luis Obispo, California, 93401, USA." Some eight thousand miles away.

The weird case of Martin Polin made me think of the late sociologist Zygmunt Bauman. Bauman wrote evocatively about the bizarre but common feeling we have when, after a period of uneasiness and dark premonition, we finally confront a danger that we can see and touch.[10] When we give shape to the things we dread, we make them manageable.

Leaving behind the shipping container library, we climbed another ridge and descended into a new valley. Here, we found Polin's bunker itself. Time hadn't treated it well. Water had pooled on the sagging ceiling and had run around the bunker to cut downhill in an unnatural rivulet. Wood pallets, plastic shards, and steel framing jutted from the banks of the channel. The bunker was steel-framed, lined with breeze blocks, and encased in poured concrete. The blast door was missing, and we stepped cautiously across the threshold into a musty antechamber. Inside, the temperature dropped ten degrees. We flicked on headlights, illuminating concrete block interior walls, and stepped into the main hallway. Our lights lent the walls a sallow hue. Water dripped through cracks and gaps, gathering in murky pools. We tiptoed over them, peeking inside rooms off of the main corridor that were meant to house a number of families. We counted twelve rooms in all, each with an embrasure covered with a hinged metal flap that could be swung open, giving defenders a field of fire on the uninhabited valley. Over each of the flaps, a concrete brow shielded shooters inside from rain and glare.

In one room, we found the almost three-inch-thick blast door: ripped off its hinges and still lined with its rubber seal, it was propped up in a corner. In the farthest room, we noticed a square hole close to the ceiling, likely the intake or exhaust for the air filtration system. Furniture and filing cabinets were strewn everywhere. In another room a lonely toilet was tipped onto its side, indicating that the place must have been plumbed. A couple of slumped and seeping fifty-gallon drums held diesel fuel for a generator nowhere in sight. One room was entirely filled with moldering cardboard boxes—for insulation, we guessed. Saturated with, and slightly overwhelmed by, the air of dereliction and decay, we stepped back outside. Looking at the exterior, we could see that the concrete blocks had been stacked inside a metal frame before the exterior concrete was poured.

Suddenly, I recalled a story that Polin's nephew Jim had told me: that the bunker had been made out of a bridge.

On January 5, 1975, during an intense fog in Sandy Bay, a bulk ore carrier had collided with the Tasman Bridge, killing twelve people. A temporary two-lane steel truss Bailey bridge, put in place while repairs were carried out, subsequently became the shell for Polin's bunker—and here it was. There was a weird logic to disaster relief infrastructure being transformed into disaster anticipation infrastructure, in much the same way that the South Dakota munitions bunkers had been converted into bunkers for people. The crippling expense of building a bunker was almost always, it seemed, subsidized through adaptation from surplus state investment.

After poking around the bunker a bit more, we walked back over the ridge, passing the abandoned security trailer we'd found on the way in, as dusk began to settle over Circular Marsh. Emboldened by our discoveries, I shouldered the door. Inside was a moldy tableau, clearly undisturbed for decades: a propane-fueled camping stove sat on the table, and on the floor there was a pile of cans of baked beans, oil, and salt next to three grimy mattresses. A single window, the same dimensions as the embrasures, looked out to the trail we had hiked in on. I imagined Polin, after fleeing from his beachside family home in California, perched in here some forty years ago, in the middle of this sparsely populated island forty degrees south of the equator, sharpshooting at nothing through the window. Our craving for adventure satiated, we navigated back to the car by the beams of our headlamps.

Though it was now a ruin, Polin's Circular Marsh bunker complex had been fueled by visions of the future. A local Tassie electrician named Roger Nutting claimed that in 1991 he was cornered by Polin, who said he was looking "for young couples with young families to perpetuate the human race" from his bunker "after a nuclear holocaust," adding that "he was constructing a shelter in his Sandy Bay home capable of withstanding a nuclear war in case he could not make it to Circular Marsh in time."[11] Here, again, was the idea of the bunker as a space of rebirth. It put me in mind of Waco, and the survivalists. Being at the same time both the end of everything and the horizon of hope, the disaster Polin imagined was a kind of hybrid formation, an apocatopia.[12] To us, forty years later, the bunker was little more than a hollow shell. Who knows, perhaps Vicino's xPoint would end up in a similar state.

But for me, the most interesting thing about Polin's bunker was its location. Rich enough to pick any spot on Earth to escape to, Polin chose Tasmania. Today, the prime location for "billionaire bunkers" is New Zealand, a short plane hop over the Tasman Sea. Polin was a trailblazer, a harbinger, one of the first preppers to use his extreme wealth to bug out to the Southern Hemisphere, and I was keen to know what that legacy had wrought.

7

Escape from California: Boltholes at the Bottom of the World

> "The most terrible misfortunes are also the most improbable and remote."
> —Arthur Schopenhauer, *Counsels and Maxims*, 1851[1]

I met Ian Clarry for dinner at Moorish Blue, a restaurant in North Sydney. It overlooked Luna Park, a small but iconic landmark with games and rides. As I walked from the Milsons Point railway station, the colors of the spinning Ferris wheel were reflected in the still waters of Sydney Harbour. Clarry, a self-styled "doomsday capitalist," had told me that his twenty-eight-year-old Swedish

125

bodyguard, Manny Ray, would "be in attendance" for our 7 p.m. dinner, and texted me a photo of Manny looking ripped at a gym, along with an image of himself driving a yacht in Ray-Bans. I wasn't sure if this was meant to intimidate or impress me—both, probably. I arrived just as the owner, Jamil, was sending the last customers out the door, closing the restaurant down for our private conference.

Clarry, a Kiwi who preferred to be called by his surname, was the Australia and New Zealand representative for Hardened Structures, a company based in Virginia in the United States that specializes in designing fortified homes, bomb shelters, and hardened military facilities. The people at Hardened Structures seemed to me to be the most elusive of the dread merchants. I'd heard that they were involved in many of the large-scale doomsday community projects that I hoped to visit: Sanctum in Thailand, Fortitude Ranch in West Virginia, Kansas's Survival Condo, the grandly named Oppidum in the Czech Republic, and some build-outs for California-to–New Zealand émigrés. However, the Hardened Structures website was a smear of vague photographs, technical diagrams, and reports that made drawing any kind of narrative about what they actually did challenging. They also advertised a backyard shelter called the Genesis (playing on the resurrection theme), but the website again provided only schematics, not photos of installed shelters. The owner, Brian Camden, when asked in an interview what they were building for, once gnomically replied that "the only thing we know for sure, is that no one knows what's going to happen."[2] The thing I didn't know was how you could build an international business on that premise. When I contacted Camden asking to see what they'd built, he simply sent me another batch of blurry photos that had no context. I was hopeful Clarry could act as gatekeeper and introduce me to Douglas Clark, the Oregon-based project manager for Hardened Structures, so that I could get on-the-ground access to one of their bunkers.

Clarry was welcoming: he'd informed the staff that I'm vegan, and a gorgeous plate of okra, hummus, beetroot, and giant couscous was set before me.[3] Clarry pushed his meal aside when it arrived. His bodyguard, meanwhile, ate a plate of salmon at astonishing speed and then started scrolling through his phone rapidly with one thumb, face aglow in the dim lights of the restaurant. As we talked, it became clear that Clarry was incredibly enthusiastic about "asset risk management," but vague about why it was necessary. His starting point was that the end of the Central American Maya people's calendar in 2012—which was meant to indicate transformative global events would occur—had caused a significant uptick in interest for bunkered space. It was obviously a thing for dread merchants: Vicino had put a Maya calendar countdown timer on his website in 2011 to encourage buyers.

"Okay," I said, spooning couscous around. "But there obviously wasn't an apocalypse in 2012." Besides—I didn't add—I knew the calendar didn't really end in 2012: it was just the end of a four-hundred-year segment in the Maya long-count calendar, another turning of the wheel.

I asked Clarry if the sustained interest in hunkering down, in the lead-up to 2012, perhaps had to do with the more incremental environmental apocalypse picking up speed. Perhaps, I suggested, the Maya calendar thing was a displaced fear over the climate crisis—an especially tangible threat in Australia.

"Global changes are obvious," Clarry acknowledged, adding that for him the cause of such changes was "irrelevant." Hardened Structures, he said, with an estate agent's brightness, "only deals in solutions." The solutions he proposed were massive, almost government-scale: evacuation plans, off-grid communication networks, and bunkers for dozens, even hundreds, of people. He told me Hardened Structures liked working with "the elite" because they didn't skimp on cost. As a rule of thumb, Clarry thought that everyone should invest 1 percent of their net worth into prepping for Black Swan events.

"If you make ten million a year," he said, spreading his hands out on the restaurant table, "would you think twice about putting a hundred thousand of that into security?" Point made, he got up from the table and vanished for ten minutes without explanation. As his dinner congealed, I tried to chat with his bodyguard Manny Ray, who Clarry had told me was a Thai kickboxing champion. Engrossed in his phone, he wasn't interested in talking.

When Clarry returned, I described the xPoint bunkers, which

were selling for a fraction of the amounts he was talking about; a range of people, I observed, seemed to be coveting hardened architecture, not just the rich. He nodded enthusiastically.

"Fortified, off-the-grid, hardened homes with shelters will become the new norm in time," he said, craning his neck around the corner, toward the front door.

"Are you waiting for someone else?" I asked.

"Nope," he responded. Other than the clinking of dishes in the kitchen, the restaurant was silent. In a back garden, the owner and two large men were smoking a hookah and sometimes looked in, as if also waiting for someone to enter. The whole scene, the sense of anticipation, was making me jittery.

Hardened Structures was overwhelmed by demand, Clarry told me. Not only were they doing "military-grade risk mitigation for high-net-worth individuals," they also had government and military contracts for prisons, schools, and shopping malls.[4] But when I asked for details of specific projects, Clarry was evasive. He told me that he'd completed "dozens" of bunkers for Silicon Valley elites who wanted a backup location in New Zealand, now seen as the most friction-free and least disaster-prone part of the English-speaking world.

Clarry wanted me to know that they were helping elites to build bunkers, panic rooms, and secure compounds, where the wealthy were parking their money in cryptocurrency outside of the nation-state, expecting its demise in a global catastrophe. They, Clarry and Manny Ray, were determined not just to ride it out but to make economic gain from the disaster.

I wanted to know: Could I visit one of these projects? Yes, said Clarry, "eventually," though maintaining OPSEC (aka operations security) was paramount. This, apparently, was also the reason for our clandestine meeting—though the veneer of secrecy was quick to wear off, as Clarry explained that he held all his meetings here, that he'd been the best man at Jamil's wedding, and that he had limitless credit. "I don't even want to know what my tab looks like," he said, laughing.

After spending a few hours with him, I began to feel that Clarry was a dread merchant without a product. The only information I managed to extract from him related to his passion for "bitcoin, bunkers and billionaires," Maya prophecies, and the ZetaTalk conspiracy website, the source of the "Planet X" pole-shift scenario.

It didn't help that as we talked, both Clarry and his bodyguard were twitchy. At one point, Manny Ray took a gym bag out to his car, saying he was going to work out later. I couldn't help but wonder what was *really* in the bag.

Though I'd arrived at the meeting feeling pretty relaxed, I grew tense and could feel my stress levels spiking. My paranoia, I realized, was partly down to spending too much time loitering on conspiracy-laden prepper internet forums, but it was also fueled by the slipperiness of Clarry's "solutions." I was frustrated, and felt I was losing my grip.

I told Clarry I had to get going, thanked the staff for the private meal, and headed out. He insisted on walking me back to the station. On the way, I asked him if he could give me some case studies of actual projects with which Hardened Structures was involved. I made sure he got the sense that I would not be returning without something substantial—and physical—that I could visit.

"Okay, I've got this covered!" he said, beaming. "I'll send a message to Jakub Zamrazil, the founder of Oppidum, and see if we can't link you guys up. Let me also put you in touch with Auggie at Chiang Mai so you can go visit Sanctum. And let's get you on the phone with Douglas Clark, the Hardened Structures project manager for the US Pacific Northwest." It seemed as though I was finally getting somewhere.

As I settled back into my office at the University of Sydney the next day, I found myself distracted, unable to focus. I was supposed to be preparing a lecture, but I kept listening to news on the radio instead, waiting for something bad to happen. I soon abandoned all pretense of working and was busily scrolling through a sequence of mildly hysterical news stories about "billionaire bunkers" built by tech giants who were going to "escape" to the Southern Hemisphere— specifically, New Zealand—when I had an epiphany.

Which was this. These stories had started taking hold back in 2012, when police raided the New Zealand property of Kim Dotcom (born Kim Schmitz), a US-born millionaire hacker and founder of Megaupload, a file sharing site. The US wanted Dotcom extradited for piracy—the Feds were being pressured by global media conglomerates who wanted the man behind bars. While his mansion was ransacked by seventy-two police officers—like the old FBI survivalist raids—Dotcom hid in a panic room he'd built. When the police finally cut their way into it, they found the six-and-a-half-foot-tall, three-hundred-pound black-clad man sitting inside with a loaded sawed-off shotgun, holding three passports under different names, a bulletproof wristwatch, and twenty-five credit cards.[5]

After being caught up in a seemingly endless battle over extradition and appeals during the next seven years, Dotcom finally told *New Zealand Herald* journalist Steve Braunias that he'd bought the land on the South Island in preparation for the Fall.[6] "New Zealand was going to be a bolthole, a bunker," he said. "I never had a plan to live here permanently until we [were] close to the event . . . [but] I may have accelerated it, because I told my friends in the Silicon Valley, and I'm very well connected." Dotcom was convinced we were approaching the end times. "Humanity is heading to a large mass casualty event simply because of the increase in population and the pressures on resources, and the political pressure that causes," he said. He fantasized about building a compound for thirty to forty people, where they could wait out the impending collapse. His arrest triggered a slew of media stories perpetuating the idea that tech moguls were all building "doomsteads" in New Zealand—all of which could be traced back to 2012, the same year as the end of the Maya calendar, the same crescendo in interest that Clarry saw for bunkered space.

The evidence for an exodus of the rich to New Zealand looks compelling. According to the 2013 census, more than half of the 2,781 homes in Wanaka (a resort town on New Zealand's South Island) were unoccupied. Many were owned by foreigners.[7] LinkedIn founder Reid Hoffman claimed that among his techno-aristocrat friends "saying you're 'buying a house in New Zealand' is kind of a wink, wink, say no more."[8] Meanwhile, then–prime minister John Key, seeing it as a boon to the economy, was cheer-leading for preppers to relocate, reiterating that New Zealand was the safest place to be in the event of Armageddon. In 2017 PayPal founder Peter Thiel was handed a Kiwi passport at an embassy in Santa Monica, California, enabling him to purchase a 477-acre property on Lake Wanaka.

Yet every journalist who flew to New Zealand attempting to drill down into these "boltholes of the rich and famous" stories came back with pretty flimsy evidence that people were burying bunkers there. For instance, a 2018 article by Olivia Carville in Bloomberg reported that seven Silicon Valley entrepreneurs had purchased two three-hundred-square-foot bunkers from Rising S in Texas and had them shipped to two locations in New Zealand: Picton, across the Cook Strait from Wellington, and Auckland's Waitematā Harbour.[9] They were supposedly buried soon afterward.

The CEO of Rising S, Gary Lynch (whom I'd interviewed, of course, in my time in Texas) claimed that he'd in fact shipped about thirty-five underground bunkers to New Zealand from the Dallas factory that I'd visited. However, local councils in New Zealand had no evidence of shipment, transport, or planning permission for these massive structures.[10] The same Bloomberg article contained the by now almost obligatory quote from Robert Vicino, who airily claimed to be getting to work on a bunker in New Zealand that could accommodate three hundred people. This was news to me.

The media hype around the Kiwi bunkers, which I'm convinced was all precipitated by the story about Dotcom's panic room, reminded me of the "sea steading" panic of the early 2000s, when Silicon Valley elites were supposedly all going to do business on floating platforms or reappropriated cruise ships in international waters off the coast of San Francisco—all to remain beyond the sway of immigration authorities, tax collectors, and labor laws. Ultimately people forgot about those plans and moved on.

The simple fact is that if people like Tom, Milton, and Mark back at xPoint in South Dakota were willing to stump up $40k to $50k to invest in their own safety by building out a remote bunker, it's easy to imagine that a billionaire might drop $20 to $30 million on protection. For Peter Thiel (net worth: $2.3 billion), meeting

Clarry's 1 percent test would mean investing $23 million in security. So, while there's no evidence that he had some massive subterranean lair at Lake Wanaka, the fact that Thiel turned his walk-in closet into a panic room in another house he had built in Queenstown an hour away isn't too surprising. In the end, having two passports and a private jet to a remote estate is a pretty solid bugout plan: you don't need a blast shelter, geography *is* the bunker.

My curious contemplation, as I scrolled through all those stories to avoid looking at my empty PowerPoint lecture slides, was whether in New Zealand the bunkers were a red herring; it was the ideology behind the bugout that mattered. The paradox in any truth behind the stories was that the tech giants of Silicon Valley—or some of them, anyway—were making a fortune from the systems they felt might trigger a disaster. Peter Thiel's stated goal in starting PayPal, for instance, was to "create a new internet currency to replace the US dollar." For someone holding the reins to an alternative currency, destabilizing existing currency could be a great investment opportunity.

Equally, as Silicon Valley execs were becoming aware, making money out of AI and robots was generating widespread anxiety and resentment among an all-too-human US workforce. Back in 2018, tech exec Andrew Yang (who ran in America's 2020 Democratic presidential primary) remarked that when self-driving vehicles stabilized into a reliable technology "we're going to have a million truck drivers out of work who are 94 percent male, with an average level of education of high school or one year of college." "That one innovation," he said, "will be enough to create riots in the street."[11] Tech moguls seem less worried about a nuclear war, an asteroid, a plague, or a pole shift than just a good old-fashioned mob of their own making, and their dread was trickling down in a way their wealth was not.

Certain quarters of "techno-libertarian" philosophy map onto prepper philosophy, where they seem to see crises not simply as inevitable risks to mitigate but as necessary and productive periods of resetting and renewal. These are times in which prudent moves can consolidate already-obtained wealth and power. One of Thiel's favorite books, a foundational text from 1997 called *The Sovereign Indi-*

vidual, suggests that the time is ripe for the morally bankrupt "welfare state" to transition into a libertarian utopia.[12] The book's epigraph is a quote from Tom Stoppard's play *Arcadia*: "The future is disorder."[13] Unsurprisingly, it's a book inhaled not just by Thiel, but by many aspiring Silicon Valley types. (Recall Facebook founder Mark Zuckerberg's now famous motto: "move fast and break things.")

One of the coauthors of *The Sovereign Individual*, James Dale Davidson, is a self-proclaimed "crisis investor." Davidson specializes in advising the rich on how to profit from economic catastrophe—essentially what Naomi Klein calls "disaster capitalism," with a twist.[14] *The Sovereign Individual* posits that the rise of cryptocurrency (keep in mind that this was written in 1997) will make it impossible for states to tax incomes, thereby causing them to collapse. Then (here's the twist), "out of this wreckage will emerge a new global dispensation, in which a 'cognitive elite' will rise to power and influence, as a class of sovereign individuals 'commanding vastly greater resources' who will no longer be subject to the power of nation-states. . . ."[15]

Thiel founded PayPal just after reading *The Sovereign Individual*. He did so explicitly recognizing its ability to erode the power of the state. The Bitcoin boom, leading to the proliferation of cryptocurrency, was well designed to do the rest. Given that Facebook is now rolling out their own currency called Libra, and countries like Sweden have all but done away with cash, it's not an implausible scenario.

The book's other author, Lord William Rees-Mogg, who died in 2012, was a British conservative, Euroskeptic, and onetime editor of the influential newspaper *The Times*. He was a libertarian who saw the nation-state as an obsolete relic. So it's no surprise that some of the tech giants of Silicon Valley were convinced by the ideas in his book and seem to be deploying their technologies to similar ends.

Rees-Mogg also had a marked influence on the political career of his son, Jacob Rees-Mogg, one of ringleaders of the Conservative Party who'd met with Steve Bannon as he pushed for Brexit. In doing so, he brought his father's prophesies to fruition, and profited handsomely from it. According to Channel 4's *Dispatches* program, his political maneuverings helped the value of Britain's currency to plummet, and Jacob Rees-Mogg made £7 million (approximately $8.5 million US) in profits by betting against the pound. In fact, all the architects of Brexit seemed to have benefited from the country's political turmoil: in particular Boris Johnson, who in July 2019 became prime minister, propelled into Britain's highest political office by a core of Conservative Party members.[16]

For many in the UK and around the world, the Brexit referendum of 2016 signaled an end to the age of global cooperation, of the sort needed to tackle worldwide crises, in particular impending climate catastrophe. In September 2019, a British photojournalist leaked details of a report, entitled "Operation Yellowhammer," that outlined grim outcomes for the country in a "no-deal Brexit," including breakdown of trade, resource shortages, and civil disruption. The leak forced the UK government to publish a watered-down version of the full report. Soon after, it was realized that "Operation Yellowhammer" was in fact not the worst-case scenario. That scenario was known as "Operation Black Swan," echoing the book by Nicholas Taleb.

Around the same time, the government rolled out a £100 million (approximately $122,000,000 US) "Get Ready for Brexit" campaign, sending pamphlets out and running ads on TV. The police advised everyone to prepare an emergency "grab bag" at home, without really explaining what it was for. Spoofing the official public information campaign, one joker in the city of Bristol wheatpasted a fake ad over a billboard that asked "Are You Brexit Ready?" and offered bunkers for £9,000 (approximately $11,000) and reduced prices on "child traps" and "flame throwers," as well as "in-store demonstrations on preparing and cooking a human body." Brexit seemed like a microcosm of the wave of neonationalist sentiment sweeping the globe, a breakdown of fragile geopolitical and social fabrics threaded over many decades. Six months previous, the UK government had activated "Operation Redfold": a defense contingency plan to house a thirty-five-hundred-person military team in a nuclear-proof bunker under the Ministry of Defence that would provide backup for the police if chaos were to take hold during the post-Brexit period.

Britain's people were quick to cotton on to, and to capitalize on, this sense of emergency. In the Yorkshire city of Leeds, one entrepreneur started selling "Brexit Boxes": disaster chests containing sixty freeze-dried meals and a fire starter for £295 (about $350 US). Another survivalist charged £250 ($300 US) for weekend courses on combat and urban survival. By early 2019 10 percent of the UK population were stockpiling food in advance of Brexit. What spooked people was not the suggestion that the international supply lines, which bring in a third of the country's food, could collapse, but a more generalized sense of uncertainty.[17]

Ironically, these preparations left some Britons better prepared for the outbreak of the COVID-19 pandemic, which put even Prime Minister Boris Johnson in the intensive care unit.

The Sovereign Individual also discusses the disruptive potential of technology like satellite-uplinked portable computers, cyber warfare, the possibility that online bots could imitate humans to propagate discontent, and the inevitability of a populist backlash against globalization. All prescient stuff, for 1997: these last two phenomena are of course central to how Trump ended up in the Oval Office. What's most disturbing about the book is how much of it had already come to pass, twenty-some years from publication. It's almost as though—if you take statements like Zuckerberg's "move fast and break things" at face value—these people actually brought this situation about.

The Silicon Valley elites' ambitions go further than simply building bug-out locations, or indeed cherry-picking the communities with which to populate the after time. Many of them share the belief, prevalent among preppers, that preserving consciousness is more important than preserving the body—and unlike most preppers, they have the financial resources to try and make it happen. If there is any chance consciousness can be uploaded onto servers or into robot bodies, cryonically frozen in their heads until they can be resurrected, or transferred through DNA reincarnation, they'll do it. But of course this data must also be protected and preserved in the bunker.

At least one bunker has already been turned into a reincarnation facility. It was originally built in 1978 by Girard Henderson, the director of Avon Products in Las Vegas and a big fan of underground living. In the middle of the first doom boom, Henderson created an exhibit at the 1964 New York World's Fair called "Why Live Underground?" and, in reciting the benefits, claimed that "underground living boasts of pure air, elimination of noise, freedom from all climate hazards and nuisances, lower heating, air-conditioning, insurance and maintenance costs, [and] more durable construction . . ."[18]

The five-thousand-square-foot, twenty-six-foot-deep bunker under Henderson's house had a swimming pool, putting green, his and her sinks in the well-appointed bathroom, and a pink-tiled kitchen and bar—all of which were in a setting constructed to resemble a landscaped garden. Pastoral murals were painted on every surface, treelike pillars loomed overhead, and mood lighting shifted from day to night to dupe the brain.

In 2018, Henderson's bunker was purchased by the Society for the Preservation of Near Extinct Species for $1.15 million. After a bit of digging, I discovered this society was connected to a company called Trans Time that charged $150,000 for the "suspension and reanimation" of cadavers. As of 2018, they had four whole human cadavers stored in the bunker, and ninety more signed up to be frozen, according to chief technology officer Steven Garan.[19] Given the disjunction between the false fecundity of the bunker's interior and the harsh reality of the surrounding Mojave Desert, it would be a confusing place to be resurrected.

At least since the Cold War, it seems American elites have been determined to turn catastrophe into opportunity. The loot reaped— if you took *The Sovereign Individual* as representative of their worldview—would not just be financial, it would be political. If you're truly committed to speculating on the apocalypse, the fact that collapse has not yet come is only further proof that the threat is still out there.[20] For the techno-libertarians of California, distance is all the shelter they need to assure it would only be an apocalypse for some.

• • •

Ian Clarry never provided me with any firm details about what Hardened Structures had built in New Zealand, as I'd asked. In lieu of this, rather bizarrely, he invited Douglas Clark to send me an assessment of Kim Dotcom's security situation. For all Clarry and Clark's apparent helpfulness, I still couldn't get any clear information about anything Hardened Structures had actually built. Finally, I got Clark on the phone, but when I pressed him for specifics, he simply told me that the company had been "shortlisted presently for both domestic and international government-scale projects, but those are all confidential and we cannot disclose any details." After our call, he sent me blueprints for a bunker under a house, labeled "Project Sedna," in an undisclosed location, where a secret staircase from a walk-in closet traversed an eighty-four-inch pipe tunnel that could be pumped full of Agent BZ (3-Quinuclidinyl benzilate gas) to incapacitate "determined" attackers. The bunker itself was standard fare, with a second escape route running to a hatch in a garden retaining wall. Given his recent experiences in building fortified domestic architecture, I sent it to my brother Pip, the California contractor, and asked him what he thought.

"It just looks like regular plans with massively thick walls. It would be ridiculously expensive to build for what it is, just based on materials," he wrote back. Clark didn't provide me with an estimate of construction costs. When I asked if I could see a photo of the finished project, Clark responded, "We did not construct Project Sedna. The client went another direction, and purchased a remote property instead."

I was deeply frustrated. Much about Hardened Structures felt like a shell game. After I told Clarry as much, he invited me to another dinner at Moorish Blue, at which I'd have the chance to interview Jakub Zamrazil, the founder of Oppidum in the Czech Republic, touted as "the largest billionaire bunker in the world," and in whose construction Hardened Structures had played a pivotal role, according to Clarry.

Oppidum offered an illusion of exclusivity that the media gobbled up. It'd been featured in *Forbes* and on CNN, CBS, and a host of other outlets. To get access to the facility's website, you had to request a secure code. Once you'd entered this code, the website disgorged spectacular representations of a bunker that rivaled even the most sophisticated government deep underground military base. The word *oppidum*, Latin for "an enclosed space," was originally used by the Romans to describe Celtic settlements. I guess the Latin was meant to make the modern version sound imposing—which Zamrazil's bunker certainly was. The website depicted this hundred-thousand-square-foot facility as being big enough for a few dozen very wealthy inhabitants spread across seven apartments. It was originally carved out of the rock by Soviet forces in 1984, intended as the ultimate fortress, geologically shielded inside a mountain at a secret location. Now made over for the private market, it had a helipad, golf course, and twenty-room bunker split over two deep levels with a command center. In the images of the command center, a sort of situation room with screens everywhere, a hologram of Earth beamed over a massive dark wood table.

"The bunker will be able to provide long-term accommodation for residents, up to 10 years if necessary—without the need for external supplies," the Oppidum LinkedIn page boasted. The endorsement of the former chief of the Czech Military Intelligence Service, General Andor Šándor, lent the project an air of solemn credibility.

After my previous experience at Moorish Blue, I arrived at about 2 p.m. with trepidation. To my relief, the atmosphere was completely different: the restaurant was buzzing. A table had been prepared for about ten people. As I chatted with Jae Wydeveld, an Australian ex–navy diver who was interested in investment opportunities, and Nina Bell, a marketing guru who was helping revamp the Hardened Structures social media feeds, *New Zealand Herald* journalist Steve Braunias—he of the original interview with Kim Dotcom—peppered Clarry with questions about what he actually did for a living besides hang out at Moorish Blue. Braunias was professorial and incisive, but he seemed to get about as much out of Clarry as I had: very little. Manny Ray, the bodyguard, was at Clarry's side as before, scrolling through his phone. Then the afternoon's VIP appeared: Jakub Zamrazil walked through the door.

Zamrazil cut a disheveled figure. He was wearing a stained, mismatched tracksuit and carried his belongings in a torn plastic shopping bag. He said he'd just come from a helicopter ride over the Sydney Harbour. He'd been excited to play tourist for the afternoon, having never been to Sydney. Braunias and I, wanting to know how Zamrazil had come to found Oppidum, got down to brass tacks.

Zamrazil murmured that he was a real estate investor, and was interested in unique properties.

Oppidum certainly fit that bill, I said, and asked about Hardened Structures' involvement in Oppidum's design. Zamrazil clutched the shopping bag in his lap, looking perplexed. He scratched the back of his neck and explained that he was here to try and sell the bunker to Clarry, or to an investor like Jae Wydeveld.

"What, the whole bloody thing, with the helipad and command center?" Braunias said.

"Oh, well, we're looking at selling the bunker in shell core stage," Zamrazil responded meekly. "Shell core" meaning empty. In other words, there was no billionaire bunker: the website, the LinkedIn page, and the "news" reports all depicted something that didn't exist.

Braunias closed his eyes briefly. Then he leaned over to me. "Brad, Clarry is a loose unit," he said. "These guys are all grifters."

We finished our lunch. Zamrazil ate nothing and left about thirty minutes later, presumably without securing a buyer for the "billionaire bunker."

Arriving back to my office, I Googled "Oppidum, Czech Republic" and reminded myself of the dozens of outlets that had run stories about it, many seemingly inviting the reader to believe it was a place that one could move into tomorrow. Journalists had enticed readers to see future plans as present realities. I was getting used to this: the media had written about Vivos bunkers in Germany and Seoul, often including the standard-issue computer renderings that looked like photos, that had never been built. At the same time, Robert Vicino had called out Oppidum. "It's a fiction!" he'd roared to me at xFest. "These guys called me trying to sell me a stake in the property they never built. Look at the photos, you can see they're aboveground, it's all a fantasy!"

Whatever their state of completeness, these bunkers they were selling were supposedly designed to alleviate dread but, to my mind, were rather perpetuating it by making such buildings seem more ubiquitous than they actually were. As I scrolled through the stories about Oppidum, it struck me—not for the first time—that the architecture of dread was a source as well as a symptom of our collective anxiety.

As a case in point, when at the beginning of 2020 the team of atomic scientists' Science and Security Board set the Dooms-day Clock to one hundred seconds to midnight, they stated that "focused attention is needed to prevent information technology from undermining public trust in political institutions, in the media, and in the existence of objective reality itself."[21] I thought about the stark realism of those articles in *Life* magazine from the 1960s: grim, yes, but they were also serious investigative journalism, in stark contrast to contemporary uncritical clickbait articles about nonexistent bunkers like Oppidum.[22]

Soon after our encounter with Zamrazil, Braunias filed a piece in the *New Zealand Herald*, titled "The Bodyguard at the End of the World." Its tone was scathing and incredulous.[23] Clarry did not come off well and emailed me constantly, seeking redemption. At one point, he confessed that Oppidum was actually a "front" for another bunker in Switzerland that Zamrazil was selling, which only made him sound even sketchier. When I asked for info on this Swiss bunker, Clarry sent the "off-market" PDF ad: it was fourteen thousand square feet, and was decorated in a way that made me imagine a 1960s alpine ski lodge cafeteria. It was priced at 140 million euros (about $150 million US), which seemed like an unfathomable sum for any private buyer. It was also almost certainly a fiction. When I looked up the address of the Czech limited liability company listed on the ad under Zamrazil's name, it turned out to be a graffiti-covered apartment block in Prague.

For all that, the charade to which Clarry had subjected me sat in contrast with the solidity of Hardened Structures' architectural plans: both Douglas Clark and Brian Camden, a civil engineer and the CEO of Hardened Structures, seemed competent enough. But by the time I was done chasing these guys around, I was left with a distinct sense that they were doing a lot more consulting than construction: Hardened Structures did their best to convey the impression that their bunkers were all over the world—but on closer examination almost all seemed to melt into air. Like many of the dread merchants, much of their business was speculative and their clients were elusive.

Clarry did eventually come through with another contact, promising that I could see an actual physical location where Hardened Structures had played a pivotal role. The contact was Auggie, who was busy building a massive luxury bunker in Thailand that he had called Sanctum (more Latin). Auggie, though, was quick to send through photos of his under-construction fortified home, as soon as Clarry connected us on Facebook. Taking a full tour of the bunker, he assured me, required nothing more than showing up. Sanctum was a chance for me to see how the technicalities, aesthetics, and ideologies of bunkers were trickling down into the domestic sphere, and how a global bourgeois class were increasingly incorporating defensibility into their everyday lives around the globe. A month later, I was on my way to Chiang Mai.

8

Sustainable Security: Thailand's Eco-Fortress

"Civilization [is] a thin layer of ice resting upon
a deep ocean of darkness and chaos."
—Werner Herzog, *A Guide for the
Perplexed*, 2014[1]

Chiang Mai is a sprawling city in the mountainous part of Northern Thailand tucked in between Myanmar and Laos. The crumbling, canal-ringed walls of its historic center, which once protected
gilded Buddhist temples, today enfold massage parlors, beer-soaked
bars blaring rap anthems, and "nomad" expats in flowing elephant-

print trousers waiting for adventure while discussing their financial travails over five-dollar vegan Pad See Ew.

The influx of *farang*, "foreigners," has extended well beyond the old city walls. Trying to get away from the chaos of the urban center, émigrés have begun settling in small villages, which they often effectively colonize, building gated communities and engaging little, if at all, with the agricultural communities they displace as they buy up their land to build new enclaves. In 2014, Thailand's military took control of the government in a coup d'état—the twelfth in a century—and suspended the constitution. But it's not political instability people fear as much as everyday crime. And it's not just the foreigners moving into these developments. Members of Thailand's growing middle class, progressively more afraid that they'll lose their newfound wealth to violence, are also fanning out. In other words, the class insecurities of the nouveau riche are running hot in Thailand. This is a story that plays out the world over; as Zygmunt Bauman writes, it's the people who live in the greatest comfort who often feel most "threatened, insecure and frightened, more inclined to panic, and more passionate about everything related to security and safety."[2]

Auggie, a Canadian from Manitoba, moved to Chiang Mai fourteen years ago to marry a Thai AirAsia hostess named Mam whom he'd met at a DVD rental shop. Pictures of them with their one-year-old daughter on Facebook are like an ad for global cosmopolitanism. With welcome transparency, Auggie wanted to give me some context for the multimillion-dollar "eco-fortress" he was building in an abandoned orchard in the tiny hamlet of Hua Thung in Nong Khwai village, about a twenty-minute drive from Chiang Mai.

"The Thai word for 'gated communities' is *moo bahn*," he'd told me over the phone. "But these"—meaning the run-of-the-mill gated communities—"are just housing estates with walls and some eighty-year-old *somchai*"—the equivalent of John Doe—"manning the gate." People think these places are safe, Auggie continued, but they're not: "The *somchai* get paid off and there are break-ins all the time. People just hop over the back fence. There are home invasions, rapes, terrible things, families get tied up." Residents in these gated communities had resorted to makeshift protection: glass shards in cement on top of walls, or rows of iron spikes. Auggie thought both were gauche. He preferred clean lines, hidden traps, and elevated, impermeable façades.

"I get that you want to feel safe," I told him, "but what is making you so anxious that you feel a need to build a fortress? Was it the coup in 2014?"

"The coups come and go." Auggie said, philosophically. "I don't know, man, I think there's a gradient of what people perceive to be the greatest threats to them, and they prep in accordance. For me, keeping my family safe and secure each and every day is what I focus on, not only during an 'event' of that kind of magnitude. Your best chance at doing so is when you take control of the parameters." What especially bothered Auggie, before building Sanctum, was that he often wasn't around to keep his family safe: he'd worked on offshore oil rigs as an underwater welder and was gone half the year on long stints. Later, he got a promotion to an inspection engineer role working with divers from a control room. It was less dangerous, but still required a lot of time away from home.

"The money was good," he said. "But I worried about my wife and kid when I was gone." He'd moved the family into increasingly secure *moo bahns*, until finally he decided they'd just build their own. At xPoint, when I really pressed Mark and Tom on their spurs to action, it eventually became clear that their wives were behind the drive for safe space. Auggie, too, was driven as much by his wife, Mam's, desire for a secure compound as his own interest in building it.

Once he'd managed to obtain the 0.6-acre plot, he figured it would make sense to build a few more structures to leverage the funds to construct his own castle, as in many end-of-days communities. He settled on four concrete block "villas" on the plot, each a detached, fortified home. The first of the quad was for Auggie and his family, the other three were business investments.

He funneled more than $60,000 of his savings into producing slick promotional materials. Rather than catering to a few paranoid billionaires, as Zamrazil had done, Auggie marketed the materials to the jet-set crowd, businesspeople who might just want a fortified second residence. Booths with pamphlets and large graphic displays were deployed at key real estate expos. He even snagged two prizes for the designs at the 2017 Asia Pacific Property Awards, when the first villa was still just a shell, following which he managed to sell two of the other three villas, on the basis of plans alone, to Bitcoin millionaires, a German and an American living in South Korea. Both were looking for an ultra-secure holiday home.

I arrived in Chiang Mai hoping to see the almost complete first villa. My first stop was the house of a colleague at the University of Sydney: Philip Hirsch, who'd retired to the forty-resident Nam Jam hamlet in Nong Khwai with his Thai wife, Tubtim. Their house—all open plan, high ceilings, filtered light, and foliage—was picturesque. It was also a twenty-minute walk from Sanctum.

Tubtim, a researcher at Chiang Mai University and an expert on class tension and urban-rural migration in Thailand, was the ideal person to quiz about friction arising from an influx of paranoid expats. As the three of us ambled over to Sanctum, Hirsch wheeling their tandem bike alongside him, I asked Tubtim what the community thought of Auggie's bunker. The only sign of his presence in the neighborhood, she said, was construction materials being dumped in the irrigation channel: apart from that, nobody knew him, though his wife, Mam, was from a nearby town. "We've all been wondering what he's building," Hirsch chipped in. Hardly a recipe for community relations, I thought.

We walked through Nam Jam toward Hua Thung—the palm-shaded streets and lush lanes heavy with the smell of overripe fruit and woodsmoke—past large houses with open front gates where people paused their sweeping to wave at us cheerily. Phil and Tubtim had become deeply embedded in the community since moving there full-time in 2017; everyone we saw greeted them enthusiastically. Most of these people, I also noticed, left their property gates and front doors wide open.

Sanctum soon loomed into view: a massive concerete block draped by hangng plants set in the middle of some scrubby fields that were once orchards. Palm trees in wooden crates sat next to it, awaiting planting. There were no windows on the bottom floor, which gave it the air of a wall around a compound rather than the outer wall of a house. It was the logical escalation of a suburban gated enclave, a residence not only defensively built but also weirdly urban—in contrast to the village—and utterly private. Just approaching it made me feel uncomfortable, and the other three villa blocks hadn't yet been built. It would be an imposing complex when complete.

Walking up to the main gate, we saw Auggie poring over plans rolled out on the hood of a brand-new jet-black Ford pickup truck, talking to one of his workers. He was in good shape. In fact, I thought, he was the healthiest-looking prepper I'd met, by a long shot. He wore a long-sleeve black shirt and had a well-trimmed auburn beard. When he saw us, he waved hello, removed his chunky black sunglasses, and shook our hands enthusiastically. We followed him into what was more or less a construction site: people were laying cement, cutting tile with screaming saws, stringing electrical wiring, and carrying buckets from one area to another.

Auggie explained that the workers on-site were Thai Yai. He described them as "the most dependable people in the world"—which may have been true, though I knew from Tubtim's work that hiring Thai Yai people (the Thai term for Shan people), an ethnic minority in Thailand, was often about keeping the workforce disorganized so they couldn't demand better wages. A lot of them lived in slapdash corrugated iron construction camps and were regarded with suspicion even by relatively poor local farmers.

The work they were doing, however, was astounding. Given a guided tour by Auggie, we saw the Faraday-protected electronic closets, an office that doubled as a panic room, and wandered up the main staircase past bamboo scaffolding where workers were installing a "living wall" to support passion fruit vines so that food could be grown inside the house. The center of the building was a sun-drenched open-air atrium, where a swimming pool in the middle would filter blue light through a submerged glass panel into the nuclear fallout shelter, which doubled as a day spa.

"We only have glass on the second and third floors, and it'll be covered in 3M ballistic-rated window film, so that even if someone comes with a ladder, they're going to have a hard time getting through the windows," Auggie told us as we ambled. The corporation 3M, I recalled, was also selling this film to schools in the United States to shooter-proof them—and making a mint from it.

In 2020, 3M stock prices spiked during the COVID-19 pandemic, since the company was a primary manufacturer of respirators and coveted N95 face masks. I'd long suspected one of the executives at 3M might be a tea-leaf-reading doomsday prepper.

"Auggie, I have to ask," Hirsch ventured. "If you're so concerned about the neighbors, how do you know what kind of people are going to move into the other villas? If everyone who moves here is suspicious of their neighbors, they probably won't be very good neighbors."

"You're right," Auggie said, laughing. "At the price I'm asking," which was about $1.5 million, "I can't be too picky about who moves into Sanctum. But I do want to know the neighbors, not just here, but in the wider village. I feel like there's three aspects to security in Thailand. First, you need physical security, which we've got here," he said, sweeping his arm over the interior courtyard. "Second, you need to be connected to *sen yai*, you know, a big noodle. So, we're paying a small fee to the local police to come here every day and check on things."

"Dude, that sounds like an extortion racket!" I interrupted.

"Yeah, well, in Canada when you call the cops they show up. Here they might need a little incentive," Auggie said, shrugging. In Thailand, if you had the resources like Auggie had, you didn't need to sweat the small stuff constantly, you just paid to deal with it.

"But the third thing, you're right, is that if we know our neighbors, we can look out for each other. Hopefully we can get around to meeting other people once this is all up and running." As Auggie took out his measuring tape and checked something, I thought it must have been strange for the people of this very sociable and friendly village to see a man they didn't know working away six days a week for three years on a mysterious project. But Auggie seemed be in his own world, oblivious. I could see him doing mental calculations as he turned back to us.

"So, what is it you're preparing for?" I asked.

"Well, it's really more about assurance in the present rather than prepping," he said. "As the severity of things that can go wrong increases, so does the difficulty of being prepared for them, but they all boil down to the same elements: food, water, and shelter, or safety. If people aren't fulfilling one of those categories, it'll be a major stressor. Sanctum kinda takes care of all of them, while allowing us to live here and enjoy it. Food is abundant here, there aren't complicated supply chains—it goes from the farm to the market where you buy it. We can also grow food in the rooftop planters or in the green spaces. The house has its own energy sources and well water and has different levels of security. Yeah, if the army shows up, I don't have a chance, it's not as secure as an underground bunker with steel vault doors or something, but for a daily house that's actually pleasant to live in, it's very secure."

The "elements" that Auggie was referring to were outlined in 1943 by Abraham Maslow, a psychologist who had researched the idea of basic human needs to achieve happiness.[3] In his hierarchy, Maslow breaks down needs into five categories on a pyramid chart. From base to tip, they are: physiological, safety, love and belonging, esteem, and self-actualization. Each of these categories builds on the others. However, in order to fulfill higher needs, a degree of vulnerability is necessary, which might mean sacrificing some of the lower needs. Conversely, focusing too much on basic needs for security and safety can be to the detriment of intimate relationships, leaving people stuck at the base of the pyramid. The higher people climbed on the pyramid, Maslow argued, the happier they would be. Reaching self-actualization, or realizing one's full potential, was the pinnacle. It felt like Auggie was striving to cover the first two—his physiological and safety needs—in building Sanctum, and was keen to expand his love for the family into a community around him—but his heavy investment in achieving financial and physical security was stilting his ability to reach toward the top of the pyramid.

Auggie was hardly alone in wanting to "protect the base": indeed, it's a phenomenon increasingly found across the globe. As a perceived sense of threat to their basic security increases, people are retreating to the bottom of Maslow's pyramid. In Auggie's case, he was privileged to be able to bug out to a rural location, where land is cheap and threats are few. But many urban dwellers simply don't have the opportunity to flee the city, and have to make do with the space that they have. At a time when what we most need is more cooperation, community support, and openness, people in cities are withdrawing into armored districts and creating two kinds of disaster architecture: buildings meant to dissuade interest through intimidation and covert territory to be accessed only by those "in the know."

I knew that the latter has evolved, especially among wealthy urban populations, through the carving out of underground "upgrades" to the home. A big part of this, as in Singapore, is about pressure on space: if you can't expand in any other direction, you dig down. But as inequality continues to escalate, exacerbating social tensions, underground spaces are also convenient places to store wealth out of sight. It's no surprise that this phenomenon should be especially apparent in the UK, where, as the geographer Danny Dorling has shown, the gap between the very rich and the rest of the population is wider than anywhere in Europe, and has reached a level not seen in a century.[4] Brits, as a result, have been literally burying their wealth.

Between 2001 and 2014, planning applications for "megabasement" developments in the boroughs of Kensington and Chelsea rose from 46 to 450.[5] Many of these projects contained cinemas, bowling alleys, spas, wine cellars, tennis courts, weapon vaults, panic rooms, and other hardened elements. Between 2008 and 2017, across all of London, 4,650 basements were approved, and included 1,000 gyms, 380 pools, 460 cinemas, 380 wine cellars, and 120 rooms for staff reaching to a combined depth of almost fifty thousand feet.[6] Since the subterranean capacity of these excavations can exceed the size of the street-level houses by several times, these homes constitute a kind of "iceberg architecture."[7]

In a 2016 study on the rise of "domestic urban fortresses," Rowland Atkinson and Sarah Blandy, both based at the University of Sheffield in the UK, suggest that the fortified architecture of contemporary ultra-secure homes tends toward two extreme types: "stealthy" and "spiky."[8] Iceberg mansions, like the panic rooms of California, or the bug-out ranches of New Zealand, can be viewed as stealth houses. They are intended to dissimulate their luxurious qualities, comprising a strategically defensive but inconspicuous architecture. This makes them a less attractive prospect to criminals. Sanctum, on the other hand, with its daunting, monolithic façade, dropped into a rural setting where you couldn't help but notice it, falls into the spiky category. It is meant to intimidate, to dissuade, and to deter. It is meant—ultimately—to present itself as a "hard target" to attackers, one that can't possibly be worth the risk of gaining access to whatever is inside. And what's inside, of course, is luxury that few Thai people can afford.

On the third level of Sanctum there was an outdoor Jacuzzi looking out over the forest, waiting to be filled with water. The four of us climbed a ladder and pushed open a hatch to check out the solar panel array on the roof. The hatch, Auggie assured us, "could be latched from the top, so if things got really bad, we could just pull the ladder and stay on the roof." He explained that this would buy them time during a home invasion. In the distance, we could just make out Wat Phra That Doi Kham, a mountaintop temple with a fifty-six-foot-tall gold Buddha in the middle of it.

Squinting at the temple, Auggie said, "You know, people build bunkers for the future, but it's easier to plan and build for the present and the future at the same time. These places where rich people buy the bunker sight unseen like Survival Condo, they've never lived in the bunker. There is a good chance they forgot things or designed them wrong for living. I just find that prepping for the here and now is more valuable than focusing all this energy on long-term survival and 'what if' scenarios. People are going to 'what if' themselves into the grave."

Taking up Auggie's offer to hang out on the construction site and watch the bunker come together, I returned to Sanctum the next day.

"So Auggie," I said, as he checked some overhead wiring, "when I met with Clarry in Sydney, he said that Hardened Structures had consulted on this project. Did they design the whole thing?"

"Um, not really," he said. He told me that Hardened Structures had looked over his plans and offered to assist if one of Sanctum's future residents wanted a full bunker designed from the ground up. The plans Auggie was working from, he assured me, were his own. Nobody from the firm had ever visited the site.

At the end of the workday I climbed into Auggie's black Ford

Ranger, and we headed into Chiang Mai for dinner. As we drove, he got to talking about a legal dispute he was involved in—with the two Bitcoin millionaires who'd bought into Sanctum. After they'd paid him deposits in Bitcoin, and he'd cashed it out, they'd tried to wrench control of Sanctum from him by purchasing the land, rather than just the villas, and then kicking him out once they had 50 percent control. During the dispute, the funding stream had dried up, and Auggie worried that he was going to have to go back to the oil rigs if he wasn't able to sell the third villa. As he'd said, he couldn't be too picky about his neighbors.

"I feel terrible because when we closed the first two deals, I told Mam that she could quit her job," he said. "Now I'm scared that I'm going to have to leave with Sanctum unfinished. Prepare as you might, you can't prepare for everything. I can't let them take this away from me, though, it's my life's project."

As we approached the built-up outskirts of the city, the traffic grew denser. Mopeds swarmed around us, stacked with teetering bundles of fresh produce from the countryside; driving them seemed as much as anything a matter of balance and hope.

"You know, Trump scares the crap out of me," Auggie offered, deftly swerving around a cluster of bikes. "I feel like we're in a second Cold War, now with China. I'm optimistic though, maybe to a fault. I imagine walking through the doors of Sanctum when it's finally finished and feeling the anxiety drop out of my body. I imagine spending time in there with my family, safe and secure and," unconsciously echoing Maslow, "becoming my best version of myself."

On my last night in Chiang Mai, I took a stroll through the city's night markets, where the streets were thick with stalls and people. Suddenly, the heavens opened, sending the crowds scattering for cover. I ducked into a used bookshop and browsed as I waited for the rain to stop. I picked up a well-thumbed, highlighted copy of Martin Heidegger's *Existence and Being*—clearly discarded by some backpacker before flying home to less philosophical shores.

The rain cleared, and I took the book to a bar. A crack in the spine marked out Heidegger's essay "What Is Metaphysics?,"[9] in which he tackles *angst*, the German word for "dread." Unlike Kierkegaard's idea of dread, which was based on original sin as sweet as it was debilitating, Heidegger saw it as a phenomenological state: a first-person experience, a state of being. For him, dread is the experience of having your world fall apart when you recognize your own insignificance, and the world—which you previously thought you'd made sense of—has no meaning at all. Dread, in other words, is the realization that we're utterly alone—but that realization also gives us freedom, from the world and from ourselves. I realized that Heidegger's words summed up the collective mood I'd found wherever I'd gone: that sense of teetering on the brink of destruction and possibility. Heidegger instructs us to embrace this sense of being on the edge: it shouldn't lead to nihilism, he says, but to joy, because to dread is to be human. He'd have made a pretty good prepper.

In February 2020, Auggie's wife's fears of everyday violence were proven justified when a gunman went on a shooting spree in an upscale airport-themed Thai shopping mall called Terminal 21. The shooter killed more than thirty people. But Auggie's financial situation had also stabilized—he'd warded off the intended coup from his two buyers—though he still hadn't finished his own home. In fact, in speaking to Tubtim and Phil, it seemed that construction of the second villa was proceeding faster than the first. Auggie ended up working on ships and oil rigs until the German Bitcoin millionaire pitched in another $100,000 to speed the final stage of construction. Meanwhile, Mam and Auggie invited Tubtim and Phil to their tenth wedding anniversary. Finally, they hung out with the neighbors.

Captain Paranoid: Fortitude Ranch

"The doomsayers are always right, eventually."
—Bryan Walsh, *End Times*, 2019[1]

A few hours' drive from the Greenbrier bunker that President Eisenhower had ordered built during the early days of the Cold War, I drove through the "unincorporated community" of Lost City, West Virginia, an Appalachian settlement where townsfolk drink on the stoops of their mobile homes in the summer. Crunching slowly up a gravel driveway through dappled shade, into a valley between two densely wooded ridges, I crept past an empty watchtower. This was the only indication that I'd arrived at Fortitude Ranch, a fifty-acre survival retreat buried in the George Washington National Forest. A man stuck his head out of a window in a large house, tracking my progress up the drive. When I parked, he called down that Drew Miller was away picking up building supplies: I could let myself in.

The journey from Washington Dulles Airport had only taken a few hours, and I had a lot of energy left for exploration. Pulling my overnight bag out of the trunk of the rental car, I noticed a buried metal culvert with an uneven concrete face: not, as I'd thought on first sight, the storage shed, but a fallout shelter. I cracked the door and the musty smell of disuse wafted out. Inside, rows of cramped bunk beds built out of particle board were tucked into the arc of the walls, bookended by twenty-five-year-shelf-life #10 cans, five-gallon buckets of other supplies, and two-by-fours holding up the roof. Plastic bags full of belongings had been dumped on a few of the beds. In the back, a wooden ladder led to an emergency vertical escape hatch that let a trickle of light through, illuminating dust motes that drifted around lazily.

Drew Miller had a grand vision for Fortitude Ranch, of which the West Virginia location was only one component. His aim was to construct a network of twelve survivalist encampments, spread across the USA, each for fifty to five hundred people, sufficient size to deter attacks by the marauding hordes that would roam the country after the Fall. By buying into the model for $1,000 a year, members could use the spaces to vacation, but then could retreat to any of the forts to escape if things started kicking off. Miller's motto was "Prepare for the worst, enjoy the present."

Once inside the gates, residents could, if necessary, retreat further into shallow underground shelters of the kind I'd just poked my head into. Shelters and basement rooms filtered against pathogens were buried under several feet of earth, which would also protect against nuclear fallout. Though there would be some stored food, this was more of a survivalist model, where crops and livestock in the compound would keep people going, behind fences flanked by guard posts and watchtowers like the one I saw on the way in. This was, of course, if the livestock weren't already contaminated by disease or radiation.

A retired colonel from air force intelligence, with a Harvard PhD from the John F. Kennedy School of Government, Miller is widely seen as one of the most practical and qualified of the dread merchants: his doctoral thesis was on shallow underground nuclear defense shelters.[2] After retiring from the air force, he also self-published a postapocalyptic novel eerily titled *Rohan Nation: Reinventing America After the 2020 Collapse.* This work of fiction, about the lives of biological warfare survivors, is described on Amazon as a story of "America's rebirth, realistically forecast in a future-thriller-action-romance novel" and steeped in "Libertarian political philosophy."[3] In the book, an electromagnetic pulse detonated in the middle of a pandemic causes "billions of deaths worldwide." The book's jacket claims the narrative is "based on sound research and analysis," but the Amazon reviews are mixed. "If you're an anarcho-libertarian horse fanatic," one reviewer wrote, "sitting in your cabin with a hoard of ammunition and a lifetime supply of SPAM, eagerly awaiting The Collapse, then you might like this book. Otherwise, it is probably not for you." In contrast to the litany of scathing reviews, for many preppers, the novel only bolstered Miller's considerable credibility as an apocalyptic soothsayer.

Most of the dread merchants prepare for multiple scenarios and a cascading ripple effect, but many also have a favorite disaster scenario to speculate on. For Miller, the Fall is all about a bioengineered viral pandemic or BVP. He's suggested in public lectures that in the coming decade a rogue scientist will release a deadly virus. In a piece he wrote for the right-wing magazine *The American Interest* he'd sent me before our meeting, he suggested that North Korea or the Islamic Revolutionary Guard Corps of Iran would intentionally unleash a BVP, and then deploy the vaccine in their respective countries before the virus looped back via global transport connections.[4] US military might, meanwhile, would be crushed by the superbug.

In another, unpublished article Miller sent me, he echoed Tom Soulsby back at xPoint where he wrote that "unlike the largely rural, resilient population that weathered the 1918 flu pandemic (a relatively low-lethality virus), our urbanized society depends on electricity, central water supply systems, and daily deliveries of food over long distances.... People will panic as food stores are quickly sold out or looted." Reading this, I felt that the cascading effects of his plague scenario seemed more plausible than its intentional deployment from North Korea or Iran. However, Miller was right that biological agents had killed more people than anything else in history—more, indeed, than all combined wars to date. Only one hundred years ago, the Spanish flu infected 500 million people and killed off 3 to 5 percent of the world's population. As the COVID-19 pandemic tore through the world's major cities in 2020, spreading contamination via international trade and travel networks, it became startlingly obvious how much *more* susceptible we are to pandemics than we were in 1918, because of the way we've built our financial systems—over the last thirty years especially—to depend upon global exchange. The virus, like capital, sought proliferation and found it through the same channels, making a mockery of biosecurity measures.[5] In other words, we built COVID-19's pathways.

Given that the outbreak also stalled, ever so briefly, our assault on the Earth by curbing travel—and thus some carbon emissions—it also corroborated preppers' assertions about the veiled benefits of catastrophe. Miller's cool contention during the pandemic was that we'd gotten off easy. He continues to suggest something far worse is just over the horizon, particularly now that foreign powers know what a powerful weapon the virus can be in crippling capitalist economies.

The guy who'd stuck his head out of the window on my way in turned out to be a swarthy barrel-chested Puerto Rican ex-marine named Zack, who acted as physical security, innkeeper, and some sort of web guy for the otherwise deserted ranch. As he showed me to my roomy lodgings, I asked him if he was there because of his own worries about the future.

"Nah, man, I'm not like Captain Paranoid," he said (meaning Miller). "I figure if shit goes down being healthy is the most important thing. I'd rather spend my time lifting weights than building bunkers out here. But hey, it's his business."

"And what is the business?" I asked. "I mean, people are buying in for a thousand dollars a year, I get that, but are they actually coming here to hang out?"

"I don't really see that side of things, man," Zack said. "We rent this place as a bed-and-breakfast and I check people in and out, but half of the people who stay here don't know what the place is. It's a cover." I wasn't sure why Miller needed a cover, since multiple articles about the facility called out its name and location. Surely the members were aware of that. Later, I watched Zack check in a German couple with a toddler staying in the bed-and-breakfast (so, not members) who indeed seemed to have no idea they were staying in a fifty-acre survivalist plague citadel.

When Miller turned up, I was photographing a black oil drum sitting on a plastic pallet. It was in the middle of a field where milk goats were grazing next to a chain basket for disc golf.

"That's where we would burn the corpses if people got infected," he told me as he stepped out of his truck. "We'd collect pictures and ID from the bodies before we burned them. We tried it out with a goat."

Miller's chestnut-colored hair was wild, sticking up at all angles. His white T-shirt and cargo pants were covered in a textured rainbow of paint flecks, sawdust, and wood chips. As I shook his hand, I noticed two of his fingernails were black: he'd clearly smacked them with a hammer. The lines on his face told a story of a life of work outdoors, and—just possibly—a deep level of anxiety.

"Is this your only subterranean structure?" I asked, pointing to the bunker I'd peeked into.

"Those are what we call our 'spartan' facilities. But the focus on deep underground bunkers is misplaced," he said. "Although the Survival Condo in Kansas is the gold standard for prepping, you only need three feet of earth for shielding from radiation fallout. Castle technology, with watchtowers defending a community, is what will get you through." He looked around with hands on hips, as if taking stock of the defenses. I just saw trees.

"Let me get my snake gun and we can walk around," he said. A "snake charmer," as they are often called in this part of the world, is a pistol loaded with small pellets rather than a solid bullet, useful for peppering fast, small creatures. As I waited for him to return, I couldn't get out of my mind the image he'd left me with: the charred goat and piles of ID collected from burned bodies.

Miller came back wrapping a gun belt around his waist, his black Labrador, Ringo, bounding alongside, trying to lick his face.

"So like I was saying, we're going to have roving gangs," Miller continued, apropos of nothing. "Not on day one, but when they come out, guards in the watchtower are going to fire a warning shot and I can't imagine getting into a firefight—people are going for soft targets first." Miller's idea was that once the gangs knew the compounds were well defended, they would move off to a grocery store or something.

Miller cinched the gun belt a little tighter and tucked in the strap. "In the first days of the collapse people are going to be pigging out trying to eat all the food that's going to go bad. But forty-eight hours in, those people will start going hungry and freaking out while we switch to more sustainable sources in here.

"Sorry I'm all over the place. Come on," he said, charging up the valley. Given his background, I'd expected a cold, calculating type. Miller was anything but.

Miller showed me energetically around the site: the solar panels and inverters for converting electricity, battery storage, propane generator backup, and a shortwave radio system. He pointed out black walnut and peach trees, brick ovens, a greenhouse, firepits, and wells. Overlooking us were tree platforms where snipers could fire on intruders, and these currently doubled as zip-line platforms; the fortifications I'd failed to notice earlier also acted as family fun park features.

"I like dual-function architecture," Miller explained. Walking up a sheer bulldozed hill drenched in a solid gray river of spilled concrete, we stepped onto a building pad and through a missing piece of wall into a log cabin that was still under construction.

"This is how I like to build shelters," he said. "It's a country club model. Upstairs you have a comfortable space with lots of light; downstairs you've got the underground rooms with separate air leading to the fallout shelter. You've got two inches of wood, a metal pan, eight inches of concrete, and three feet of earth."

He would cap each ranch population at five hundred people, because any more than that would be hard to defend, and to control.

"In an emergency situation, people don't make sensible decisions," he told me. "We will be making decisions for them. That's in their best interest."

"What if someone wants to leave?" I asked.

"Then they're not coming back in," he replied brusquely. "I'm not having the ranch infected because someone wanted to go on a supply run. So, anyway," he moved on briskly, past the unspoken question of what would happen to the excluded resident, "you've seen the spartan shelters. This is the economy model down here," he said, looking around. "If you want a luxury membership, you get to sleep upstairs in the log cabin."

On the far side of the rooms downstairs, currently framed by LED lights dangling from the ceiling, another door led to a large concrete box—the fallout shelter, which was currently awaiting a roof. It all looked a long way to completion. There was one other worker there, a guy chain-smoking in a sleeveless shirt, doing what looked to me to be preternatural woodcrafting, but Miller was doing much of the work himself—often, as I would find, late into the evenings.

It was all a bit of a letdown. As with xPoint, the vision and plans, as well as the representations of the community in the media, were out of joint with the reality of the preparations. This isn't to say Miller didn't believe what he was telling me, or that what he'd built wouldn't work as planned. But there was a vast discrepancy between media depictions of a sweeping cultural zeitgeist metastasizing into a "second doom boom," of a kind that would match early Cold War preparations, and the material realities of these places. Miller's dream, optimistically depicted online, of twelve ranches dotted around the country that could be used as resorts for recreation and family staycations until the collapse hit, seemed a long way off, despite the weird prescience of his fictional narrative in *Rohan Nation* that America would be crippled by a pandemic in 2020. If Miller's other (nonfiction) predictions can serve as a guide, he should have hundreds of hands on deck in order to be ready in time. The reality was that construction at Fortitude Ranch was proceeding at a snail's pace. The only other "ranch"—in Colorado—consisted of a single building and a stacked-rock sniper blind on a hill. The airy claim on Miller's website, that a few sites would be completed each year, seemed unlikely to be fulfilled.

We had lunch in the main building, after having assembled a forlorn selection of carrots, olives, and crackers by rummaging through the cupboards and fridge. It struck me as odd that there was nothing to eat in a doomsday prepper camp. As we ate, I thought about the food stores in the bunkers. In an emergency, I knew I'd be looking for them within a day or two. In three days, I'd definitely hurt someone to get at them. I wondered how long it would take for people to start picking around in the body-burn pit for scraps.

Meanwhile, Zack was watching a documentary about El Chapo's tunnel prison break in Mexico assisted by the Sinaloa drug cartel. The German couple came in to ask for directions to a supermarket in the next town over. Miller provided the directions in German. As they chatted, I got the gist that he was letting them in on the secret that they were staying in a doomstead, pointing out the sniper platforms. Clearly confused, they left quickly to go and find supplies outside the compound.

"People don't get it," Miller said, after they closed the front door. "Experts will tell you we're overdue for a pandemic, they're not rare occurrences, they happen with regularity. It takes one person and no money to engineer and release a pandemic. Somebody is going to see it as the moral thing to do, they'll justify it by arguing, at least in their own minds, that Earth has to be saved from people." Miller was dismissive of other prepper theories, which he found both far-fetched and counterproductive. "I'm sick of all these conspiracy theories, the Mayan stories and Planet X and the FEMA concentration camps. All that stuff does is discredit the prepper community when those prophecies don't come true." Pandemics, on the other hand, Miller assured me, punctuated history with horrifying regularity and efficiency.

Even before the COVID-19 outbreak, I knew Miller wasn't off-base. Around the end of the fifteenth century, 60 million people—or about 10 percent of the world's population at that point—were living in North and South America. Within a hundred years, this was reduced to just 5 or 6 million through disease spread by colonization. If we had any doubts about human impacts on climate, killing off all those people also cooled the Earth significantly, creating a "Little Ice Age."[6] A similar event now, released naturally—or, Miller opined, intentionally by an environmental activist as an act of retribution and attempt to stave off climate disaster (a scenario imagined in Terry Gilliam's 1995 film, *12 Monkeys*)—could ravage today's urbanized populations. Researchers at the University of Oxford's Future of Humanity Institute concur with Miller, seeing a genetically engineered pandemic, or what they call "synthetic biotech," as a threat outstripped only by the inevitability of dangerous artificial intelligence.[7]

Another pandemic scenario I'd read about involved the release of long-dormant bacteria and viruses, trapped in now melting ice and permafrost. Remnants of anthrax were recently found in corpses buried in mass graves in Alaska's tundra.[8] Smallpox and bubonic plague are also locked in the ice, along with microbes from the Pleistocene, the last Ice Age. If they were released, we wouldn't have the biological resistance required to fight these contagions, just like those 55 million people wiped out in the Americas five centuries ago.

Miller was also very concerned about a foreign power hitting the USA with an electromagnetic pulse (EMP). He told me that he was a former intelligence officer and directed me to an article by former CIA director R. James Woolsey that outlines North Korea's capacity to explode a single warhead as an exo-atmospheric detonation some twenty to three hundred miles over the USA. This would, Woolsey claimed, black out the national electric grid for more than a year, killing 90 percent of Americans through starvation and societal collapse.[9]

"We need to harden our infrastructure against EMP attack," Miller insisted. "This could save American civilization and hundreds of millions of lives. Until the government takes that threat seriously, it's up to us to build resiliency. I worked at the Pentagon, Larry Hall at Survival Condo was a spook, too, he worked on classified military contracts, and you know Dave Jones, the EMP guy, who has a spot on the ranch, works at Mount Weather, right?" (Mount Weather being the 180,000-square-foot US government bunker fifty miles from Washington, DC, that congressional leaders got evacuated to on 9/11.) "The people calling this stuff out are not outliers."

I hadn't yet met Larry Hall or Dave Jones, but these statistics struck me as massively overhyped. When I later reverse engineered the 90 percent figure, I ended up at a transcript from the 2008 US House Committee on Armed Services. In it, one Dr. William Graham, chairman of the Congressional EMP Commission, says he obtained the figure from the postapocalyptic novel *One Second After*. The novel had a foreword penned by former House speaker Newt Gingrich, who suggested that an EMP attack would "destroy our complex, delicate high tech society in an instant and throw all of our lives back to an existence equal to that of the Middle Ages. Millions would die in the first week alone . . ."[10] Fiction and fact, it would seem, were pretty blurred in this instance.

The US government, however, is convinced by the EMP threat. In 2011, it formed an Electromagnetic Pulse Caucus on Capitol Hill; more recently, it authorized a $44 million expenditure on a HEMP- (high-elevation electromagnetic pulse) and blast-protected antiballistic missile interceptor system in Alaska—housed, naturally, in a massive underground silo.[11] In March 2019, President Trump signed an executive order directing federal agencies to coordinate defense against an EMP about the same time he was proposing deep cuts in the budgets of the Centers for Disease Control and Prevention (CDC) and National Institutes of Health (NIH), two agencies crucial to coordinating the pandemic response.

Miller's anxieties struck me as a fairly classic example of dread. In Sigmund Freud's lectures in *A General Introduction to Psychoanalysis*, he defined dread as a "neurotic fear . . . a general condition of anxiety, a condition of free-floating fear as it were, which is ready to attach itself to any appropriate idea, to influence judgment, to give rise to expectations, in fact to seize any opportunity to make itself felt. We call this condition 'expectant fear' or 'anxious expectation.' Persons who suffer from this sort of fear," Freud continued, "always prophesy the most terrible of all possibilities, interpret every coincidence as an evil omen, and ascribe a dreadful meaning to all uncertainty. Many persons who cannot be termed ill show this tendency to anticipate disaster. We blame them for being over-anxious or pessimistic."[12]

Freud's analysis could have been written about today's dooms-day preppers. His point is that it makes far more sense to see the "neurotic" individual as a person rationally responding to an uncertain situation. Their tendency to "ascribe a dreadful meaning to events" may be triggered by external conditions as much as by psychology. Freud makes a clear distinction between fears, phobias, or anxieties, which have objects, and boundless states such as neurotic fear, dread, and hysteria. These overwhelming feelings are often vocalized by preppers, and channeled by dread merchants. In my previous encounters with the latter, I had never quite believed that they genuinely suffered from dread. Their concerns were too smoothly expressed, too practiced, and always ended up coming across as sales patter. With Miller, "Captain Paranoid" himself, I was unsure. He had the deep conviction of someone who knew time would vindicate him.

Late in the warm evening, reading on the porch of the main building by the light of my headlamp, I heard a saw biting into wood at the under-construction log cabin and wandered over. Miller was slicing through a cluster of two-by-fours to make space for an electrical conduit.

"Hey, hand me those yellow wire cutters, will you?" he said, pointing to a table. As he worked, Miller told me that he hoped I was going to write about ripple effects, situations where one event triggers another event, like dominoes falling. He thought the trigger event was less important than what came out of it. In his mind the tail end of most disasters involved a mob, which he felt able to handle at Fortitude Ranch. Other, more far-reaching catastrophes—an asteroid impact that blots out the sun, say—he thought just weren't worth preparing for. Once the ranch lost the ability to grow food, and their solar panels went dark, they were dead in the water.

Impact events were a growing obsession among preppers. Back in Sydney, astrobiologist and space scientist Michael Dello-Iacovo had told me about asteroid strikes, their probability and impact. Although, he reassured me, a catastrophic strike is not likely in the near future, small meteors burn up in the Earth's atmosphere every day; this fact is probably where the fears stem from. He told me of one asteroid that did make it to Earth, in 1908, flattening almost eight hundred square miles of forest in Tunguska, Siberia. A 2018 US government report found that if a Tunguska-sized asteroid hit New York, it would obliterate virtually the entire city and kill millions of people. Somebody else who knows an awful lot about asteroids is the British cosmologist Martin Rees, Astronomer Royal and cofounder of the Centre for the Study of Existential Risk at the University of Cambridge. The Earth, he says, is hit by asteroids 160 feet in diameter about once per century. Taking this, and other factors, into account, Rees estimates the probability of human extinction before 2100 at around 50 percent.[13] "That's a pessimistic view," Dello-Iacovo opined laconically, "but not an unscientific one."

Miller and I talked about this as he worked. "Look," he said, "people might survive in places like Survival Condo under those conditions, but then, those people are investing millions in those preparations." As I watched him strip insulation off some wires, I wondered what would keep the security guards from simply taking over the bunker in those long-term lock-in scenarios.[14] Being trapped underground with a bunch of people after the sun has winked out creates a serious set of social complications, particularly if there is no exit in sight.

So Survival Condo wasn't a competitor, because they were prepping for different things. Miller wasn't bothered by the likes of Hardened Structures, either. "Hardened Structures caters to the rich, and the rich aren't interested in building communities, for the most part." I handed Miller his electric screwdriver while he put in the socket box.

"Now, you've been out at the Vivos bunkers in South Dakota, haven't you?" he asked. I nodded and asked what he thought about Vicino's plans.

"What, all that crap about Planet X and magnetic-pole shifts or whatever? Well, what I think is that we've got enough real threats in the world, we don't need to make shit up." Miller suggested that most companies in the business, like Rising S or Atlas Survival Shelters, were just putting pipes in the ground: they had no interest in building the communities necessary for long-term survival.

"Have you seen any communities that look viable to you?" I asked.

Drew shrugged. "I also don't know if Trident Lakes in Dallas ever took off, but I always wondered why the hell you would put a fifty-foot statue in a survival community, it makes no sense at all."

"How many people do you have in this community now?"

"About a hundred people have bought in, most here, some in Colorado where we've got what we call pioneer memberships," he said. Miller had recently started selling cryptocurrency—Fortitude Ranch Tokens—to keep the funding stream wet. The idea was that tokens sold in the initial coin offering (ICO) could be used as proof of ID to gain access to a ranch, but were also a good investment because they would "skyrocket in value after an event."

Miller was also concerned about nuclear strikes—especially on Washington, DC, about a hundred miles away from Fortitude Ranch. He'd prepared for fallout from such an attack by digging a trench around the lodge. Fallout, being heavier than air, would collect and slough off down the trench—or be shoveled out by the members. I wondered where you would find your cryptocurrency after such an event. Would people really be firing up laptops on solar panels to trade crypto in a post-state disaster zone? Although Miller had scoffed at Vicino's wilder theories, his scenarios, in their own way, seemed equally far-fetched.

And yet. As Miller built his future-proof fortifications in front of my eyes, I appreciated that his response to those theories hinged on solutions and action. The spaces preppers are creating are more resilient, more sustainable, and in many ways more realistic than living in a stucco suburban condo, being dependent on a car to get you to a grocery store or on Amazon trucks to deliver supplies to your house for basic survival. These bunkers might require a lot of up-front investment of time, energy, and resources, but they were built with resiliency in mind. The problem—as ever, in the precarious world of the dread merchants—was in attracting the population to keep up their maintenance when times were good.

As I sat on the porch that night, I made some notes about survival. The people who would fare best in a disaster would be those who had never bought into consumer culture in the first place. A few years ago, I drove across Australia from Sydney to Perth with my friend Wayne, a geographer, poet, and polymath. Our midway point was the opal mining town of Coober Pedy—which supposedly means "white man in a hole"—where some million-plus vertical shafts have been excavated in the last hundred years by people looking for the precious stone. Eighty percent of the town's population lives underground in houses called dugouts.

On the way there, in the middle of the outback, hundreds of kilometers from any settlement, we saw an Aboriginal man sitting on a termite mound next to the highway. As we drove by, he appeared not to register our passing. In town that night, we had a similar sense that many of the Aboriginal people there were, in Wayne's words, "looking past the place, not waiting but present." It dawned on us that a people who'd been living here for at least 50,000 years, or 2,000 generations, would view the last 230 years, or 12 generations, of foreign settlement, as a weird catastrophic blip. Also, for indigenous people, in the words of philosopher Donna Haraway, "the idea that disaster will come is not new; disaster, indeed genocide and devastated home places, has already come, decades and centuries ago, and it has not stopped."[15]

Disease outbreaks, global wars, environmental catastrophes, nuclear disasters, and colonization are all apocalyptic events that humanity has survived but that left our cultures forever changed. For those who survived and endured these events, it was the end of the world they'd known. The residual effects on those who remained have been described as postapocalyptic stress syndrome, in which an entire culture suffers from post-traumatic stress disorder (PTSD), and must rebuild their cultural story in the same way that an individual suffering from PTSD must rebuild their sense of self after experiencing a traumatic event.[16] It's suggested that looking to past events should give us hope, because human beings can and do survive events like those that are unfolding.

Germaine Greer has argued that "catastrophe is the natural human environment, and even though we spend a good deal of energy trying to get away from it, we are programmed for survival amid catastrophe."[17] Much of our migration across the Earth over the last few million years, indeed, has been driven not by a desire for exploration but by necessity, as animals were killed off, sustainable environments were exhausted, or conflicts with neighbors broke out.[18] There is ample evidence to suggest that *Homo sapiens* experienced a population bottleneck about a hundred thousand years ago, bringing down our numbers to just thousands of individuals.[19] This event was possibly due to climate change after a volcano called Toba, on Sumatra, in what is now Indonesia, spewed a 650-mile stream of vaporized rock into the air, dimming the sun for six years and causing temperatures to plummet.[20] In other words, in 70,000 BCE, humans almost became extinct. But they didn't. Instead, early humans pushed into new areas in the course of fleeing the volcano, so that the eruption encouraged, and rewarded, exploration. We are now, as Vicino's friend Jerry told me at xFest, hardwired for survival—or so it would be nice to think.

For this reason, I found Fortitude Ranch oddly affecting. In his own way, Miller was building to solve practical problems, in the way humans have always done. This may require tactical retreating, retooling, and re-skilling—a mastery of everyday survival. I liked that Miller didn't fear that. All prepping, in the end, is born from hope: after all, only those who believe there will be a future prepare for one. Still, I felt sorry for Miller—living with such anxiety must be a constant burden. My sympathy, though, waned as I reminded myself that he was also making a living out of capitalizing on other people's apprehension.

I was able to see that process play out in January 2020, in the early days of the COVID-19 outbreak. Weeks before the World Health Organization deemed it a public health emergency of international concern (PHEIC) and two months before it was declared a pandemic, Miller sent out his monthly newsletter in which he warned all Fortitude Ranch members that "this will become a worldwide pandemic." Miller advised ranch members to keep their vehicles' tanks full and to keep extra fuel on hand to make it to the ranch, should the virus escalate. He sternly admonished all residents: "Do NOT go to gas stations or supermarkets if this pandemic does erupt and there is panic buying—you want to stay out of public areas to avoid the virus and to avoid possible looting/marauding which can happen immediately." He also counseled stocking up on ammunition and viral face masks and not to touch anything in public. Miller's sense of vindication was palpable as the outbreak confirmed his earlier assertion that "we're overdue for a pandemic." But perhaps more importantly, by February 2020 Miller had announced that there were no more rooms available at Fortitude Ranch Colorado, but the cash injection from the spike in memberships meant that he could open a new "Viking Lodge" there in the spring.

10

The Antibunker:
Bloom Where You're Planted

"Great self-destruction follows upon unfounded
fear."
—Ursula K. Le Guin, *The Lathe
of Heaven*, 2001[1]

Heidi was waiting for me in a golf cart on a highway verge bordering the Great Smoky Mountains National Park. Turning off the
road after she waved me down, I followed her down a narrow
gravel track in a community of well-cared-for mobile homes tucked
into a slope amid poplar and mimosa trees. Her bright red Mazda

Miata convertible had been backed into the carport. Heidi was a quick-witted middle-aged woman with curly blond hair who sold medical equipment for a living. As she walked me through her verdant front garden, she explained how she had embraced a life of sustainable self-sufficiency, engineering self-watering systems for plants, and canning what she couldn't eat.

Over home-baked bread and honey collected from a neighbor's hive, we sat on the patio and listened to the locusts beginning their evening chorus. Heidi said she was shocked when she discovered how little people knew about growing, canning, harvesting, and hunting. She thought it symptomatic of a larger problem. "People don't know how to think for themselves anymore," she said in a languid, calculated Southern drawl, shaking her head.

"Now, for instance, I'm a Christian but I don't think that means I have to be a conservative, especially when Trump's integrity blows with the wind," Heidi said, venting. "Republicans these days will pound a lie into the ground until it's the truth. That's why you can't watch the news anymore. Half that stuff doesn't pass the sniff test. People don't have time to check facts anymore. News has lost its dignity."

I noticed she had a TV inside and asked if she watched it. It was hooked up to the internet so that she could watch YouTube videos, she explained, but she had little interest in TV. "You have to find your own facts and your own way of living, a simpler way. Plans with too many moving parts never work out."

As dusk fell, fireflies surrounded us, illuminating the porch in gentle pulses. The peace was intense. I slept in Heidi's spare bedroom, surrounded by ration jars and the ubiquitous twenty-five-year-shelf-life #10 cans. There were also survival manuals, cookbooks, and boxed wine bladders filled with water and a teaspoon of bleach for preservation.

In the morning, we drove the golf cart down the road to a store called Tennessee Readiness. On the way, I noticed Heidi had supplies in the cart, including a collapsible bow and arrow stored in a pouch.

"Yeah, you've got it, this is my bug-out vehicle," she said as the morning sun flickered through her translucent pink visor onto her sunglasses. "I can play 'the old woman in the golf cart' and whizz right through with my everyday carry kit. These hills up here in the Smoky Mountains, they're full of caves. There are plenty of places for us to hide out. And we're going to need to—these preppers that think they're going to fight the army from their bunker are full of beans."

Heidi's community in Cosby, Tennessee, was remote. It was thirty minutes to the grocery store, with no trash pickup. It was the kind of place where you had to rely on your neighbors and trade for what you needed; it was a town with a history of people distilling liquor in garden sheds.

Tennessee Readiness had a spacious wooden front porch with a swinging screen door leading to a shop floor of meticulously organized preparedness equipment. Heidi introduced me to Carey, who was chain-smoking hand-rolled cigarettes in a rocking chair on the front porch, and her cousin and business partner, Sonya, who was cutting up boxes from an earlier delivery for the recycling bin.

Carey squinted at me. "Yeah, that's right, buddy, we're middle-aged women running a survivalist store—not what you expected?" She loosed a belting laugh that turned into a chesty cough. As she rocked violently in the chair, Sonya shook her head and crumpled a piece of cardboard. Recovering, Carey went on: "You're going to be surprised by all sorts of shit over the next few days, man, especially if you go see those militia people over the mountain."

The "militia people" hung out at another shop, called Carolina Readiness Supply, just over the state border. I gathered they took a rather more militant stance on prepping.

"We're what you call homestead preppers or prepsteaders over here," Carey said as I took a seat. "We spend more time thinking about growing and making things, building up skills, than building walls. We've got no interest in getting into a firefight with some paramilitary fuckers after it all falls apart."

I asked her how she got started prepping. "Dude, I'm going to blow your mind," she said, raising her eyebrows.

"See, the way I see it, the window between science fiction and reality is narrowing. I've been a prepper since Reagan started talking about the New World Order and I realized that conservatives were drinking the same Kool-Aid as liberals. Bunkers aren't saving anyone in the New World Order. In the first couple of weeks there might be confusion and even altruism, but then those United Nations blue helmets will be here trying to get you to go to a Walmart where supplies are being handed out and they're going to put an RFID [radio-frequency identification] tracking chip in your arm."

Though her suspicion about corporate entanglement in government suppression was a relatively new phenomenon among preppers, Carey's brand of antigovernment sentiment was in line with that first stoked during the Cold War and carried through into the populism of the 1980s with groups like Almost Heaven, CUT, and the Branch Davidians. The response of the government was to ratchet up surveillance on these groups, which only deepened people's anxieties and hardened their belief that there was a conspiracy at play quashing grassroots organization. Now, with ready access to almost any perspective online, paranoid people can dredge up any evidence they need to reinforce those anxieties.

Fiddling with her phone, Carey beckoned me closer to listen to what sounded like a radio broadcast. It was a crackly feed from the US National Parks Service, the kind of thing road signs ask you to tune in to as you're approaching a park. A voice was announcing that the Yellowstone Caldera—a super-volcano in the Wyoming part of the park—had blown, and that all visitors were being asked to evacuate the park immediately. This, I knew, was a serious incident. A 2017 FEMA report called "Preparing for 'The Big One'" had suggested that the total financial damage to the United States from a Yellowstone super-volcano eruption could top $3 trillion, or about 16 percent of the country's GDP.[2] Yet when I tried to search for news of this disaster on my own phone, I found nothing. I suspected she was playing it from a prerecorded upload somewhere on the internet.

Carey, however, suggested that the fact that there was no evidence of the event in the mainstream news only confirmed a cover-up. I tried to imagine who would create such a bogus emergency, and for what reason. All I could come up with was that it was a foreign power sowing chaos through misinformation, just as Russia had done during the 2016 presidential election. The seeding of fake news had become a powerful geopolitical tool for countries hoping to expand public discontent in the US. For those who completely distrust the government, any alternative narrative bolsters their beliefs.

I wasn't sure how to respond to Carey's sincerity about the "broadcast." Here, even in the most practical of prepping communities, the information streams on which they relied were polluted with garbage from the internet. Indeed, as Heidi's decision to avoid the TV and rely on information from YouTube videos showed, it seemed people were deliberately putting themselves in the path of everything from unverifiable news and rumor, to conspiracy theories and propaganda. Heidi and Carey were making decisions based on completely different information from the other half of the country, and yet I couldn't fault their sincerity of belief, or the value of their practices. I asked how one might prepare for an event as cataclysmic as a volcano eruption.

"What's going to save you in a disaster like that is faith in God, being surrounded by people you trust, and being able to get out of here and take care of each other," Carey said, thumbing behind her toward the mountains. Shelter could be sought in those hills, she told me. During the early days of the Cold War, Tennessee's civil defense director estimated that about eight hundred thousand residents could be housed in the extensive network of underground caverns stretching under the state, many of which could be accessed from the national park.[3]

I asked if the general sentiment in Appalachia was that bugging out was better than hunkering down. Sonya, now sweeping up the remains of the packaging, looked up. "We had a guy come in here who was building a bunker and he bought a whole pallet worth of food," she said, wiping her forehead with a sleeve. "And on his way out he stopped and looked around at our shop and said, 'You know, after the shit hits the fan, we're not going to be hunters and gatherers, we're going to be gatherers and takers. So y'all keep gathering this stuff so I can take it.' "

Heidi nodded vigorously. "People tell you who they are if you listen," she said. "I've shed a lot of friends who made very clear whether or not they would stand with us, even if they didn't mean to."

The women told me they'd created the store to bring a community together. They'd stashed supplies, had bug-out bags ready, and would escape to secret gardens where they were growing food in camouflaged food forests in the Smoky Mountains. They could wait events out there.

"What about the shop?" I asked.

"We built it as a gift for the people left behind," Sonya said.

"Even that guy who wants to take everything?"

"He can have it," Carey responded. "We're not militia—those guys are crotch grabbers. And we're not survivalists taking a one-way trip into the forest with an INCH [I'm Never Coming Home] bag. He can clean out the store and then someone else will probably clean him out. Then we'll come back and rebuild."

For these homestead preppers, who believed bunkers were a foolish waste of resources, time nevertheless remained a crucial factor in a breakdown of society. Sonya had lived in Florida before moving to Tennessee and had been through Hurricane Andrew in 1992. "In the first few days after the hurricane, grocery stores were handing out everything perishable and writing it off—we filled the entire back of a pickup truck with food. I've never eaten as well as I did during that 'disaster,'" she said, putting air quotes around "disaster." "But once people were down to canned food, they got irritable." Once the canned food then ran out, the logic went, if you couldn't hunt or grow, you might become the hunted. Which was why for these women, self-sufficiency, not self-defense, was the key to survival. So, too, was operations security, so—as Bushy, the prepper in Melbourne, had put it—you didn't become "a supermarket for other people."

Hurricane Andrew was a Category 5 storm with 165 mph winds. It destroyed 63,500 houses, caused $27.3 billion in damage, and was classified as "catastrophic." As I ambled through the well-stocked shop, looking over knives in display cases, jars of food, spools of paracord, flashlights, and fire starters, it struck me that a natural disaster has clear boundaries in space and time; we know there will be an end to it, that there will be an "other side" to make it to. Sonya and her friends took advantage of that disaster in Florida because it had parameters. They assumed law and order would be restored after it was over but that in the interim, they could get away with being a bit naughty, taking food they didn't have to pay for. Amorphous, cataclysmic disaster provokes a more panicked response.

I'd previously spoken on such topics with Daisy Luther, the Organic Prepper. Daisy is a homestead prepper based in Virginia. She told me she was working toward finding sustainable solutions to problems by breaking out of fragile commodity supply chains. Living for a while in California, she'd found it a lot easier to prep there because the growing season lasted longer—but then acknowledged that as a prepper you have to "bloom where you're planted": we don't all have the luxury of choosing where we live, or the ability to flee to a remote location. Even in cities—which, like so many preppers, she described as urban death traps—she said the key was to find trustworthy, self-sufficient people and stick with them. In short, she'd agreed with Sonya and Carey's view that sustainability, self-sufficiency, and community were the keys to survival.

"Stockpiling guns and food buckets is only going to get you so far," Daisy told me. "Soon you'll need people who know how to build things, grow things. We've all become consumers that don't produce anything," she said, echoing Heidi. "We've got to flip that logic on its head."

"Who wants to live in a bunker anyway?" Daisy stated sternly. "I want to be able to have my opinions, I don't want to kowtow to some dictator—and you know one will emerge in that situation—I want to live in a community where people can be themselves but look out for each other. I want to see people building gardens, not bunkers . . . that's how we're going to weather the storm." The only thing differentiating Daisy and the other prepsteaders, I thought, was distance. These were people who would find a place anywhere, people who would make do regardless of circumstances.

The next morning Heidi and I took the hardtop off her bright red Mazda Miata convertible. Having loaded it up with a handgun, the collapsible bow and arrow, and a bug-out bag, we drove over the mountain to meet the "militia folk" at Carolina Readiness Supply. Their store was packed with manual grain mills, rope, stoves, water purification systems, camouflage bags, freeze-dried fruit, cans, buckets, and bags of rice, beans, and corn. Every aisle was a smorgasbord of militant camping gear. A few bearded men poked furtively around, collecting supplies.

The owners, Riley and Jed, perched behind a front counter covered in militia patches and stickers, were edgy and evasive, clearly the kind of preppers who didn't appreciate strangers just dropping in. Jed said that he'd started prepping after the election of Barack Obama to the presidency in 2008. He said people needed to prep because "liberal elites were ruining the country," which seemed like a dated narrative, given Donald Trump had been the president for years. The contrast with Heidi and her chirpy homestead prepper friends was marked.

I went to browse Riley and Jed's hearty selection of canning guides, wilderness survival manuals, patriotic nonfiction by James Wesley, Rawles, and postapocalyptic novels including *One Second After* and *World Made by Hand*. It was prepping in microcosm: science fiction and reality blurring almost imperceptibly. People reached for fictional accounts of apocalypse almost as instinctively as they sought practical guides on how to deal with it.

As we drove back over the mountain, Heidi said she wasn't surprised that the owners of the shop were terse—most people were these days. "I'm telling you," she said, "you'd better hold tight, I think we're going for a wild ride in 2020. I can feel it in my bones!" As with Drew Miller's prognostications, her words took on a grotesque quality as time passed.

That night Heidi had a group of six prepsteaders over to her house for drinks and homemade blackberry pie. We gathered in the living room, in a haphazard circle on a couch, a recliner, small stools, and chairs pulled in from the kitchen, arranged like an Alcoholics Anonymous meeting. One of the homestead preppers, an ex–intelligence officer with close-cropped hair and stern confidence, told me as we poured coffee that she'd learned things while working for the government that she wished she hadn't. That was when she started prepping. Each person in turn expressed dismay over what the government was keeping from them, lamented the excessive connectivity and demands of the modern world, and expressed disdain and frustration over inequality. As a group, they were committed to building complementary skill sets, in order to stay afloat when the powerful checked out and left them to die. For them, community was paramount. They were clearly grateful that they'd found each other—largely through Heidi, who enjoyed her role as the group's hub.

For all their determination to survive, no one seemed particularly perturbed by the idea of death. Outside on the porch after pie, in a drizzle that tapped lightly on a patio umbrella we were all huddling under, the homesteaders made clear they were devout Christians. They believed that signs were aligning that indicated the end of days. Carey felt—like Drew Miller—that pandemic might be the likely cause, but, she opined, the years in which the pestilence would ravage the Earth might actually be the rapture itself.

Heidi and the homestead preppers had most of the hallmarks I'd come to expect: the stores, the guns, the faith in breakdown. But their attitude was almost convivial: they seemed to take great joy in the sense of community they were able to cultivate around prepping and planning. It was easy to imagine them, in the post-apocalyptic world, hiding up in the Smokies, playing music, hunting, growing, drinking moonshine, and generally thriving, while all the "crotch grabbers" fought over what they'd left behind. It *would* be a kind of rapture, with the wicked left behind to fend for themselves in a world full of demons.

11

Community Nourishment:
Utah's Mormon Citadel

"There are more things . . . likely to frighten us
than there are to crush us; we suffer more often
in imagination than in reality."
—Seneca, *Epistles*, Vol. I[1]

Many of the sixteen million members of the Mormon Church of
Jesus Christ of Latter-day Saints (LDS) are prepared to ride out
catastrophe. Like evangelical Christian eschatology, a conservative
wing of LDS doctrine is millenarian: it forecasts the end of our age
as foretold in the Book of Revelation, which depicts a period of
tribulation that will need to be traversed before Jesus will return to

Earth. LDS Church members are admonished to be ready for this time by living debt-free, keeping alive skills of self-sufficiency and crafting, and stockpiling supplies. For fundamentalist Mormons, involvement in these activities is driven by a vision of an apocalyptic scenario, but for a wider swath of the Church, preparations have a more practical, community-solidarity vibe: they're about constructing an agreeable life in the present that also acts as a bulwark against what's coming down the road. It's what many call "practical prepping" and has a lot of overlap with the practices of homestead preppers, especially in the core principles of sustainability, self-sufficiency, and civic care.

Just over a decade ago, the LDS Church president Thomas Monson admonished parishioners that "We live in turbulent times. Often the future is unknown; therefore, it behooves us to prepare for uncertainties. When the time for decision arrives, the time for preparation is past."[2] An earlier Church president, Gordon B. Hinckley, quoted *Doctrine and Covenants 38:30*, a key piece of nineteenth-century LDS scripture, in his observation that "it was not raining when Noah built the ark. But he built it, and the rains came. The Lord has said, 'If ye are prepared ye shall not fear.'"[3] It's precisely this sentiment that Vicino echoes in his signature tagline "No one believed Noah until it was too late." Both warnings suggest that a leap of faith needs to be taken to prepare. This leap is the crux of survival.

Fascinated by the LDS Church's fusion of these principles of sustainability, community, and apocalypse, I'd come across a piece of writing by Mette Harrison, a novelist based in Salt Lake City who's been publicly candid about her years spent as a Mormon prepper mom. Mette, who was diagnosed in 2017 with high-functioning autism, had been a committed prepper. In addition to storing a year's worth of food in her basement, she regularly practiced for the realities of doomsday with her family: periodically, they would subsist only on what they had in storage to test the preps. Reflecting on this strange, intense period in her life, she wrote in the piece that in hindsight aspects of her life seemed out of control, and prepping was one thing she could control. More than that, it made her feel superior to others, both materially and spiritually, and it gave her a thrill to "think about the horror, defeat it, and then feel triumphant."[4]

I had to meet Mette. Luckily, the largest prepper convention in the world, PrepperCon, was going to be held in Salt Lake City, which gave me two reasons to make the trip. I booked a cheap house on Airbnb and hit the road.

Salt Lake Valley was an obvious place for Mormon settlers to stop in 1847: it's a natural fortress, barricaded by the snowcapped peaks of the Wasatch Range on one side and protected by the flat, shallow, seventeen-hundred-square-mile Great Salt Lake on the other. Downtown Salt Lake City is a checkerboard of LDS buildings, civic architecture, bustling brew houses, and religious bookstores lining wide, clean streets. As I drove through it, I used as a navigation point the gilded statue of an angel blowing a trumpet toward the east, standing tall from a spire in Temple Square.

Mette met me at a Himalayan restaurant for lunch. She was short and muscular, brown hair pulled into a tight braid over a puffer jacket. Mette had covered some bases. An award-winning novelist, she also had a PhD in Germanic Languages and Literature, worked as a professor at Brigham Young University, was an Ironwoman triathlete, and was raising five children. Mette wanted to make clear straightaway that although she'd moved away from prepping, she still thought it was prudent, to a degree. She reminded me that even the Department of Homeland Security advises US citizens to prep by storing nonperishable food in every household, and she told me that prepping in this way was pretty customary in Utah.[5]

The Church encourages adherents to keep food stored—most Mormon houses have basements that double as storage areas—and to calculate preps by the length of time one can survive on them, not by food volume. The time people need to be self-sufficient, as stipulated by the Church, has ranged from three months to five years at different periods in the past. Crucial to this belief is that these stores are not just for the individual or the family, but for the community. Although, if cataclysm struck, LDS Church members might seek shelter in their basements—bunkers in all but name—they would be expected to emerge and contribute to the common good as soon as was practicable. So Mormon prepping is not about escaping the emergency, at whatever scale it happens to be unfolding, but about being prepared to hunker down, then go into the post-emergency zone to do good works. All of which is part of a greater vision that includes their foreign aid agenda, which has converted millions of people around the world through relief supply efforts. Fifty-seven percent of Mormons now reside outside the United States, many of whom went into disaster areas and stayed.

Mette explained how the act of building her food stores had helped her feel she was living according to Scripture and in accordance with the guidelines being passed down by Church leaders. But over time, it dawned on her that she was spending more and more of her time in the present preparing for a hypothetical future threat. In doing so, she'd neglected to tend to her family's current needs. She began to notice the negative impacts of the practice on the mental health and well-being of her children. They were getting spooked. As a high-functioning autistic, Mette didn't register her family's discomfort as quickly as someone who's neurotypical.

"Two of my kids, who are now in college, suffer from anxiety which I think was caused, in part, by performing doomsday scenarios," Mette told me. Her children's anxieties stirred deeply buried memories from her own Cold War childhood, itself saturated with stories of apocalypse. As a child, the noise of plane engines scared her: she was convinced that every aircraft she heard was carrying the Bomb. Unwittingly, she'd immersed her children in a similar environment—and realized that she had to do something about it.

It was hard for her to break out of that mentality, because "Church services often contained messages about prepping, and emergency preparedness drills were taking place in schools within the communities." Disaster preparation was baked into Mormons' lives in other ways. "Classes were offered for women where prep food is cooked, using recipes for food stores. It was meant to be eaten, cycled through." Even the stored food of the deceased, dug out of basements when clearing out their houses, would be distributed among family members, recycled in the community.

Mette had, she told me, noticed a change in recent years from a focus on crafting and practical preparedness toward increasing militancy. She was concerned about an upswing in groups she called "gun Mormons," who watch Fox News constantly, subscribe to often repressive socially conservative beliefs, and are vocal in Church about the importance of storing weapons as well as food in their basement.

"I don't know, or want to know, those people," she told me. Mette remembered something like this happening before, decades ago, that had fueled the scare stories of her childhood.

Back in the early sixties a Mormon named Ezra Taft Benson rose high in the community and in the US government, serving both on the Quorum of the Twelve Apostles, the governing body of the Church, and as the secretary of agriculture under Eisenhower. In his latter role, he was the administrator designate of the US Emergency Food Agency, a group formed in 1958 to serve in the event of a national emergency. Benson also aligned himself with the John Birch Society, an advocacy group supporting anti-Communist activists, whose members included many of the far-right-wing survivalists of the time. Benson, who clearly had survivalist leanings himself, encouraged LDS Church members to read up on the New World Order conspiracy theory and, at the Church's general conference in 1963, called on Church members to "come to the aid" of anti-Communist "patriots, programs and organizations." Many did so.

By 1986, up to a million Americans were actively serving in militias and as many as 3 million Americans were involved in survivalism.[6] In 1991, some Mormons began predicting a global financial collapse followed by rioting and natural disasters. Their prognostications reflected the febrile national mood at the time: this, after all, was the year Elizabeth Clare Prophet had addressed the Rotary Club in Montana, and when Martin Polin had advertised for couples to populate his Tasmanian bunker.

The militancy came in waves. Every few decades, there seemed to always be some group or another of militant millenarians emerging from the Church, transforming the idea of prepping for communal good into prepping for apocalypse. In 2015, the Church distanced itself from a doomsday diviner named Julie Rowe, who claimed to have had a near-death experience in 2004 in which she visited the LDS spirit world and saw visions of the end times. A charismatic public speaker, Rowe claimed that seven years after the 2008 global financial crisis, a greater crash would launch the period of "tribulation." With few LDS Church members publicly vocal about their deeply held beliefs, the media leaped on Rowe. Unsurprisingly, she was a favored guest on right-wing news programs whose hosts hawked survival products.

In an interview with Fox News, Rowe said that the time had come to "build a righteous army" to "defend the Constitution."[7] This was language that survivalists understood. In 2019, when Rowe was excommunicated from the Church of Jesus Christ of Latter-day Saints, another breakaway LDS group emerged. Calling itself the Mormon Transhumanist Association (MTA), it sought to align Mormon teachings and the technological singularity, where human and machine consciousness merge. The ascension from the body in LDS Church doctrine—the entrances into the "spirit world" Rowe spoke of—they argued, might mirror the beginning of the Novacene, the machine age.

Mette was quick to explain, however, that these were marginal stories grossly inflated by the media, rather than the everyday reality of Mormon life.

"The Church leadership has really been moving away from apocalyptic talk of late," she told me. For a church already suspected by many Americans of being cultlike, having those fringe actors working inside the Church was not an option.

Trying to detour me from these eccentric stories, and wanting me to get a sense of what Mormon prepping was all about, Mette recommended that I drop in to the Bishop's Storehouse, a place where those in need can go to obtain food and supplies. The Salt Lake City storehouse, built in 1938, is one of 138 across the world.

At the Bishop's Storehouse, I was warmly greeted by the immaculately dressed manager, Joel Moriyama. Moriyama introduced it as a welfare facility. Though it looked like a grocery store in many ways, much of the food was stored in twenty-five-year-shelf-life #10 cans produced by Deseret Food Store, the Church's own distribution company. These cans, which each hold about a US gallon, are distributed nationally and are pervasive among prepping communities: I'd seen them in Miller's "spartan" bunker, and in Heidi's house in Tennessee I'd slept surrounded by piles of them.

The facility is intended for Church members who have hit hard times, but it's technically open to anyone whom an LDS bishop deems worthy of receiving aid. "Although we prefer for a bishop to give a referral to come in, we would never turn anyone away," Moriyama explained as I perused the stock. It was very well organized: the can labels were so meticulously arranged, they even lined up perfectly in my photos.

"Okay," I said, "so I can just walk in here and walk out with a week's worth of food, and no money will be exchanged?"

"I'll give you some right now," Moriyama said, smiling. He then loaded my arms with a giant bag of pasta. "But you might consider doing some volunteer work in exchange," he said as he walked off down the aisle. Indeed, the entire storehouse was run by volunteers. Moriyama introduced me to a retired couple from Devon, England, who'd been traveling missionaries. When they stopped off at Salt Lake City, they "found their calling here in the Bishop's Storehouse," as Moriyama put it. Ten months later, they were still there stocking shelves.

"The Church has people putting in 4.3 million volunteer hours every year," Moriyama said. "We've got thirty-nine farms, four fruit orchards, four ranches, and a turkey farm, but we also have five hundred million pounds of wheat in storage. All of that would be made available in an emergency at any scale, from a family member losing a job to a natural disaster." It sounded as if the Church would fare well in a total collapse. I asked Moriyama if he'd be able to cope with the inevitable influx of people from outside who'd come looking for help after a cataclysm.

"We'd welcome them," he said. "In fact, we send our stores to emergencies now. During Hurricane Harvey in the Southeast," a Category 4 hurricane in 2017 that caused $125 billion in damage and during which eighteen people died, "we sent two hundred trucks filled with food supplies."

Though the Bishop's Storehouse—indeed the entire LDS community—was geared to emergency relief, Moriyama was clear about the everyday practical value of prepping: "It doesn't always have to be for doomsday, it can be for today or tomorrow." As if to emphasize his point, he handed me a glossy pamphlet the size of a shirt pocket, detailing how to accumulate a year's supply of food for less than $500.

My next stop was Neca Allgood's house, a stucco four-bedroom affair in an unassuming suburb north of the city. Neca greeted me out front. She was willowy and fair, with short brown hair and eyeglasses hanging from a neck strap around a turtleneck sweater. Her husband and three boys, one of whom was transgender, weren't home. Taking me outside to show me her garden and solar oven, she explained the principle that underlay her prepping: the simple idea that the power has gone out.

"Let's also assume tap water isn't flowing," she continued. "FEMA tells us we should have seventy-two hours of supplies on hand—but what if you have to wait longer than that? What if my neighbors run out of water?" Walking me downstairs into the chilly family basement, she explained that she took a "deep larder" approach: "This might look like a bunker but I'm not locking my door to anyone. We have a phone tree system to make sure every person in this neighborhood is accounted for in an emergency." She flicked on a light, revealing dozens of five-gallon buckets. She pulled one out, labeled "5 Bean Mix," and opened the lid to sift her hands through the dried beans and pulses. Next to the buckets were bottled preserves, canned goods, and even a manual wheat grinder.

"I am not a fan of the paranoia that drives many preppers," Neca stated emphatically. "I stock up because I want to be a responsible steward of the resources I have. Knowing we have our supplies covered gives us peace. In the meantime, we just cycle through it." Mette had mentioned this, too: LDS members see preps less as emergency supplies than as food stores that are used regularly. It's a practice encouraged by FIFO storage, meaning the first thing in is the first thing out. It also ensures the preps are as fresh as possible.

On the way back to my lodgings, I spied a cluster of matte-white grain silos emblazoned with a Church of Jesus Christ of Latter-day Saints logo, and pulled over to take some photos. The gate was open, so I drove in and parked near the administration building. After a few minutes of snapping, the front door of the facility opened and a guy in a hairnet waved me over: "Do you want a tour?" Soon, I was also wearing a hairnet and walking through the Deseret Mill and Pasta Factory with Clancy, an enthusiastic guide who explained that Deseret, as the generic Church label, wasn't just a food brand, it was also the name of a publishing house and a range of other industries.

The scale of this expansive facility was impressive. It was staffed by volunteers who were mixing, slicing, canning, wrapping, and shipping an endless supply of pasta, wheat, cheese, and bread. Watching the coveted #10 cans roll down a sterile steel-roller assembly line, filled with "spaghetti bites" or "pancake mix," then sealed and labeled, was strangely satisfying. I imagined people walking away with them from the Bishop's Storehouse—and preppers all over the country stacking them in basements next to their AR-15 rifles. On the way out, as we passed a sea of pallets stacked with doomsday-proof food wrapped in plastic, ready to load onto trucks, Clancy grabbed some stray bags and filled my arms with food. He was all smiles.

Salt Lake City has a private long-term food industry whose expansion mirrors the Church's own. The next day, I visited Wise Company, a private business that produces dehydrated food in buckets and bags made of Mylar, an opaque, metalized polyester that lasts even longer than #10 cans and endures better in humid climates. Aaron Jackson, the company's former president and CEO, helped catapult Wise Company into an everyday brand at a national scale after coming to the realization that while more than half of American homes had first-aid kits, fire extinguishers, and flashlights on hand for emergencies, food was missing from their kit. In a 2017 interview with Bloomberg, Jackson said that his food was a staple "that every American household in this age of uncertainty should have."[8] Certainty, in this case, could arrive courtesy of Wise: on a pallet of black plastic buckets delivered to your front curb for $7,870.99, containing a three-meal-a-day one-year food supply for a family of four.

When I turned up at the low-slung office block that housed Wise Company's HQ, the current CEO, Jack Shields, greeted me with a firm handshake and welcomed me into his office, a functional affair with low-pile gray carpet and venetian blinds. Shields had a silver mustache that matched his hair and a gold signet ring with gems in it. Describing the scale of Wise Company, he explained that he looked forward to US presidential elections, because people tended to stock up when change was imminent. While many of Wise's core customers were preppers and Mormon households, customers were increasingly American citizens of every kind, united by a common concern with environmental, social, and political instability.

Survival food sales in the US total about $400 million annually. A competing company called Shelf Reliance reported that from 2010 to 2013, sales of long-life foods surged over 700 percent.[9] Picking up the torch in 2014, Wise's annual retail sales more than doubled in three years. Such is the company's exponential growth that in the aftermath of the devastating Hurricane Maria in 2017, FEMA approached them to deliver emergency supplies to Puerto Rico. This association with the federal government gave the brand unprecedented visibility and a massive spike in sales, pushing turnover to an annual $75 million. Shields felt that the US government should be more interventionist: specifically, in offering tax credits for prepping, so that the state would reward people for being prepared, which would alleviate pressure on FEMA when disaster did unfold (and which would, in the process, enrich Wise Company and their private market competitors through publicly subsidized consumer spending).

As in so much, the private emergency food business was filling in for the state. In an age of accelerating catastrophe and cuts to government spending on social welfare, the federal government was not only failing to protect its citizens, it had become a primary client of private companies that were making millions in profits from disasters (which, despite all its undoubted altruism, included the LDS Church).

"All preparedness is about an unknown event in the future," Shields conceded—but, he qualified, "unknown doesn't mean unlikely. There are few things I guarantee in life, but I guarantee these things: South Florida is going to get hit with a hurricane, there will be wildfires in the West, there will be tornadoes in the Midwest, and California will have an earthquake. I have no clue when those things will happen, but the majority of the people in the United States live in an area where some sort of a natural disaster is likely to occur within the next ten years and they need to be prepared." A few months later, when California was hit with a magnitude 7.1 earthquake, his words echoed in my mind. The earthquake's epicenter was two hours from where I grew up.

Wise Company, I knew, had preceded a vast luxury market around doomsday prepping that had sprung into being in recent years, aimed squarely at liberal urbanites. A Southern California National Public Radio station started airing a show called *The Big One: Your Survival Guide*, which mixes dramatic performances and ominous music to instill in listeners fear about the next big quake before turning to a word from the podcast's sponsor—a company that sells three-day emergency bug-out bags for $495. The same company was featured on Vice's show *Most Expensivest*, where the rapper 2 Chainz unboxed the $4,995 Prepster Black Ultra Emergency Bag, which includes a solar-powered radio charger, satellite communicator, chocolate, and gold bars to trade after economic collapse. The snarky assessment of the bag from 2 Chainz was that "having a ten-thousand-dollar bag clearly gives you a higher level of survival instinct."[10]

Wise Company's success provides overwhelming evidence that the private market for preparedness has gone mainstream: its buckets can now be bought at Kmart and Bed Bath & Beyond. Costco has a page on their website dedicated to "Emergency Food by the Pallet," advertising one year of food storage—3,986 servings for $4,999, or 1,986 calories per person, per day, of grains, fruits, vegetables, proteins, and dairy. Costco is also selling a two-person, seven-day bug-out bag on wheels for $179.99, which the savvy novice prepper can weigh up against a three-day "tactical assault" bag available on Amazon for $49.99.

In showing me out, Shields also presented me with some freeze-dried food: now I had food for a week. I drifted around Salt Lake City for a few days hiking in the Wasatch Range, eating for free, and waiting for PrepperCon, the largest preppers expo in the world, to kick off. Twelve thousand preppers were expected to attend

PrepperCon from across the country, including hundreds of vendors. They included Milton, the burly vape-smoking xPoint resident, who'd been dispatched by Robert Vicino to hand out flyers for the second annual xFest. Vicino clearly saw this as a prime opportunity to attract new residents. Other attractions included talks by Dave Jones, "the EMP guy"; an ex-military expert on nuclear, biological, and chemical attacks; and Dr. Drew Miller from Fortitude Ranch.

"Dude, you can help me hand out flyers and pick out an oven for my bunker," Milton told me excitedly over the phone in the middle of one of my hikes. I couldn't refuse. Neither could I refuse Milton's request to let him crash on my couch.

12

PrepperCon:
The Business of Survival

"Extinction is the rule. Survival is the exception."
—Carl Sagan, *The Varieties
of Scientific Experience*, 2007[1]

PrepperCon was staged in the Mountain America Expo Center in Sandy, Utah, at the south end of Salt Lake City: a twenty-
six-thousand-square-foot facility with orderly walkways and a
good view of the eleven-thousand-foot mountain peaks behind
it. Walking up through the convention center doors, Milton and I
were pulled aside by a representative from the Three Percent militia

in a black "tacticool" paramilitary-looking outfit covered in clips, pockets, and patches. "You guys look like you're up for defending the Constitution," he said, waving a flyer at us, "check this out."

Named after the myth that 3 percent of the US population was in the battlefield during the American Revolution fighting the British, the Three Percenters claim that it will, equally, take 3 percent of the current population to bring about the "restoration of the Founders' Republic"—or, in other words, a return to a utopian past. Though they're a long way from these numbers, the group is the largest civilian militia in the United States today, with perhaps ten thousand members, and recruitment is on the rise.

As Milton chatted with the guy, proselytizing about xPoint, I ducked into a room in which retired US Army veteran Dave Jones, "the EMP Guy," was talking about the bombing of Nagasaki. Jones was a superstar in prepper circles and the room was packed. I lingered near the door.

Looming over his audience, wearing a baseball cap with a "Veteran" patch stitched on the front, he pointed to a slide behind him: "A twenty-kiloton nuclear bomb like that," he said, "is going to create one-thousand-degree heat a couple of miles out, and the fires are going to burn for weeks." His pronunciation—"nuke-u-lar" rather than "nuclear"—reminded me of George W. Bush. On a table set up next to him, Jones was selling something called "reactive skin decontamination lotion" for chemical attacks. I imagined the leap of faith needed to slather his lotion over my burning skin after a terror incident in a shopping mall or something. As with all this stuff people were selling, including bunkers, if it didn't work as promised you'd be dead, so I guessed it was a pretty low-risk marketing for the sellers.

Jones spread his hands wide. "The real disaster," he proclaimed, "would be from a high-altitude nuclear explosion. The resulting electromagnetic pulse is going to wipe out communication." Settling into his theme, Jones told his audience about Starfish Prime, a 1962 nuclear test conducted by the US government in outer space, two hundred fifty miles above the Johnston Atoll in the northern Pacific Ocean. The explosion created an EMP that fried electronics on the atoll and knocked out three hundred streetlights in Hawaii, almost nine hundred fifty miles away. Communications between Kauai and the other Hawaiian islands were also severed.

The other threat from an EMP, Jones explained, is natural. Coronal mass ejections (CMEs) from the sun—giant clouds of magnetized plasma—hit Earth's magnetosphere all the time, creating the geomagnetic storms we see in the Northern Lights. During the 1859 Carrington Event—named after one of the British astronomers who witnessed it—Earth got hit with a CME that knocked out Quebec's power grid and electrified telegraph lines across North America. People in Cuba saw the Northern Lights.

He explained that if such an event were to happen today, it could short out electricity networks and kill off refrigeration, medical equipment, car electronics, gas pumps, and ATMs. The internet is a Cold War technology built as a rhizomatic network for surviving nuclear war, meaning that if one node goes down we don't lose the whole system, so we wouldn't lose the backbone or bunkered server data, but the end point connections could be fried. A National Academy of Sciences report Jones referenced indicates that the economic cost of a Carrington-sized event today could exceed $2 trillion: twenty times greater than the cost of Hurricane Katrina in 2005.[2] Like Drew Miller, Jones didn't rely on conspiracy theories or outlandish scenarios to sell his product, he relied on historical precedent. I could see why he'd thrown his lot in with Miller and bought space at Fortitude Ranch.

"Now, how many of you have basements?" Jones asked the crowd. This being Salt Lake City, about a quarter of the audience raised their hand. "Okay, that's good, that's going to cut radiation by 90 percent. But you're going to need to shield your electronics from the EMP, so I'm going to show you how to make a Faraday cage for your electronics that can block an EMP, from a steel trash can, two yoga mats, and some duct tape." Not wanting to get dragged into an extended craft session, I wandered back out to find Milton.

The main hall of PrepperCon was a frenzy of activity: stalls with screaming people hawking survival paraphernalia of all kinds, a main stage featuring a panel discussion among celebrity survivalists, a selection of bug-out and assault vehicles, people starting bow-drill fires with sticks and twine, and crowds and crowds of people milling about with drinks in plastic cups and hot dogs. There were people handing out self-published pamphlets about constitutional law over hoisted mustard-colored "Don't Tread on Me" flags and racks and tables of "POW/MIA" and "MAGA" hats, and guns, clips, knives, hatchets, spears, and samurai swords everywhere. One weapons booth had as its emblem an image of Thomas Jefferson in a bulletproof vest, wielding an AR-15 rifle with a sardonic grin. The effect of the whole scene was overwhelming. I followed Milton to the booth of a company selling Dave Jones–endorsed EMP-proof solar panels, and from there to a vendor selling battery bank systems, which could be wired to the panels.

While Milton was handing out his xFest flyers, I spied Ron Hubbard from Atlas Survival Shelters. Having missed him during my visit to the warehouse, I went over to say hello. He sat in a virtually empty booth, in a low-slung plastic chair, drinking a forty-four-ounce Big Gulp soda next to a stack of brochures. Behind him hung a banner for his signature BombNado backyard shelter—the one I'd seen being loaded onto the trailer in Dallas. Clean-shaven and dressed in spotless sneakers and a button-down Hawaiian shirt, Ron's appearance contrasted starkly with that of most of the other exhibitors, who were all tacticool gear and camouflage. He had a healthy tan and a droll smile that looked as if it might have been induced by a spot of nip and tuck.

"I was supposed to bring one out," he said, pointing his thumb to the banner behind him. "A BombNado. But it was too much work to load the thing onto the trailer, so I'm just here." He took a drag on his giant soda, through a straw tucked into the side of his mouth. I asked Ron if there'd been any call for BombNados in Salt Lake City.

"Yeah, I did an install here of three bunkers linked together for fifty people. It was a huge job." While he was talking, Ron looked over my shoulder, avoiding eye contact. I explained who I was and thanked him for lining up my visit. Ron shrugged and then launched into his new obsession: the Denver International Airport. There were, he said, far more people passing through the airport than could possibly be traveling. "It's the New World Order airport, man. They've got satellite images of endless trucks of dirt coming out of there—there's a bunker under it. The government has their bunkers, and you need to think about what it might mean that the elites have this bunker in place for when Tribulation begins." I told him I'd take a look.

The airport was opened in 1995, and came in $2 billion over budget. The official reason for this massive overspend was an underground baggage system that involved twenty-two miles of tracks and conveyor belts and was supposed to be automated, but which was never functional. The airport on view to the public is just plain weird. It's filled with disturbing art including images of cities in rubble and people fleeing from disasters. Pride of place is given to a thirty-three-foot-tall electric-blue horse with glowing red eyes—dubbed "Blucifer" by locals—that greets passengers on arrival. The statue toppled over at one point, killing the artist who was creating it by severing an artery in his leg. Finally, as if all this weren't odd enough, on display in the airport is a concrete box with a time capsule inside it. There's a plaque on the box—dedicated to the Freemasons—which says the airport was funded by the New World Airport Commission—an organization that doesn't exist. There is no rational explanation for this extraordinarily bizarre stuff. If it's not an Illuminati headquarters, it sure looks like a deep underground military base that will one day be declassified. It's also totally possible that I had bought into a conspiracy theory sold to me by a guy sipping a Big Gulp in front of a BombNado banner at a doomsday prepper convention.

Wandering around the main hall at PrepperCon, I stopped at a stand selling vehicles. Plan B, from Ogden, Utah, rehabs ex-military hardware into supercharged disaster bug-out trucks, mobile four-wheel-drive shelters, and overland rigs capable of crossing continents. The founders, Tom Broome and Dan Coleman, a pair of gearheads dressed in business casual, market them as useful bug-out vehicles for emergencies including earthquakes, hurricanes, blizzards, tornadoes, financial collapse, wars, pandemics, and political unrest. "These rigs," I overheard Dan tell a customer, "can get your family out of harm's way."

There was another, more altruistic side to Coleman and Broome's spiel. Both were Mormons, and proposed that their vehicles should be used to bring supplies to affected areas and people in need of rescue. They themselves, they now told me, had participated in relief efforts during Hurricane Harvey, with a Mormon hope of saving souls as well as bodies: theirs were rescue rigs with missionary zeal. The Plan B model made sense in terms of the Mormon prepper ethos, which Mette and Neca had explained to me: this was about building community and sharing what you have, with a bit of rugged Western individualism thrown in. It was also, apparently, a thriving business model; Coleman and Broome said they'd barely made it to PrepperCon because their staff was overstretched by back orders.

Milton strolled up just as I was clambering into a six-wheel-drive recreational vehicle (RV) called Big Red. We marveled at the three king-sized beds, shower, and underfloor heating stuffed into a two-hundred-fifty-square-foot box trailer with a safari rack, solar panels, and a two-hundred-gallon water tank sitting on an M939 five-ton military truck chassis. Milton and I climbed into the cab, sank into the bucket seats, and looked out over the showroom floor, debating the merits of a mobile bunker against being dug in in South Dakota. Milton thought that, ideally, you'd have one of these rigs to get to the bunker. The orange five-hundred-horsepower Humvee next to Big Red, I argued, was a better bet to get there quickly during an event. Broome and Coleman, sensing my excitement, invited me to their workshop to test-drive one of the trucks. I got their address and promised to stop by.

In the afternoon at PrepperCon, the advertised highlight was a talk by Drew Miller from Fortitude Ranch. It was standing room only, and Miller had dressed for the occasion, in a khaki shirt with a patch over the breast pocket that gave him the air of a Cub Scout leader. He said "nuke-u-lar" like Dave Jones. The slides he flipped through were a ginned-up representation of what I'd seen on-site. They didn't seem especially representative of where he was at with the project.

After the talk, back in the main hall, I chatted with a group of guys in their twenties who were building a social media app called Bunker Days, which will help you find like-minded people to build a community, wherever you are. I also spoke to a contractor in Arizona who was building panic rooms, secret hatches, and escape chutes, who said he was looking for big government contracts and that "school hardening" was a "good area to move into." The hardening of schools, he explained, is a suggestion that came from the National Rifle Association's (NRA's) School Shield Task Force. It's a policy that essentially aims to turn every school into a bunker. Given there are almost a hundred thousand public schools in America, the contractor suggested, "It's great the NRA lobbied the Trump administration for new laws to mandate hardening." This, he felt, was bringing the building of hardened architecture into the mainstream of the construction industry.

I rendezvoused with Milton at a café for the first of many beers, which I needed. We sat at a large table with two women, one of whom, a heavyset fifty-four-year-old with a plastic visor, told us she was a preacher and a prepper. "We have a society that's unraveling, a president that can't keep his mouth shut, and glaciers melting up in Alaska," she said. "The emergency is all around us, you can feel it like an undercurrent."

Milton gave her some of his xFest flyers, which she scrutinized. "I like what you're doing out there," she told Milton. "You're working on human time, not on God's time. No one can work on God's time. People spend time worried about what they can't control instead of building with their hands. Fate isn't subject to our wishes."

Milton turned and looked at me wide-eyed, clearly not knowing how to respond. "Well, I don't know about that, lady, but you better get your bunker now before the prices go up."

On our way out of the café, Milton and I dealt a few more flyers onto the tables like poker dealers. Suddenly, we were surrounded by five people, including a police officer and an elderly man with a stained beard and a cane.

"See?!" the bearded man screamed, pointing at the flyers with his cane, shaking. "They're conducting unauthorized business on the premises." Apparently, beardy man was the guy running PrepperCon. The police officer watched while beardy man's henchmen gathered up and trashed our flyers. Then everyone left, except the police officer, who sat down and started scrolling through his phone. I asked him if the expo had been busy for him. He looked up briefly from his phone and wrinkled his nose. "This is the only action I've seen here, fella, other than *Candy Crush*," he said.

The beer made me introspective. By the time I got to a booth selling bulletproof backpacks for schoolchildren, my unease had started to bleed into despair. The representative explained to attendees that "active shooter situations in schools are our everyday reality now, and the best we can do is armor up."

That evening, I attended the PrepperFash fashion show with Milton and Ron Hubbard, watching models sashay down the runway in tactical outfits and demonstrate "quick draw" techniques from purses and backpacks with concealed carry compartments. When two children walked onto the stage to model the bulletproof backpacks in front of a stall selling AR-15s, I got up and left.

I checked my phone. There, in my Twitter feed, was breaking news that a seventeen-year-old student had murdered ten people and wounded thirteen others in a school shooting at Santa Fe High School in Texas. It was the twenty-second mass shooting in the US in five months: at San Bernardino, Orlando, Vegas, and many, many more. I wish I could say that was a strange coincidence, but it really wasn't. According to the Gun Violence Archive, a Washington, DC–based online archive of gun violence incidents, there had been as many mass shootings as days in the year. I'd reached my limit of what I could handle for the day and headed back to the Airbnb.

I tried to wind down by kicking back on the couch in the living room and watching some TV. It was a mistake. I ended up watching President Trump giving a press conference on the school shooting, "determined to do everything in our power to protect our students, secure our schools, and keep weapons out of the hands of those who pose a threat to themselves and to others." The news report then replayed footage from a press conference three months earlier, after the Marjory Stoneman Douglas High School shooting in Parkland, Florida, where Trump had suggested that the best solution was to arm more people, including teachers and campus security—and to harden school architecture to curb the body count.

Before I knew it, I was on my laptop searching for more. In a federal school safety meeting with state and local officials four days after the Parkland shooting, Trump explained, "I don't want to tell my son, 'You're going to have to participate in an active shooter drill.' I'd much rather have a hardened school."[3] Soon after this, Congress passed the STOP School Violence Act, which allocated an annual budget of $50 million per year to help schools fund such expenditures, which in turn boosted the private hardened structures market with public money. Business is increasingly lucrative: schools are buying everything from bulletproof calendars and whiteboards, to door shields and gunshot detection systems, and redesigning building layouts. Teachers, students, and administrators need training by expert contractors in these emergency systems and situations.[4] This was what the Arizona contractor had mentioned. Turning schools into bunkers was where the serious money was at.

According to the *Washington Post*, a 2012 report issued by the NRA's National School Shield Task Force suggested "a single point of entry to a school's grounds with fencing preventing access elsewhere. Shrubs should be kept away from the buildings and trees planted at a distance, to prevent an assailant from climbing to gain entry via upper windows or the roof." Specific entryway schematics were provided to maximize sight lines and minimize the ability of a shooter to get past without confrontation. Ballistic glass was recommended for interior windows, and "steel plating" for entrypoint desks.[5] The implementation of ballistic glass and steel plating around a campus, in combination with the arming of campus staff, creates defensible space from which to hide from or attack an attacker. These suggestions seemed to be the baseline for the STOP legislation.

Following the report's recommendations, in one exceptional case, Healdton Public School in Oklahoma installed in classrooms six $30,000 eight-by-eight-foot bulletproof boxes that they purchased from a company called Shelter-in-Place. The term "shelter in place," I knew, originated from the Cold War, from a 1957 House subcommittee hearing, in fact. The words used to encourage sheltering in a bunker from nuclear fallout, but have since become common language during emergencies ranging from pandemics to hurricanes to mass shootings. In other words, in the event of an "active shooter situation," kids were meant to climb into these boxes and wait it out.[6]

The report also suggested that, like the duck-and-cover drills of the Cold War, students should practice active shooter situations. The US Department of Education took this seriously: in the 2015 to 2016 school years, 95 percent of schools practiced lockdown procedures. Many schools staged expensive mock attacks with high production values: blanks fired from real guns, fake blood spilled over "victims," and simulated bombs tossed into classrooms by masked-up teenage actors. At one Indiana school in 2019, teachers were marched into a room, told to get on their knees, and were "executed" with a pellet gun.[7] The effect of these simulations on students was predictable: some fainted, others lost control of their bowels. Many students, unsurprisingly, are reported to be exhibiting signs of PTSD stemming from the constant expectation of something horrible unfolding in a random future moment.

I'm sure the violence I experienced growing up in Southern California had long-term effects on me, but they weren't all negative. I'm an anxious adult, but I'm also wary, adventurous, and relatively resilient to conflict, because I have a realistic view of violence. But I worried that what people were reacting to at PrepperCon, and generally in the United States, was not an increase in violence as much as an increase in the *perception* of violence. According to a 2018 report by researchers at Northeastern University, the overall number of students killed in shootings at schools has actually decreased from the early 1990s, when I was a teenager.[8] David Ropeik, a consultant in risk perception and communication, has said that the likelihood of a public school student being killed by a gun in school between 1999 and 2018 was about 1 in 614 million.[9] This isn't to say the US isn't a dangerous place, or that school shootings aren't horrific, but it does suggest it's the media coverage of these shootings that is driving the bunkerization of everyday life.

Milton returned from PrepperCon soon afterward, and we lounged on milk crates on the front porch in the warm Utah night eating Chinese takeout. I asked him how it was all coming together at xPoint.

"It's sweet, man, it's full of good-hearted people and it's filling up now," Milton replied. Three more bunkers, including the now completed show bunker, had been sold recently. The guy that bought the show bunker also bought the one next to it. Milton told me that he had plans to dig an El Chapo–style escape tunnel between them that could be traversed by pulling on a rope to winch a trolley down a set of greased tracks.

"We're going to have a great reset, Brad, but you have to be a visionary to see it, you have to kill the noise, you know?" It was hard for me to imagine a "reset," a catastrophe, being great.

His upturned face illuminated by a streetlamp, Milton let out a contented sigh. "I just love my bunker," he said. "I close the door and stay in there for a few days and then I can think again. I've been off-balance and I think it's because of everything around us. But you know, after the reset, we won't even need laws, just the respect we already have for each other. I can't wait for that."

13

Rolling Territory:
The Mobile Bunker

"The unlimited escalation of control is a hopeless response to the predictable breakdowns of
the system."
>—The Invisible Committee,
> *The Call (l'appel)*, 2004[1]

Dan Coleman from Plan B Supply, the Utah-based company building custom assault vehicles and bug-out rigs, looked all-American:
a sleepy-eyed mechanic in a greasy baseball cap and a T-shirt. Tom
Broome was slender and taciturn, more of a polo shirt kind of guy.

Both seemed thoroughly wholesome, the kind of people you'd ask to keep an eye on your kid at a ball game while you grab a snack. Their YouTube channel was full of earnest chats with each other about preparedness, and hijinks. In one video, Tom steals Dan's phone and runs over it with General Lee, the five-hundred-horsepower slant-back orange Humvee we saw at PrepperCon; in another they sink a Humvee into a mud pit and have to drag it out with a five-ton truck's winch. I did not get the sense that these guys put much stock in apocalyptic rhetoric: they were having too much fun and making too much money to care about end-times prophecies.

Plan B Supply is located in an industrial business center in Ogden, forty minutes from Salt Lake City. You can't see much from the road, but around the back of the building stand rows of Humvees, giant trucks, monster machines, piles of spare parts, and crates everywhere. It's like an army depot junkyard. Coleman and Broome invited me inside the workshop where half a dozen workers were pulling engines, welding rack systems, and zipping lug nuts off with air wrenches. Their office was a cramped room connected to the massive work floor. We closed the door to be able to speak, and they graciously ignored constantly ringing phones while we chatted.

Coleman and Broome had mentioned to me at PrepperCon that they were members of the LDS Church. I told them about my meetings with other members of the Church, and that I thought the idea of sheltering a community to weather a crisis was affecting the methodologies of preppers more broadly.

Coleman agreed that the "lone wolf" days of survivalism were passé. "We actually have a Plan B Disaster Response Team, or DRT," he said. "Every person who buys a vehicle, we ask them if they'd be willing to help in an emergency, and if so, we put them down for the DRT."

"Sometimes they end up helping even if they don't sign up," Broome said. "We did our first extended cab rig for a guy in Houston. He just bought it for fun. Then during Hurricane Harvey, we were watching the news and we saw the rig driving through five feet of water going to help people!"

Broome explained that their last DRT trip was to the 2015 flash

floods that destroyed three hundred fifty homes and claimed thirteen lives in Wimberley, Texas. As they were preparing to leave, a private contractor got in touch with them and wanted to buy all their vehicles on a FEMA bid, to support disaster response work.

"They wanted thirty trucks the next day," Broome said. "We didn't even have thirty drivers. We lined it all up anyway, because we wanted to be of service, but FEMA didn't extend the contract and it all fell through. We couldn't believe it." Luckily, private individuals stepped in. A doctor who owned a chain of dialysis centers told Coleman and Broome that his patients were trapped inside their homes by the flooding. They could be dead in four days if they couldn't get them on dialysis. It had become a YOYO (You're on Your Own) situation.

"He called us and said 'Screw FEMA, I'll buy the trucks and go take care of it myself.' Those were his exact words," Broome said. "Another guy that sells diesel generators, he bought five vehicles. We pulled up and parked them and he jumped in immediately to go and help people. So those trucks that we got ready for the FEMA contractors, we put them into private people's hands." The guys said that they'd learned through that experience "not to trust the square wheels of government." In another flood event they told me about, FEMA actually tried to prevent the DRT crew from acting. Their response, typical of preppers, was to drive right past the FEMA officials, into door-deep floodwater, to ferry dozens of stranded people to safety. By the time FEMA was actually ready to step up, they were no longer needed.

The California-based author Rebecca Solnit, who has written extensively about disasters, suggests that the biggest issues in most disasters actually arise from the attitudes of politicians, police, and the military, who fear that their hold on power will slip in an emergency.[2] Social scientists call this "elite panic." They fear, in other words, precisely the cycle of change the preppers have anticipated—and, in some cases, hoped for. During Hurricane Katrina in 2005, police shot and killed unarmed people on the Danziger Bridge in New Orleans. They then engineered a cover-up story for the murders, it was later revealed in court. Stories like this reinforce the sense preppers have that the social contract between citizens and those in power has been shattered. Many of the resilient citizens of New Orleans saw the destruction of the city as part of a cycle of renewal that reminded those who have lost faith, or who never had it, that capitalism is a fragile fiction and that ultimately their first allegiance is to their community, not the state. Many of those whom Solnit spoke to in the aftermath of Katrina, people who lived with injustice on a day-to-day basis, on some level welcomed a crisis that had laid bare those abuses of power for the world to see.

The government's relationship with disaster capitalism takes on a particularly insidious form with the provision of emergency materials. Police forces have become bolstered and militarized in recent years, even as funding for other public services has been cut. The police now often spend more time quelling angry citizens than protecting them. This leaves the private market to do the work of disaster relief organization and logistics while the cops run around "keeping everything under control."[3] Coleman and Broome are part of that budding civilian market, but are also aping the militarization of authorities, creating a kind of arms race.

The vehicles Plan B Supply are refurbishing are ex-military rigs that are between fifteen and fifty years old. The Humvees at the back of the lot had been auctioned off, because the US Department of Defense (DOD) is phasing in a far more aggressive truck. The DOD is spending $1.7 billion on about seventeen thousand joint light tactical vehicles (JLTVs), built by Wisconsin-based Oshkosh Defense. The JLTV can run on two flat tires for six hundred miles after taking small-caliber fire to the fuel tank, engine oil reservoir, or coolant system. These vehicles also have a remote-operated weapon station that allows for machine-gunning people from the comfort of the cabin.

As the JLTV comes in, two other trucks are going out that will soon to hit the private market. The "Growler," a small four-wheel-drive truck first used in 2009 by the US Marine Corps as a utility, scout, and fast-attack vehicle, with automatic tire inflation, is being retired, as is a seven-ton cargo truck. The latter is a C12 diesel, four-hundred-ten-horsepower monster that can ford five feet of water and traverse a 60 percent gradient. Both are being auctioned off on

GovPlanet, a private website for used military equipment similar to Australian Frontline Machinery in Sydney.

These intimidating vehicles—which will no doubt soon be driving down the wide streets of Salt Lake City—continue to escalate the militarization of private transport. Maybe they'll save lives when government aid completely vanishes in our libertarian future, though in the process they might kill us anyway: new research shows that SUVs were the second-largest contributor to the increase in global CO_2 emissions from 2010 to 2018, beating heavy industry, aviation, and shipping.[4] But at a time when every decision feels like a bad one, DIY people like Coleman and Broome just press forward.

"We're here to put capable vehicles in the hands of people who are willing to take action," Broome told me. "It feels great to know your trucks and the things that you're doing every day can actually have that effect." He clearly had this response memorized. It was a marketing bromide that could have come straight from Facebook.

"But there's also a practical component, too," Coleman said. "There's a lot of things in life now where we are at the mercy of whoever designed it. Your phone's broken? Well, after a hard reset that's the limit of your ability. Now you have to take it to the Genius Bar or whatever and they can't even fix it, they just hand you a new one.

"The world is being designed in a way that feels unsustainable," Coleman continued, leaning back in his creaky office chair. "Education, the market, the products we use, the way that we're living, the way we're spending, and the way that we think, well, it's like we're all kind of turning inward. People feel lonely but they're surrounded by other people. It's all so superficial. That's why we like building things with our hands here." By inference, Coleman suggested their vehicles were an open book, the kind of asset friends could wrench on together on weekends. This assumes, of course, that the people buying them have a basic working knowledge of mechanics.

Coleman and Broome couldn't ignore their phones anymore and handed me off to Mike Christiansen, the plucky Plan B sales manager, to go wander around the warehouse and see what they were building at the moment. Christiansen had an army crew cut and wore a black Plan B Supply polo shirt with denim cargo shorts and an old-school Casio watch. He was a no-nonsense kind of guy.

Big Red, the two-hundred-fifty-square-foot six-wheel-drive RV with three king-sized beds in it, that I'd admired at PrepperCon just a few days earlier, was parked in the middle of the warehouse, being cleaned up for sale. Despite being the height of a single-story building, Big Red looked to scale in the cavernous workshop: the place was so big you could do donuts in the truck on the shop floor if you wanted to. I climbed inside to admire it anew.

"This truck will go off-grid for quite a while. It's all yours for $185,000," Christiansen called up at me from the shop floor. Around him, workers were busy breaking down and building up vehicles. Plan B Supply can transform ten to twelve vehicles a month, and have up to ten complete conversions ready to go for buyers who walk in with cash and want to drive away that day.

"Mike, how is this street-legal?" I called down.

"Ah, well, Utah is pretty relaxed when it comes to registering vehicles. Once it's got Utah plates, switching it over to another state is pretty simple. Unfortunately, though, when the military sells us anything, they take the armor off, so we have to put the armor back on. Check this out," Christiansen said, walking over to a jumble of parts on the floor and holding up what looked like a fender. I climbed down from Big Red.

"We've developed this armor kit in hopes that if people have Humvees and they want to prep, well, they can just bolt this on and bug out," he said. "We're just getting around to putting these on the website."[5]

Christiansen set me up to test-drive "the Hulk," a custom-built extended-cab six-wheel-drive truck with an 8.3L turbo diesel engine and a sunroof, retailing at $95,000. The tires were waist-high, and I had to swing myself up into the truck using a handrail. After a few whiplash-inducing lurches while I got a feel for the brakes, we turned onto a back road next to some freight tracks and he told me to punch it. The Hulk rumbled into a pace that was anything but "turbo"—but which would most certainly pull you over the top of a police cruiser. On the way around the block I asked Christiansen if he was Mormon, like Coleman and Broome.

"Well, yeah," he said. "The business started with wanting to provide trucks with purpose for people with purpose—whether they feel it's their religious duty to be prepared, or whatever. I can't speak for all LDS preppers, but there is certainly a mentality of 'I am going to have this vehicle ready built so I can help out' as opposed to going to 'I'm going to armor this thing so I can run over zombies.' But hey," he continued, grinning at me from the passenger seat, "we sell vehicles to both those groups. I'll show you a doomsday rig when we get back."

Like the bunker, the bug-out vehicle (BOV) went mainstream during the Cold War. At the same time people were leaving cities for the suburbs, the US government produced a pamphlet entitled *Four Wheels to Survival*, which noted that "the car provides a small movable house. You can get away in it—then live, eat, and sleep in it in almost any climatic conditions, if needed, until a civil defense emergency has ended."[6] The BOV—whether this be Nick's boat in Sydney, Bushy's Humvee in Melbourne, or Heidi's golf cart in Tennessee—is generally thought to be a crucial component in the bug-out plan. If bunkers are the contemporary iteration of the medieval castle, then the fleets of SUVs and Hummers parked in the hardened garages of these self-contained bunkers are the modern-day rowboat in the dead of night.

The US government has its own bug-out vehicles as part of FEMA's Mobile Emergency Response Support (MERS) network. From 1982 to 1994, FEMA built and tested three hundred response support trucks around the country: high-tech mobile command bunkers crafted out of eighteen-wheeler tractor-trailers. Each unit is a serious doomsday truck that, stocked with food and supplies, can operate for a month without support. They're equipped with long hoses that can suck diesel out of abandoned gas stations as they roam the country, mobile off-grid communications, and an independent power system capable of firing up a three-story airport terminal (should the need arise).[7]

In the *FEMA Director Battle Book* (leaked online in 2013), an undated response manual for biological, chemical, explosive, and radiological/nuclear attacks, as well as earthquakes, floods, and hurricanes, the updated MERS fleets are described as being able to provide mobile telecommunications, life support, logistics, operational support, and power generation from five bases around the country in a total grid-down situation.[8] The trucks have been updated with new technology to allow for filtration of brackish and salt water, satellite communication systems, and the ability to provide heating, ventilation, and air-conditioning for a sixteen-thousand-square-foot building.

During the Cold War, governments tackling the possibility of nuclear apocalypse were concerned almost exclusively with the survivability of government rather than the general population. In addition to the MERS fleet, since 1974 the US government has kept a fleet of four Boeing E-4 planes—dubbed by the media of the time as "doomsday planes"—ready to get into the air at short notice. These $250 million aircraft cost the taxpayers $160,000 *an hour* apiece to operate. With eighteen sleeping bunks, six bathrooms, a conference and briefing room, and space for 112 people, the planes have analog flight instruments capable of withstanding an EMP, and can serve as a survivable mobile command post in which—were the US to be hit with a nuclear strike, pandemic, or some other serious catastrophe—the president and his or her cabinet could continue to govern from the air.[9]

The US has another fleet of planes that are able to transmit launch commands to US ground-based nuclear missile silos in the event that the ground launch control centers are rendered inoperable. They can also communicate with and order launches from one of the eighteen Ohio-class submarines—those slyest of doomsday machines, which, with their twenty-four Trident missiles, would be submerged under a shield of water until the time was right to surface and respond.

In the year 1957—the same year the House subcommittee first uttered the term "shelter in place"—the mobile bunker really became a crucial asset. This was the point at which ICBMs could theoretically annihilate cities anywhere on the planet without geographical constraints. "Worldwide delivery in 30 minutes or less, or your next one is free," one poster inside the Minuteman II Launch Control Center in South Dakota boasted, imitating a pizza delivery ad.[10] In the decades that followed, mobile bunkers and weapons systems—"hardened mobility"—became increasingly central to government planning, and subsequently, to prepping more generally. The reason North Korea started putting its nukes on ninety-ton mobile launch vehicles instead of building ICBM silos is that bunker locations are fixed, they're static systems. In other words, in a world where most things can be seen and known, mobility is defense: possession of territory is about movement and circulation as much as control of geospace.[11] The idea, in both government and civilian prepping, is that a mobile target is a hard target. Ideally you would have both options. But if you must choose one—whether to "bug in," as at Fortitude Ranch, or "bug out," as Nick Sais planned to do back in Sydney—bugging out offers more flexibility in planning. In years to come, private survival might rest not so much on isolation and "hardened architecture" as on the ability to keep in perpetual motion, whether by foot, wheel, sail, or wing.

Back at the workshop, I pulled in next to a fully armored black truck with a V-shaped plow. Metal mesh grating covered the windows, as well as portholes that could be swiveled open to fire a broadside volley from the vehicle. It had a gangplank that could be extended into a second-story window, defeating ground-floor building security, and an external speaker system. This put me in mind of the sonic warfare tactics utilized by both federal and Texas State law enforcement when trying to flush out the Branch Davidians at Waco by playing a twenty-four-hour stream of Tibetan chants, Christmas carols, bugle calls, and Nancy Sinatra's "These Boots Are Made for Walkin'." I also thought about Sanctum, and Auggie's fear that someone would come with a truck and ladder to get at his shatterproof windows. It struck me that a global prepper battle royale would make for an amazing reality show, with the production company paying for all the preps and damages and then letting the competitors loose.

Coleman and Broome emerged from their office. "That's a special case," Coleman said, walking over. "That used to be an armored Brinks security truck for cash transport. The guy also had us build a five-ton truck with a big armored box on the back and a swivel turret on top, and he's already got an armored Humvee. He's gearing up for civil war, I think." Broome nodded sagely.

The purchaser—whom, perhaps unsurprisingly, they wouldn't name or put me in touch with under any circumstances—owned thousands of acres and a lake in South Carolina. He wanted (or so Coleman said) to build up a fleet of armored rigs, so that when martial law was implemented and the government installed checkpoints, he could blast through them to go and pick up his friends and family and bring them to his property, where he could support a thousand people fairly comfortably. He believed that most cars would be wiped out by a government EMP—but in his rigs he would breeze past, or even over, them.

"Yep, we've got people coming in here telling us they're all having dreams about civil war," Broome continued. "People from all over the country, having the same dreams, like collective anxiety. They all see the same thing—that those people that are all gung-ho are going to get slaughtered. You've got to hang back and take stock, protect your people."

"That's right," Coleman concurred. "You have all this political turmoil, the world is in all kinds of commotion, and people are having these religious or spiritual experiences and visions, and it's all tied together. And here we are at the center of it building these EMP-proof mobile bunkers. It's crazy," he added, with perhaps a little too much enthusiasm, "we can't build them fast enough." All of which was in stark contrast to most of the dread merchants—who seemed to be working overtime to get people to buy into their doomsteads.

Imagining the breakout moment of the Brinks truck reminded me of another story one state over. My partner Amanda's dad had a cabin that she used to visit just outside the seventeen-hundred-person town of Granby, Colorado. There, just before 3 p.m. on Friday, June 4, in 2004, locals heard a deep rumble coming from a shed on the property of a muffler shop on the western outskirts of town. Moments later, the wall of the shed crumpled to the earth under the grinding treads of the "Killdozer," setting out on its first and only mission.

A thirteen-foot-tall, four-hundred-ten-horsepower Komatsu D355A bulldozer weighs in at forty-nine tons. This one, reinforced with poured concrete and three-inch-thick bulletproof windows, was sixty-one tons. Inside, it was equipped with an air conditioner, a front and rear camera system streaming to video screens, a stockpile of food and water, a gas mask, and several weapons, including a Smith & Wesson .357 revolver and a Kel-Tec P-11 pistol. A .50-caliber Barrett M82 anti-matériel rifle was mounted to the front of the vehicle, and an FN FNC NATO assault rifle and a Ruger Mini-14 protruded from portholes on the vehicle's sides, all protected by half-inch steel plate. Inside the Killdozer, fifty-four-year-old Marvin Heemeyer, a brawny two-hundred-forty-pound, six-foot-four mountain man with a gray goatee, was fueled by fury, determined to destroy the lives of those who, he contended, had destroyed his. Heemeyer was a prepper pushed over the brink.

At a sauntering five miles per hour, the Killdozer made its way to a concrete plant down the road, where Cody Docheff, the plant's owner, tried to upend it with a front-loader tractor. Docheff was pushed aside with ease just before bullets began streaming from the Killdozer's embrasures, chasing him off into the woods.

The neighborly bone of contention was as follows. Heemeyer's muffler repair shop had had its access cut off by the construction of Docheff's concrete plant. To add insult to injury, the plant's construction also prevented the muffler shop from connecting to the municipal sewer, for which Heemeyer was fined by the city government. When he signed the $2,500 check for the fine, he wrote "COWARDS" over it before putting it in the post. For Heemeyer—like many preppers—the social contract itself was a kind of latent disaster, thwarting his ability to survive by his own talents and merits.[12] Having developed an acute sense that his freedom and livelihood had been under siege from bureaucracy for years, he'd finally arrived at the point where he felt he had nothing to lose. He was determined to take revenge, even if it cost him his life.

Over the next few hours, Heemeyer systematically demolished a dozen buildings in the center of town, including the Liberty Bank, the *Sky-Hi News* headquarters, the library, the town hall, and the home of the former mayor.

During this time, officers from the Sheriff's Office, the Colorado State Patrol, the US Forest Service, and a SWAT team all attempted to stop Heemeyer, but the Killdozer proved immune to small arms fire and even explosives. The homemade tank was sealed so tightly that Heemeyer couldn't see much outside through his tank vision.[13]

At one point, Granby undersheriff Glen Trainor scrambled up the shell of the Killdozer and found it was coated with oil: Heemeyer had anticipated this tactic. Trainor nonetheless made it to the top and shot thirty-seven rounds from his service pistol into the plating. His colleagues watched as he then slipped off the greased shell into the road, defeated. Just after 5 p.m., two hours after setting out on its mission, the radiator burst on the Killdozer and Marvin Heemeyer made one last push, into the Gambles Hardware Store, where he got stuck, then shot himself in the head with his .357. It took twelve hours of cutting with an oxyacetylene torch, and a tug from a crane, to crack the armored hatch that Heemeyer had welded shut.

In the aftermath, as teams were clearing through the rubble of an entire town now transformed into a crime scene, a note was found in the shed where the Killdozer was built that simply said, "I was always willing to be reasonable until I had to be unreasonable. Sometimes reasonable men must do unreasonable things."

While the Killdozer rampage seems a bizarre, isolated incident perpetrated by a man pushed over the edge, much about it reflects wider societal pressures and anxieties. Heemeyer, indeed, was hardly alone in appropriating construction equipment, and even military vehicles, to mete out street justice. The stories proliferate, whether about an Australian civilian making off with armored personnel carriers to take revenge for perceived injustices, or a US Army vet going on a rampage in a stolen M60A3 Patton Tank.[14] The catalyst for these Mad Max–style acts of violence was almost invariably societal: increasing work hours driven by "always on" technology, stagnating wages, skyrocketing rents, and a massively expanded police state—one area, funnily enough, which rarely sees government cutbacks.

Heemeyer's case, though, was especially unusual. Welding himself in, he clearly never intended to exit his bunker. Like the Idaho Mountain Boys at Almost Heaven, LaVoy Finicum at the Bundy Malheur Wildlife Refuge standoff, and the hundreds of school shooters who have turned campuses into war zones, he became obsessed not with preparing for a disaster but with bringing one about. He had morphed from a prepper into a domestic terrorist, having more in common with a martyr driving a car bomb than a prepper determined to survive at all costs.[15] Same methodology, different ideology.

As SUVs become larger and more hardened, people are beginning to envisage stockpiling and armoring the bug-out vehicle as the ultimate form of prepping, a way of bugging in and out at the same time. *Grand Theft Auto*–come-to-life stories, like Heemeyer's suicidal wrecking spree, help drive this vision; so, too, as I saw at the Plan B warehouse, does a consumer market that serves up ever more luxurious armored vehicles to meet demand. The evolution of the exclusive apartment to the gated community to the bunker-burb is being mirrored by the move from trucks to SUVs to urban assault vehicles.

The military jeep was the first SUV, a World War II rig built to carry troops with a mounted heavy machine gun. In the decades after the war, it was converted into a vehicle for the domestic market which promised both freedom and safety: one ad from 1971 said of the Jeep Renegade: "She was born to run free, far from the pavement." Then, in the 1990s, after the first Gulf War, the SUV market exploded. It was dominated by the Ford Explorer (most driven) and the Humvee (most sought after), the latter marketed as an "urban assault vehicle."[16] In Utah, people began referring to SUVs as MAVs, or Mormon assault vehicles, in the same way Londoners used to call them "Chelsea Tractors," after the exclusive area of southwest London. Each iteration of the SUV was bigger than the last, promising not just the possibility of escape to the wilderness but also the fulfillment of "the need to be prepared to move through the burning city," according to one ad.[17] If the most elementary and obvious form of success is to remain alive, urban assault vehicles offer the physical embodiment of people's concerns with survival and reproduction, in which the driver is transformed into a trooper, combating an increasingly dangerous world: in this vision, the urban environment is dangerous, alien terrain to be negotiated, combated, protected from.[18]

All of which jibes with Auggie's concerns in Chiang Mai, and middle-class anxieties in general. If survival is about outlasting others at any cost, if the death of others gives meaning to our success because we are still alive, then hunkering down in a bunker or bugging out in an armored SUV are both valid survival plans.[19] (However, while the SUV may protect you and your family to a greater degree, it is also twenty-nine times more likely to kill someone in a traffic collision.) Like other forms of prepping, buying into that sociopolitical narrative is a self-fulfilling prophecy, reinforcing class barriers and a sense of individualism, and exacerbating inequality by cutting people off from the communities around them. In the same way that ownership of a bunker provides peace of mind, the sense of security offered by driving the SUV continues when it is not being driven: its presence in your life offers—to borrow a phrase of Vicino's—a "life assurance solution" but also suggests to others that they may as well give up.

Recall that more than 1 percent of the United States population, or 3.7 million people, self-identify as preppers. This is a substantial market to whom these vehicles are promoted directly as consumable mitigation for their dread. Fear of death is an infinitely renewable resource and a huge market.[20] Many buyers profile as educated liberals: the types who might profess to think of prepping as being faintly ridiculous and backward—the kind of thing they do in the "flyover states"—but nevertheless leap into their Humvees to drive the kids to ballet class and the farmers' market. One of the taglines for the Hummer H2 reads: "When the asteroid hits and civilization crumbles, you'll be ready." It would not be a stretch to suggest that these ads actually create prepper culture: they are easy entry points into the aesthetic of preparedness, which may blossom into broader preps.

It certainly did for me. Once Amanda and I had purchased our Jeep in Sydney, and fortified our camping supplies for weekend adventures, there was no reason not to keep the vehicle stocked with supplies, so that we could bug out even from the parking garage at work if need be. Breaking down the preps on weekends—unpacking all the boxes and bags to stress-test, refill, and replace worn-out items—to be ready for an "anytime evac" became a small anxiety-relieving ritual, like buying groceries for the week, paying all the bills, or giving the house a deep clean.

In 2017, the prepper aesthetic achieved some kind of perfectibility in a vehicle simply called Tank, released by Southern California–based automobile manufacturer Rezvani. The custom vehicle, brainchild of Iranian-American entrepreneur Ferris Rezvani, boasts a five-hundred-horsepower V8, Kevlar ballistic armor, run-flat tires, bulletproof glass, and even a thermal night vision system, all on a Jeep Wrangler frame. Meanwhile, the four-hundred-horsepower V10 Karlmann King, the world's most expensive SUV, hand-crafted by a workforce of eighteen hundred people under the guidance of Italian designer Luciano D'Ambrosio, goes for between $1.8 and $3.5 million. For around the $2 million mark, you get a bulletproof body on forty-inch all-terrain tires, a 4K flat-panel TV hooked up to a PlayStation 4 (so you can play your *Grand Theft Auto* inside and out), satellite navigation, mood lighting, a refrigerator, and a coffee machine. In this vision, the mobile bunker is a capsule of excess consumption in an uncertain world: no longer simply (or primarily) a means of moving from one gated community to another, but an enclave in and of itself.[21]

Even Canada, which Americans tend to think of as having a far more tepid social and political climate, is getting in on the business. Toronto-based INKAS Armored Vehicle Manufacturing started off in 2000 building armored limousines of the sort John Eckerd's old company made. From 2015, they started selling sixteen-seat armored personnel carriers, SWAT-style trucks and rescue vans with hand-grenade blast ratings.

I was surprised by the extent of the civilian market, that we'd reached this level of bourgeois paranoia. But what surprised me even more, though perhaps I should have expected it, was that the government was buying these vehicles from civilian suppliers. It's an act that seems to close the loop on this kind of disaster capitalism. Taxpayers' money was spent on military equipment that was often never used; this government surplus equipment was then auctioned off to the private sector, where it was bought by entrepreneurs to be upgraded and sold back to the government at a vastly inflated price. If, as Jack Shields from Wise Company said, sales of survival food spiked during social and political turmoil, the same was true for the companies building rolling territory. Even in the

1960s, during the first doom boom, *Newsweek* magazine wrote that "civil defense is basically a crisis to crisis proposition."[22] Then, as now, this shadow economy was slowly slipping into the mainstream economy. It felt, at times, as if most of the wealth in the United States was being generated by either preparing for or repairing damage from an emergency.

As Mike Christiansen walked me out of the Plan B Supply warehouse at the end of the day, we came across a young family packing up a huge white-and-gray rig for an "overland trip": an extreme version of a family road trip that crosses multiple continents and in every type of conceivable terrain, on and off road. There were hundreds of empty Amazon boxes next to the truck. Matt and Jane had been posting them to Plan B to hold until they arrived to put everything in place. They'd both retired at forty from dot-com jobs, and their son Wolf was going to be homeschooled (or, rather, rig-schooled) while they drove around the world for a few years in a custom truck that Plan B Supply had built for them. Their first stop would be an Overland Expo in Flagstaff, Arizona, where, I gathered, they would meet thousands of like-minded owners of apocalypse-ready RVs. Seeing the family off with a wave, Dan Coleman walked over and left me with some parting words.

"You know, in any disaster, it's always been an interesting phenomenon to see who flees and who goes in," he said. "My own experience is that I see really good people that freeze or get scared and run. Then the dirtbags of the world turn and go help. There's something inside of some people that clicks into place in an emergency and I have faith in that. Now, don't get me wrong, we've met a few people I'd call sick. But most people we get coming through here are preparing for the worst and hoping for the best. These are good people."

"I have to ask before I go, do you guys have a bunker?" They both laughed.

"I've got a couple of years of food for me and my family," Coleman responded, "but we don't need a bunker—that's the purpose of the truck, it's a mobile bunker. I don't know if I want to be in a particular area, or if I'll want to get in my vehicle and leave. Or go in and help, if possible."

As with most preppers I'd encountered in Utah, faith drove Dan's and Tom's response to emergencies. Coleman explained to me that "salvation" in any situation would come first from "ourselves, then families, neighbors, and finally government, in that order." Like so many religious communities in the USA, Mormons equate freedom of religion with freedom from government.

The bug-out vehicle industry seemed to be thriving and serving an increasingly affluent client base. But the fixed bunker industry was fighting back, in the form of one of the most technically sophisticated of all bunkers: underground cruise ships, built to traverse dangerous times.

14

Life in a Geoscraper:
The Survival Condo

"We are reaching the limits of our ecosystem,
and we are therefore reaching a phase of permanent catastrophe."
　　　　　—Lieven De Cauter, *The Capsular*
　　　　　　　Civilization, 2004[1]

"Mechanical Level," "Medical Level," "Store Level," the voice
announced as the elevator descended into the Earth. I'd entered at
Parking Lot Level, the building's apex. I was traveling through an
inverted skyscraper—a geoscraper—climbing floors as we plumbed
the depths of the building. Larry Hall stood next to me, whistling

223

a tune, black shirt tucked into blue jeans that clashed with his box-fresh white sneakers.

When the elevator doors opened, I couldn't suppress a laugh. In front of us, four stories underground in Central Kansas, was a supermarket complete with shopping baskets, shelves, cold cases, an espresso machine behind the counter, and a middle-class-America aesthetic.

Hall turned to me and smiled. "It's good, isn't it?" A hulking, barrel-chested man in his late fifties, he spoke with the confidence of someone who's planned for every eventuality. He waved his hand at racks of #10 cans stretching down one wall.

"On the original blueprint for the renovation it said 'stores' on this level," he explained. "The psychologist we hired to consult on the project took one look at that and said 'No, no, no, this needs to be a general store. This needs to feel like a miniature Whole Foods supermarket, we need a low black ceiling, beige walls, a tile floor, and nicely presented cases, because if people are locked in this silo and they have to come down here and rifle through cardboard boxes to get their food, you'll have depressed people everywhere.' "

So, Larry continued, he'd followed the psychologist's advice. "But," he added, "there are a few rules: you can only shop in lockdown, everyone has to come shopping, and you can only take food for three days. Shopping is a social event, and if we're planning for five years and then we find half the cans have walked out of here when we need them and are under people's beds or whatever, we're going to have strained relationships."

I was inside the most lavish and sophisticated private bunker in the world. The Survival Condo was once a Cold War US government Atlas F missile silo. Constructed in the early 1960s at a cost to the US taxpayer of approximately $15 million, it was one of seventy-two "hardened" missile silo structures built to protect a nuclear-tipped ICBM one hundred times more powerful than the bomb dropped on Nagasaki.[2] The bunker was made of three feet of epoxy-resin concrete stainless-steel mesh, mounted on spring shock absorbers. According to the Brookings Institution the United States spent $5.5 trillion on its nuclear weapons development program over the course of the Cold War—notwithstanding which, many of these silos were blown up and buried after decades of disuse.[3] But not all of them.

As the founder of this extraordinarily opulent project, Hall was overwhelmed by media requests. I'd spent nearly a year badgering him for a visit before he extended an invitation.

My trip to Survival Condo from Utah took me back across the flat expanses of southern Wyoming, bordering xPoint country, and I recalled my freezing visit there. Now, though, the weather was warm, and I drove with the windows down, music blasting. Reaching the windswept crossroads that was our rendezvous, I followed Hall's pickup truck down a dirt road through corn and soybean fields, past a giant wind turbine, and through a military-grade chain-link fence rolled open by a camouflaged security guard with an assault rifle. As the gate closed behind us, I watched in my rearview mirror as the guard scanned the road for a tail. I climbed out of the car and followed Larry, who slipped through one of the eight-ton armored blast doors nestled into the artificial hillside, his cat Lollipop in his arms. We were eighteen miles from the geographical center of the United States.

Hall wasn't the first to reuse one of these Cold War relics. One silo in Wamego, Kansas, was raided by police in 2000. They discovered a massive LSD production facility inside that was generating up to a third of the country's supply. Another silo near Roswell, New Mexico, had been turned into an extraterrestrial communication facility that flashes binary code via laser beam into the cosmos. A third silo was funded by William Shatner (Captain James T. Kirk of USS *Enterprise* fame) to become a commercial research facility for studying the viability of colonizing Mars. Yet another in Abilene, Texas, is now a scuba diving training facility called Valhalla. Some have been turned into residential housing, including Subterra in Topeka, Kansas; one on a twelve-plot subdivision in Plattsburgh, New York; and another in Kimball, Nebraska, which from the real estate ads looks like the set of *The Brady Bunch*.[4]

Of all the projects that blossomed in the spaces vacated by the state, Larry Hall's is arguably the most gobsmacking. An ex–government contractor, property developer, and doomsday prepper with a master's degree in business, he had the perfect amalgam of attributes to build what had never been done before. In the 1990s, Hall had worked for the private defense contractor Northrop Grumman, where he'd designed the weapons database for an air force surveillance plane, among other things. In the late 1990s, he transitioned into constructing hardened data centers. At first, he'd planned to build a data center in a silo, but he quickly realized there was another, emerging market in doomsday prepping for the super-rich.

He quickly got started, buying the $15 million silo in 2008 for $300,000. By 2010, Hall had transformed the two-hundred-foot-deep silo into a fifteen-story luxury bolthole, where a community of up to seventy-five individuals could weather a maximum of five years inside the sealed, self-sufficient bunker during a doomsday event. When the event passed, residents expected to be able to re-emerge into the postapocalyptic world to rebuild.

It's not that difficult to imagine living underground in an environment that can sustain life, technically and materially. The basics of survival at the bottom of Maslow's hierarchy-of-needs pyramid— food, water, shelter, and security—are relatively easy to provide for over a short-term lock-in. What's rather more of a challenge is to create a psychologically and socially tolerable environment— in order, not to put too fine a point on it, that the members of this newly troglodytic community don't murder each other.[5] And the creation of such an environment was something that Hall was deeply interested in. Indeed, it was central to his vision of life in the Survival Condo.

During the early days of the Cold War, governments, military, and universities conducted numerous experiments to see how long people could withstand being trapped underground together. In a 1959 government study in Pleasanton, California, just outside of San Francisco, ninety-nine prisoners were confined in underground lockdown for two weeks. When they emerged, "everyone was in good health and spirits," according to a spokesperson for the group.[6] In a later study conducted by the University of Georgia, researchers locked groups of men, women, and children aged between three and seventy in fallout shelters six times between 1962 and 1964, for varying periods, during which they had to subsist on a nine-hundred-calorie-a-day diet of bulgur wheat crackers and water. They had no bathing water, bunks, or blankets. The researchers "found that no deleterious psychological or social effects occur from two-week periods of group confinement under austere conditions."[7]

It seemed people could adapt and make do—just so long as they knew the situation was temporary. It was like a period of submergence in a submarine: cramped and uncomfortable, but tolerable as long as a plan to surface was in place, a destination in time plotted. The Georgia study suggested, ultimately, that when citizens needed to hunker down, the preparation required for the lockdown was less important than the need to "prepare them for immediate adjustment to the post-attack world upon emergence."

Another report, published by the US National Science Foundation in 1960, suggested that extended time underground "may involve many physiological deprivations and adverse environmental conditions. Many of these stresses have significant effects on behavior. These include decreased efficiency in performance, difficulties in concentration, irritability, depression, and personality disturbances. Special groups such as children, pregnant women, and the ill would be particularly affected. A common element in the various environmental stresses is frustration. Common reactions to frustration include aggression, depression, regression, and withdrawal."[8] In other words, people might survive underground, but they wouldn't thrive. It would only be a matter of time before disquiet, and worse, started rippling through the group as different people were affected differently by the experience.

In total, in the early 1960s, some seven thousand people volunteered to be locked in spaces with groups ranging from the size of a family to more than one thousand people as part of the US government's attempts to assess the psychological/behavioral impact on people and communities.[9] While these studies yielded interesting information up to a point, they all had numerous shortcomings. Two were glaringly evident: the studies were for a set time period, and people knew they were a performance. If such studies were truly to assess the psychological impact of bunker life, they would have to embrace a realism that was clearly impossible to simulate:

they would have to involve a diverse range of inhabitants, with differing needs, who genuinely believed that they were sheltering from a catastrophic event whose outcome was as yet unknown to them; and that their immersion underground had no clearly defined end point.

Larry Hall, however, thought he'd worked out a solution to these two potential obstacles. The key to well-being underground, he told me, could be about creating an illusion of "normal," above-ground, pre-event life. Even just from seeing the grocery store and hearing him talk about how much he'd thought through the social dynamics of lockdown, to me his vision seemed refreshingly complete in comparison to the ill-conceived plans at places like Fortitude Ranch, where Drew Miller seemed to expect residents to act with perfect rationality and obedience in the midst of an emergency.

"So," Larry said, "we'll have people baking bread and making coffee, people can advertise their yoga class on the café blackboard, and we're going to stack this deli case full of three different species of tilapia that are grown in the aquaponics facility next door." The nitrates from the fish droppings would fertilize soil for the plants in the FDA-certified aquaponics facility. The fresh produce from there would end up in the general store. Leftover vegetable matter and fish heads and bones would be put through a grinder to become food for the residents' dogs and cats—including Lollipop, who was now happily roaming around the silo four stories above us. The sense of assurance the compound provided was as real as the reinforced concrete pillbox sitting on top of it. The bunker was unassuming, unassailable, and extremely comfortable.

"It's critical that we encourage people to come down and shop and be social," Larry was saying, "because obviously everything in here is already paid for."

Money, in other words, would have no value in the Survival Condo. Which was just as well, given the bankruptcy-inducing prices of buying into the facility in the first place. Half-floor apartments here were $1.5 million; full-floor apartments $3 million; and a two-level thousand-square-foot penthouse had sold for $4.5 million. In total, fifty-seven people currently had living space in twelve apartments, each paying an additional $5,000 a month in residents association fees. One of these apartments, purchased with cash, was designed to feel like a log cabin, with a loft looking down on a fake fireplace flanked by a six-screen 4K display of a snowcapped mountain range.

None of those buying into the project were currently in residence. Other than me, Larry, Lollipop, and the on-site maintenance guy, Mark Menosky, there was no one else inside the bunker. Unsurprisingly, the residents were elusive and tight-lipped. One resident was Nik Halik, an Australian from Melbourne and a self-described "thrillionaire" adventurer and wealth strategist.[10] Another resident, a real estate developer from Florida called Tyler Allen, had been quoted in the New Yorker as saying, "They don't put tinfoil on your head if you're the President and you go to Camp David. But they do put tinfoil on your head if you have the means and you take steps to protect your family should a problem occur."[11] Both, clearly, had the means.

On level eleven, about one hundred sixty feet underground, we visited a well-appointed full-floor eighteen-hundred-square-foot condo. It felt similar to walking into a bedroom in a clean, predictable hotel chain. The apartment had never been used. It had a Southwest print rug, a cushy white living room set, and a stone electric fireplace with a flat-panel TV mounted over it. A marble countertop extended to a bar that separated the living room from the kitchen, which was filled with high-end appliances. I looked at one of the windows and was shocked to see that it was dark outside. My instant, physiological reaction was to assume that we must have been underground for longer than I thought. Then I realized my mistake.

"Got you," Larry said, laughing. He picked up a remote control and flicked on a video feed being piped into the "window," a vertically installed LED screen. The scene depicted was the view from the front, surface-level entrance of the silo. It was daytime, breezy, and green outside. I could see my parked car through the rustling branches of an oak tree. In the distance, the camouflaged sentry was standing in the same place as when we arrived. But when this video had been made was not necessarily obvious—maybe there was a time lapse, and I was watching a prerecorded past I was convinced was the present. The thought sent a prickle of unease down my spine. Whereas many of the other dread merchants I'd met were selling visions of bunkers that didn't actually exist, Hall had created a real bunker in which life outside seemed a distant simulacrum. Survival Condo was a capsule, meant to exclude the hardships of a hostile surface. The grimmer the reality outside the walls, the more pressing was the need to maintain—and promote the desire to stay within—the simulation of the capsule.[12] Creating an illusion of reality through the screens, necessary to uphold stability after an event, was clearly part of Larry's plan to maintain order.

The whole project put me in mind of a science fiction novel by Hugh Howey called *Wool*, in which the world's entire population lives in a 144-floor buried cylinder. The only direct knowledge of the "outside" the silo's inhabitants have is streamed from cameras onto massive screens that fill the walls of the upper story. The novel was published the year before Survival Condo was completed. I asked Larry if he'd read it; he assured me he hadn't. I also later met Howey, who knew nothing of Survival Condo. Knowing this only made the situation eerier.

Not for the first time since my baptism into the world of the bunker at xPoint, I felt a decoupling of my consciousness from sense experience. How do we know that we're not *all* in a bunker already, some giant controlled experiment to see how long it takes us to destroy the environment that sustains us, or each other? Isn't that what so many religions hypothesize, that there is a being up there keeping score of all the poor decisions we're making? More than ever, I felt that the theory put forward by philosopher Nick Bostrom that we live in a computer simulation made an awful lot of sense.

"The screens can be loaded up with material or have a live feed piped in," Larry said. It was a comment that drove home to me how much Survival Condo depended on Larry setting the rules and controlling people's experiences belowground. After lockdown, he could choose precisely which material to share with the other occupants. Their sense of context, of reality, of what was happening aboveground—whether or not the end times had indeed arrived— would be entirely in his grip. "Most people prefer to know what time of day it is than to see a beach in San Francisco, though," he said casually, flicking the feed off again. The screen went blank.

Larry was not just experimenting with new technology, he was thinking about how to control people's thoughts and reactions. Though on a superficial level his vision seemed less domineering than that of Vicino or Miller, the amount of power he might wield in this space was truly terrifying. I knew Hall had been "a spook," as Miller had described him, and that he'd worked as a government contractor. I wondered if this whole thing had actually been funded by the Department of Defense as a human petri dish, the next iteration of those Cold War human experiments. Not telling the residents they were partaking in an experiment would be the key to its rigor.

Hall told me that he'd lived in the bunker for a month before the "window system" was installed. When the system was up and running, he realized the impact having no windows had had on his psychological state, because he'd been living in a space divorced from the natural rhythms of the sun, moon, stars, and seasons. He described it as something like an existential rather than a sensory deprivation; it had been, he said, like living in a casino. Unable to confirm that the passing of time correlated to what his clocks were telling him, or who was coming or going outside of the bunker, he'd felt totally isolated. The window system changed all of this, by reintroducing a circadian rhythm.

There is a science that encompasses these issues, known as chronobiology. This field of study was massively advanced in the early Cold War years by a thickly bearded French caver named Michael Siffre, who conducted a number of experiments to test the long-term effects of underground isolation on the human body and perception. In 1962, aged twenty-three, he rappeled 435 feet into a cave in the French Alps. There, he lived with a flashlight as his only light source for 58 days and 17 hours, which was as long as his body could handle. Without clocks or natural light, his physiological functions were his only time references. Over the course of 1,409 hours underground, he "lost" 25 days, adjusting to a schedule that seemed to be internal to the body. In other words, freed from the circadian rhythms created by the planet spinning in its orbit around the sun, he found that we have a different sense of time within us.

In a subsequent interview, Siffre described how he experienced a gradual loss of short-term memory underground. "When you are surrounded by night," he said, "your memory does not capture the time. You forget. After one or two days, you don't remember what you have done a day or two before. The only things that change are when you wake up and when you go to bed. Besides that, it's entirely black. It's like one long day."[13] A decade later, and now sponsored by NASA, he went underground for six months beneath the Balcones Canyonlands Preserve in Texas. There, the caver found that his body moved to a forty-eight-hour rather than twenty-four-hour cycle. Around eighty days in, he began to experience suicidal thoughts after his record player broke. This mental break may have been due to his age, now at a remove from the perceived invincibility of youth. Nonetheless, knowing the experiment had an end point, Siffre pushed on and emerged after a full six months with weakened eyesight and a permanent squint.

The physiological effects of these experiments indicate our thresholds for staying underground under extreme conditions. Siffre himself suggested, in his astonishing book *Beyond Time*, that "the problems with which my mind and body were confronted are among those posed by life in a hermetically sealed capsule," and hoped his experiences could be useful for thinking about the effects of being locked in a fallout shelter. He wrote that in order to survive in such conditions, people must "school themselves daily in self-control, which is a form of willpower. . . . Adaptive power is important in an epoch when the domestication of the atom with its consequent powers of destruction may oblige mankind to take refuge in underground shelters."[14] Reading this, I thought of Auggie becoming his "best self" inside Sanctum.

Siffre was not the only one considering the effects of underground living. A German scientist, Rütger Wever, conducted 418 studies with 447 human volunteers between 1964 and 1989, in a bunker constructed just outside Munich. Wever's experiments involved leaving people in a controlled and isolated bunker environment; his results reinforced Siffre's findings that internal rhythms are disconnected from circadian rhythm. Living underground more or less permanently, in other words, would require rethinking time, calendars, and the structure of our lives.

Siffre's work deals with the nature of time and our relationship to it. It's clear there's a disjunction between outer and inner time. Living in a subterranean space, a biodome, or a space station or colony, creates its own time-space milieu. Technically and physiologically, living underground is feasible; whether we can adapt to that milieu seems to be an existential question—it's a matter of will.[15] The question for dread merchants—who by necessity must have faith in technology duping human physiology to assure safe passage—is whether new technologies can extend our capacity to cope long enough to reach, say, five years: the maximum period that Larry has built for.

One of Survival Condo's residents, the one with the two-story "penthouse," had bought into this idea. She had videos filmed of Central Park from her Manhattan loft (her everyday dwelling), during all four seasons, day and night, together with the cacophonous sounds of urban life. To accommodate the projection of this year-round recording, Larry and Mark ground down the cement wall of the silo and slathered it with reflective paint. Then they built a balcony with a railing and, using a $75,000 short-throw projector, made it appear as if she could step onto the balcony to look over the city through sliding glass doors. The doors could even be closed to dampen the sound of the "life" below. Whether the simulation would be enough to distract this resident from the fact that she was likely to be staring at images of people killed in an event was an experiment that couldn't be field-tested.

"The thing the psychologist drilled into me was that my job as the developer was to make this place as normal as possible," Larry told me. "All the security and infrastructure, you want people to know how it works and how to fix it—but no one wants to be reminded all the time that they are basically living in a submarine. Come on, I'll show you the life-support system."

We took the elevator up to the Mechanical Level just below the surface, where Larry waved me over to a reverse osmosis filtration system. Water was pumped out of forty-five 325-foot-deep subterranean geothermal wells before being put through a four-step sterilization process. Ten thousand gallons of water a day could be filtered into three electronically monitored tanks that each held twenty-five thousand gallons.

"What keeps the pumps working after an event?" I asked.

"Power to the bunker is supplied by multiple redundant systems that alone cost five million dollars . . . and for good reason, because losing power would kill everyone in the facility," Larry said, evoking the prepper axiom: *three is two, two is one, one is none.* "We've got a bank of 386 submarine batteries with a storing charge life of fifteen years." He showed me a digital display on the bank. "We're currently running at fifty to sixty kilowatts, sixteen to eighteen of which are coming from the wind turbine." The second silo, he assured me, would have a turbine twice the size.

"Wait, what second silo?" I asked.

"Don't worry, we'll get to that." He batted my question away breezily. I had no idea Hall was building a second silo. "Anyway, we can't do solar here," he continued, "because the panels are fragile and Kansas is, after all, in tornado alley. At some point we know that wind turbine is going to go down, too. It can't make it through five years of ice storms and hail if we can't go out to do maintenance, so we've also got two hundred-kilowatt diesel generators, each of which could run the facility for two and a half years."

"Would a serious tornado be a threat to the facility?" I asked.

He laughed. "Brad, this was a bunker with a live nuclear ICBM inside of it; it was designed to withstand a one-megaton warhead being dropped within a half mile that would produce a two-thousand-mile-an-hour shock wave. So, believe me when I tell you that a three-hundred-mile-an-hour F5 tornado wouldn't scratch the paint on this place. The sixteen-inch-thick dome above us is also an effective EMP shield—nothing is coming near this battery bank or any of the electrical components." I recalled Dave Jones's yoga mat, duct tape, and trash can Faraday cage at PrepperCon, meant to shield fragile household electronics from an EMP, the tiny sibling of this cylinder.

The filtration unit for the condo was located in a small maintenance room. Hall described it: three military-grade filters that each provided two thousand cubic feet per minute of filtration, capable of filtering even weaponized nerve gas like Agent BZ.

"The things were thirty thousand dollars a pop," Larry sighed. "I put twenty million dollars into this place, and when you start buying military-grade equipment from the government you wouldn't believe how quickly you get to that number." It made me wonder again who, or what, was behind the Survival Condo. An individual investment of this magnitude seemed implausible and risky. Plans at this sort of scale were meant, in my mind, to be executed by architects playing with other people's money or urban planners with grand visions for humanity that required big budgets to create sweeping experiments in urban living. But, I had to remind myself, that's not the world we live in anymore. Today, a private visionary with $20 million in the bank can clearly achieve the improbable.

I thought of Le Corbusier, the French architect who considered buildings to be machines for living in, and who opined that "we must use the results of modern technical triumphs to set man free."[16] Le Corbusier would, you suspect, have thoroughly enjoyed thinking through the orderly functioning of this bunker once the blast doors were shut. Given the severe limitations of underground living—much like a skyscraper, where physical expansion isn't really feasible—anything extraneous has to be eliminated; all space must be used as efficiently as possible. The entire building had to be thought of as a single unit, where the actions of each resident inevitably impact all the others.

But the elimination of external infrastructural support—and potentially external reality—makes the bunker more like a Mars colony than a tower block: the umbilical cord must be severed, the blast doors slammed shut, in order to set the time machine in motion. Le Corbusier endorsed what he called a "theoretically water-tight formula" for urban planning. I imagined the joy he would have found in the theoretically airtight bunker: a clean, functional, distraction-free environment that would allow for analogous thinking, where waste had no place.[17] The Survival Condo was a modernist, technophilic utopia. And like any utopia, it required suppression of dissent to function without friction.

We moved down to level three, where Larry keyed a code into

a thick steel door. He opened it to reveal something like the scene from *The Matrix* when Neo and Trinity zap into the boundless arsenal to choose their wares.

"This is one of three armories," Larry announced proudly. "In each one we've got sniper rifles, ARs, helmets, gas masks, first-aid kits, and nonlethal weapons like military-grade pepper spray."

But, he continued, "the armories might not even be needed. You remember that pillbox you saw at the entrance? Inside that is a .223 remote-controlled rifle. You can kill people like it's a video game." Even the security guards might be a redundant feature. Hall opened up another key-coded bulletproof door to reveal a massive bank of screens and a control panel with a joystick. He explained that they had thermal, night, and full-spectrum cameras both inside and outside of the entire facility. The rifle could be put into automated defense mode with a kill zone and would fire three-round bursts at anything that came into the field of view.

"We can also hit them with three-round bursts of paintballs," he said, "which is going to make pretty clear what comes next if they keep moving toward the condo."

The joystick was part of a larger multiscreen control panel called Kaleidoscope. It was a basic AI system capable of closing off parts of the bunker automatically in the event of, say, a fire. If that puts you in mind of *2001: A Space Odyssey*, and the possibility that Kaleidoscope could start trapping people in parts of the bunker and hitting them with three-round bursts, you're right in sync with me at this point. Weirdly, however, Kaleidoscope was born out of legal necessity. From inception, the bunker had to conform to the International Building Code for Underground Inhabited Structures, which requires that if a fire broke out the air-conditioning system would shut off, because in an airtight structure everyone would suffocate if the smoke got circulated. There were ninety-seven fire dampers in the building that could create firebreaks and hot spots would be hit with sprinklers. Even if no one was alive, awake, or available to operate them, Kaleidoscope would do the job as long as there was power. From there, it was a short step to a surveillance and control system of panopticonic proportions.

Bunkers like Survival Condo, Sanctum, Trident Lakes, and xPoint are being built as a hedge against the fragility of overpopulated and interconnected cities, and yet the bunkers are themselves dependent on the same technology to function. In a way, they create the perfect techno-surveillance state in a box. Maybe this is why Silicon Valley elites are so engrossed in the idea of the apocalypse—one day the world would be remade in the techno-bunker's image. If we aren't already in it, of course.

"Larry, you couldn't build this without modern technology, could you?" I prompted.

"Nope," he replied, shaking his head. "The self-sufficiency we can achieve through sustainable technologies is just as important as defense in the condo. The whole idea was to build a green doomsday structure that someone could use as a second home that also happened to be a nuclear-hardened bunker." He paused and took a deep breath.

"Look, the fact is, this was not a space of hope; the defensive capability of this structure only existed to the extent that was needed to protect a weapon, a missile," he said. "This bunker was a weapon system. We've converted a weapon of mass destruction into the complete opposite. This is a safe, self-contained, sustainable experiment in architecture—it's a subterranean equivalent of the University of Arizona Biosphere project. People try to build systems like this on their farms and they get infiltrated by bugs, they get crop burn from solar radiation, and they get rain and wind damage. We've removed all those factors. This is as close to a closed system as we'll ever get."

Biosphere 2, also known as the "Greenhouse Ark," was an experiment in environmental sustainability and one of the most ambitious projects in communal isolation ever orchestrated. In 1991, in the town of Oracle, Arizona, a crew of eight—four men and four women—locked themselves inside a glass dome, to see if they could survive in a closed system for two years.[18] The experiment, which took place under a three-acre complex in seven "biomes" under glass, was fruitful, but plagued by social division, poor oxygen levels that led to extreme fatigue, and even banana theft after disappointing crop yields in multiple biomes that led to rationing, which sounds funny until you imagine food vanishing while being locked in a building with starving people.[19]

Biosphere 2 taught us a lot about how humans act under these extreme pressures. Paradoxically for a project in ecological sustainability, it was funded by oil money. It was taken over before the second mission by none other than Steve Bannon, Trump's former chief strategist, who carried around with him a copy of *The Fourth Turning*, the book by William Strauss and Neil Howe about apocalyptic rebirth. Abigail Alling and Mark Van Thillo, two of the "passengers" during the first mission, eventually snuck back in and broke windowpanes to sabotage the seal on the dome in protest over the way the project was being run. It was clear why Hall was so intrigued by Biosphere 2: both for the technological advancements it heralded, and as a litmus test for how social networks break down under lockdown.

Both Biodome 2 and Larry's silo, I realized, might signal a pivot in architectural history. Both were outliers that pointed toward the "normalization" of the bunker experience. Rather than being just for an "event," these technologies, and the social systems needed to keep them humming along, were being integrated into our everyday lives.

The tour continued. Like a burly Willy Wonka, Larry led me past the climbing wall, air hockey and Ping-Pong tables, and a pet park complete with Astroturf, sandwiched between a fake tree and a sunny mural set in the Rockies. He opened a door and flipped a light switch to illuminate a fifty-thousand-gallon indoor swimming pool flanked by a rock waterfall, lounge chairs, and a picnic table. A mural of a beach was painted on the wall behind it. It was a scene from a resort—with no natural light.

"This," he said with a dramatic flourish, "is our little piece of the Mediterranean right here in Central Kansas." My mouth must have been agape. "Yeah," he nodded, "it's one of the things you have to see to believe."

Survival Condo was the only place I'd seen on my journeys that not only lived up to but surpassed the media hype surrounding it. Unlike many of the other dread merchants I'd met, Larry had put his considerable financial heft where his mouth was. I wanted to know what he thought about some of the other bunker projects in development. Vivos, for instance.

"Well, sure, Vicino has built some stuff," Larry said. "The South Dakota model at xPoint is interesting, but I don't know how anyone is going to get there. I told Robert that we're on opposite ends of a bell curve. He thought he could make up the difference by building low-end bunkers and filling them with more people. But those people's expectations are too high. They want to pay twenty-five thousand dollars to get into the bunker and they want it to be the Taj Mahal." Larry's approach—which was clearly paying off—was to set a price to match the expectations of his high-net-worth clients: "I'm selling these bunkers for two to five million dollars, and the people who are buying them wire me the money and we just get going. If they want a sixty-five-thousand-dollar freezer in here, I say fine, have it delivered, and we'll install it."

The only competition to Hall's project—on paper at least—was Oppidum in the Czech Republic. "It's just a big scam," Hall said when I mentioned it, shrugging his shoulders. I could understand the frustration at having his silo, which he'd spent millions of dollars redeveloping, compared to a CGI rendering in media articles.

When the conversation inevitably turned to Hardened Structures, Hall told me a story. When he'd first bought his silo from the US government, he invited Hardened Structures out to do a feasibility study on turning it into a condo. The president, Brian Camden, told him they were well placed to do so, since they had already fitted out five Atlas F missile silos. Surprised, Hall asked to see one. He was told that they were classified. After months of getting the runaround and being offered nothing more than blueprints to look at, it became clear to him that "they'd never built a single one of them."

"Now, don't get me wrong," Hall was quick to qualify. "They've done some civilian stuff for ultra-high-net-worth individuals that's impressive." He described two such developments: a $30 million compound in the Pacific Northwest, and one for a banker in the

Catskills outside of New York City with a geothermally heated runway capable of taking a Gulfstream jet that could then pull straight into a $120 million two-hundred-twenty-person mountain bunker.

"I've never personally been to those bunkers," Hall said, "but those are serious projects. Unless," he considered, "they faked the photos." He described how his relationship with Hardened Structures had ended. After a few phone calls, Brian Camden worked up a feasibility study without having a written work order in place. Out of the blue, Hall says he received a bill for $80,000, which he refused to pay. Bill collectors and lawyers got involved. Hall never paid the bill. "But you know," he concluded, "he's just a businessman, so no hard feelings."

As far as Camden was concerned, the sentiment was not mutual. When I later emailed him to clarify what had happened, Camden wrote back immediately in far from complimentary terms about Larry Hall and his "Survival Condo," which Camden called a tomb. He explained that Hall had approached Hardened Structures to arrange a site visit and report, which Hall had liked and paid for. He said that Hall had asked them to do design work and be a part of his team, at which point Hall included them in his promotional literature. Hardened Structures then, according to Camden, "spent time doing planning and programming, but [Hall] ran out of money and just refused to pay. . . ."

Larry Hall and I got back in the elevator and hit the button for the cinema level. "Going down," the elevator said, taking us to almost two hundred feet below the surface of the Earth in twenty-some seconds, zipping past a dozen condos on the way, including Larry's own on level five.

The cinema was the penultimate level, sitting atop water pumps and storage. It had terraced leather recliners facing a large screen. We settled in and raised the leg rests on the recliners as Larry cued the opening credits of *Skyfall*, his favorite of the 007 franchise. He shouted over the soundtrack that we were immersed in 7.4 THX surround sound and a 4K video projection. After a few minutes of this, Larry ushered me into the adjoining aircraft-themed bar, equipped with a keg system. One of the residents had donated twenty-six hundred bottles of wine from her restaurant to stock it.

"I mentioned the overlap with what we're doing here and Biosphere in Arizona," Hall said, leaning on the bar. "Well, the psychologist we hired did work on that project. She went over everything in meticulous detail. From the frequency to the textures to the colors on the walls (reminding me of the green paint in the Berlin bunker meant to obscure bloodstains). Even the LED lights in the bunker are set to three thousand degrees Kelvin to prevent depression. People want to know why residents need all this 'luxury'—the cinema, climbing wall, table tennis, video games, shooting range, sauna, library, and everything—but what they don't get is that this isn't about luxury. This stuff is key to survival. I've got nothing against Rising S and those sorts of guys building backyard bunkers, but the time you're going to be able to spend in those things is limited because it's abnormal. If you don't have all this stuff built in, your brain keeps subconscious score, and you start to get varying degrees of depression or cabin fever."

Larry expanded on his theme. "In fact, everyone needs to work generally. People on vacation constantly get destructive tendencies. That's just human nature. You need to have a four-hour minimum workday and rotate jobs, so people don't get bored and break things. Whether you're woodworking or just taking the dog for a walk, it's crucial that people feel they are living a relatively normal life," he said. "You want good-quality food and water and for everyone to feel safe and to feel they're working together towards a common purpose. This thing's gotta function like a miniature cruise ship."

During the course of this exegesis, we'd hopped back into the elevator and gone to level thirteen, to the gym, replete with yoga space and gender-separated saunas, and then up to level twelve, to the library and classroom, which was filled with solid-maple handmade custom-curved bookshelves. I was unsurprised that the majority of the books were science fiction and fantasy.

The tour over, we headed back to the surface. As we exited the silo, the first thing I noticed was that the cars and the security guard were in the same place, stuck there in that same "window" screen configuration. After only a few hours in that hermetically sealed environment, the warm sun on my face and the smell of the trees and grass gave me an overwhelming sense of having walked into a painting animated through some mysterious force.

"So, there you go, Brad," Larry said, with the air of a satisfied real estate agent. "A dozen apartments over two hundred and one feet and fifteen floors with everything you need to survive and thrive inside nine-foot-thick concrete walls protecting families instead of a nuclear warhead. We even have a Pit-bull VX truck, armored up to fifty-caliber, ready to pick up the owners within a six-hundred-mile radius. We've thought everything through here." We hopped back in our cars, and the guard nodded as we drove out, stepping into the gap beween the rolling gate behind us, dead-eyed and rifle-ready.

The second bunker was about twenty minutes away in another identical Atlas F missile silo. Before I hit the road, Larry agreed to give me a sneak peek. He'd pumped 1.3 million gallons of water out of it: mostly agricultural runoff, and full of pesticides. After draining it and then hoisting out the old rusting fixtures, the silo was a viable "shell core" for a second geoscraper. Construction of the floor levels and stairs was complete. I poked my head over the edge and peered down the empty elevator shaft into the almost two-hundred-foot drop. Seeing the bunker in its shell core state made the whole project even more surreal. The refitting was a monumental undertaking. After passing through a series of rusty corridors and rooms still dripping with water, where incomplete electrical circuits hung limply from the walls, we met one of Larry's workers. He was busy trying to dry out the shell with industrial fans so that they could spray fireproof lining on the circular walls.

Hall told me that a Saudi prince had recently flown over to see Survival Condo and offered on the spot to cut a check for $30 million for the second bunker. "But, see, that's not gonna work," Larry said, inspecting some rust on a door. "I'm not building a bunker for this guy and his family." It wasn't simply that Larry didn't want his work to serve as someone's trophy. In his view, it had to do with the social well-being of the inhabitants. He was building the bunkers in accordance with a social structure defined by British anthropologist Robin Dunbar—called Dunbar's number—which calculated the number of meaningful relationships a human being can sustain.[20]

"We need a group of more than twenty people but less than one hundred and fifty that share common space and a common goal," Larry said. "With fewer than twenty, you don't get your societal needs met—and you really don't want those people to be family members, because you also need to interact with strangers." This, according to Dunbar, satisfied a human need for exploration and novelty. "With over one hundred and fifty people, cliques inevitably start to form," Hall continued. "The first bunker is a fifty-four-thousand-square-foot facility with a common goal of survival. In terms of sociability and productivity we've got the optimal setup. Even though we can support seventy-five in this facility, the current owners only make up fifty-six people, which is great."

Larry told me that two doctors had already bought into the new bunker—precisely the kind of clients he was looking for. They were close to retirement, and for them the silo was something between a storage unit and an insurance policy until that time. They planned to bring in state-of-the-art medical equipment, ready for use during an event. In the meantime, they were going to travel the world and see everything they could before it all fell apart, riding out retirement until it was inevitably cut short by disaster. They'd also asked Larry to incorporate real beach sand and a gas poolside BBQ into the condo's pool area, giving it a seaside resort vibe. I imagined them down there flipping burgers in flip-flops, chatting with the residents in the second silo over video link, as the bodies piled up around the pillbox outside.

It wasn't long before I was back on the Interstate, speeding through cornfields at sunset, headed due east to find a hotel somewhere. I needed to write up my notes, prepare a lecture, process expense forms, and call my family to help with computer problems—the many moving parts of life. I longed to turn the car around and descend back into the simplicity of the bunker. Luckily, I had a standing invitation to visit Vivos Indiana, Robert Vicino's only complete and fully occupied bunker, so I would be back underground in no time.

15

The Concrete Cave:
Vivos Indiana

"Being human is not about individual survival
or escape. It's a team sport."
—Douglas Rushkoff, "Survival of
the Richest," *Medium*, June 2018[1]

I woke up with a terrible headache. My mouth felt as if it were full of sand. I was in the top bunk and morning light was filtering through a vent above the door, painting elongated scars onto the wood veneer wall paneling. I had a hazy recollection of waking up earlier and seeing the light in the same place. As I came to, I was puzzled why the light hadn't moved, and then realized why. It wasn't sunlight.

I was dozens of meters underground. According to my watch, it was eleven in the morning, meaning I'd slept for eleven hours.

Opening the bedroom door, I stumbled out into the living room to find Blake lounging on a cinema recliner scrolling his phone, one leg draped over the side. In his skinny jeans, floppy high-topped American flag Converse sneakers, and a brightly striped strappy tank top, he didn't fit the demographic I'd had in mind when I'd arrived at Vivos Indiana, a bunker somewhere near Terre Haute that had once served as a node in a hardened government communications infrastructure during the Cold War.

"Dude, I told you that you were going to sleep well; humans are meant to sleep underground. People that have stayed here have missed flights and everything, it's like crawling back into the womb," he said, never lifting his eyes from the phone.

"What?" I croaked.

"The bunker, dude, it's the like sealing up the cave with rocks in old times. It's silent, there's no light, you're in the Earth and the energy is coming through you from the core to the surface. It's fucking rad. I don't know how people sleep surrounded by glass."

The bunker had the air of an upscale family home, sans windows. One of its residents, Blake, was my host for a few days underground. His pistol was on the kitchen table in his shoulder holster. We'd drank a lot the previous evening, and in the muffled night down here he'd been waving the gun around at some point, telling me how he was going to decapitate the neighbors.

"In fact, you know what?" he said, standing up and stretching. "Fuck caves, this is better than a cave. I've got a buddy who's got a cave, but you can't trust those places not to blow, they're like open wounds. Going to Yellowstone is like touring cancer."

He looked straight at me and narrowed his eyes. "You look super hungover, dude. Those IPAs sneak up on you, right?"

Ah yes, the 8.2 percent India pale ales. The dehydrated vegetable stew we tried to cook and couldn't eat, burning our hands on the plastic cups we filled with boiling water to rehydrate the bland mix shaken out of a #10 can. The wine we found somewhere in the food stores that we drank in his RV surrounded by fireflies. . . . The haze was lifting. Time made weird moves inside the subterranean ship.

It had taken me some time to coax an invite to the Vivos Indiana shelter out of Vicino, but my burgeoning skepticism about these projects had made me dogged. The ennui of Trident Lakes, the caginess of Hardened Structures, the funding problems at Sanctum, the revelation that Oppidum was little more than a CGI rendering, and the understanding that Fortitude Ranch was more or less a bed-and-breakfast with half-finished buildings and watchtowers had turned me into a communal bunker cynic. Of all the organizations and people I'd encountered, Larry Hall seemed like the only dread merchant that had any chance of pulling off his ambitious plot to pilot a terrestrial submarine full of a couple dozen people through a crisis at a moment's notice. I held out hope that Vicino had taken so long to set up a visit to Vivos Indiana because he was protecting the location, and not because it was more bluster.

I'd met Blake in a parking lot outside Terre Haute, a city of sixty thousand just over the Illinois border. I ran late, and when I'd pinged him to let him know, he texted me back, "Take your time. It's not like it's the end of the world. LOL."

When I finally arrived, pulling into a parking lot that looked like it had been shelled during a war, he greeted me like we were doing a hostage handover, asking me to step into the back of a window-less van. It wasn't much of a welcome. In one of his emails to me, he'd written that "I will continue to investigate who you are just so I know who is riding in my car." Unfortunately, I'd been too busy to execute the same due diligence and so ended up in the back of a stranger's van being transported to an unknown destination. I appreciated the need to keep the location secret, but this rigmarole seemed excessively paranoid on Vicino's part.

We bumped along a badly maintained road, slamming into muddy ruts as I bounced around in the back of the van. When it finally stopped, twenty minutes or so later, I heard Blake pull a chain through a fence and then the creaking of hinges. Then the van doors were opened, and the sun rippled through his sandy-blond bangs that swept across one eye. He flipped the hair back with his hand. "Welcome to Vivos Indy, man!"

I stepped out into a gravel road sloping up from the fence through a lot filled with tall grass surrounded by a dense pine copse. Atop the hill was a small structure with a cream-colored RV parked next to it. As Blake unlatched the unassuming front door to this spruced-up Cold War telephone exchange, I thought that he cut an unlikely sentry: he was having too much fun. Over one shoulder a pistol dangled, which he admitted to me later he'd never fired.

As we toured the facility, Blake alleviated my apprehensions: both of the bunker being another of Vicino's pies in the sky, and of being murdered and dumped in a hole. It was an impressive and well-planned facility for thirty-five people, and long sold out; each resident had paid $35,000. This buy-in might have been a hair too much for preppers moving into xPoint, but it wasn't in the fantasy realm of Survival Condo; it was the Goldilocks bunker. I followed Blake down a flight of stairs, past a pair of camouflaged quad bikes and a crane basket for lowering heavy machinery, through a blast door decorated with a Vivos doomsday clock sticker, into a surveillance room. While we flicked through camera feeds, I could see the reflection of a rack of gas masks and knives behind us. Under the screens, I noticed a switch panel with a printed label on it that said "Do not turn on unless needed for crowd control."

"Blake, what is that?"

He broke into a maniacal cackle—a characteristic response to questions, as I quickly found. "That's the PA system, dude, it'll bust your eardrums. It's our motherfucking sonic weapon." He sang the word "weapon," accompanying himself on air guitar.

We did the tour of the now familiar accoutrements of sepulchral living: the air filtration system, medical area, laundry facilities, diesel generators, and well-appointed kitchen. Opening the pantry, I was greeted by six shelves packed with #10 cans: muffin mix, rolled oats, vegetarian bacon bits, cream of chicken soup, and elbow macaroni.

"I know what you're thinking," Blake said behind me. "Thirty-five people ain't gonna last five years on that. Check this out, though." He grabbed a ladder on the floor of the cinema room next door, set it against the back wall, climbed up, and beckoned me to join him. He shoved a wall panel aside and we squeezed into a hollow crawl space over the bedrooms. In every direction were rows of paper towels, sealed five-gallon buckets from Lowe's Home Improvement, hand soap, oats, and more #10 cans. It was like staring down a four-foot-tall grocery store isle, a very deep larder indeed.

"Five years and then some, bro," Blake said, smiling at me in the dark.

"Have you tried to live off the food yet?" I asked.

"Fuck no, there's a pizza place down the street. I'm not eating that shit."

We went to the pizza place for dinner, the need for secrecy apparently having been abandoned after meeting me properly. In the summer-evening heat, we rolled past rows of derelict houses and run-down businesses. Occasionally, a barking dog pierced the hum of cicadas. Beyond the humid summer stink of urban entropy, I could make out flat green expanses dotted with brightly rubber-wrapped bales of hay. The traffic was sparse. A morbidly obese shirtless man in earmuffs cruised by on a riding mower and waved listlessly as he passed.

Over dinner, Blake told me he'd put me in the back of the van to test my nerves: "Actually, it was just to fuck with you." Cue the maniacal laughter, which sent the waitress scurrying away from our table. "But seriously, don't write about the location, or we'll kick your ass."

As he slid a piece of pizza off the tray to his plate, mounded toppings rolled off. "Other than that, I don't give a shit what you write about. I'm totally honest. There're about five residents here I trust, who are going to be useful in the after time, the rest can kiss my ass." What did he think of Vicino? I wondered aloud. "Robert and I get along because I don't take any of his shit. We all agree that at times with him it's all about the money and I've told him that."

"And how does he respond?"

"Look," Blake said, considering my question, "I don't care what his motivations are. There's a conflict between being a prepper—believing that the ship is sinking—and running a business. It's his business, not mine. I don't care if he makes money, as long as he provides us with what we bought: a serious motherfucking bunker." Like Milton at xPoint, Blake seemed to be the only person living in the bunker—the warden, as it were. Whether he got some sort of a discount, or special privileges beyond cash payments to host people like me, was unclear.

This tension ran throughout the dread merchants' projects. On the one hand, there was the need to keep locations covert, hidden, and out of view so that they appealed to preppers; on the other was the need to advertise their wares to keep accounts in the black.

As we talked—or, rather, as Blake talked and the beer took hold—anger and aggression poured out of him in a torrent.

"So aside from those five residents you trust, are the rest of the owners not serious preppers?" I asked.

"It's like a time-share, you know what I'm saying?" Blake responded. "There's more of a real estate thing going on here. There're two classes in this bunker: the people who bought in and the residents who are keeping it going. It's not going to be that way in the after time, though. There can't be a hierarchy, and if half the people don't know how to survive, they're a fucking liability."

He punctuated his monologue with a raised index finger and a swig of beer. "For instance," he continued, "we had a woman buy in who was talking about how she was going to give food to people if they rolled up to the bunker hungry. I mean," he expostulated, outraged, "what the fuck? If a family of four rocks up here, I'm killing the boy, the girl, the mom, and then dad, in that order. It's survival—look the word up!"

"You're not worried about repercussions?" I asked.

"It's the after time, bro, there's no law; if cops come up to the gate, I'm going to smoke them, too, and take their weapons. I'm going to kill you, steal your stuff, and take it all back to the bunker. That's who you gotta be."

Some of the anger in Blake, I found out as his life story started to unspool, was situational. Now in his early forties, he had until recently been dating someone who'd taken care of him financially. They went scuba diving in the Bahamas, flew around the world in a private jet, and generally, it sounded, burned the candle at both ends with a blowtorch. Blake even got his pilot's license so he could fly the jet himself.

Blake had thought the life he'd been living during those years was blessed, until it all fell apart when his partner left him for another man, just a year before I met him. Now he was working as a delivery driver, often with no knowledge of what he was delivering. He'd been approached multiple times to use his pilot's license to smuggle drugs in a private jet, but he wasn't interested in getting shot down in a Central American jungle for his cargo, by a cartel. Alone in the bunker, he'd had a lot of time to brood about all of this. Unsure if Blake's anger had a tipping point, I tried to redirect him back to discussing practicalities.

"Blake, I really wanted to see this bunker, to know that it exists," I told him. Then, as artlessly as I could, I asked him whether he knew of any other bunkers Vicino had built, or whether they were still all at the conceptual stage.

"Nah," Blake replied. "Vivos Indiana is the only thing he's built," and, he added conspiratorially, "some residents are not happy with it. There's actually a lawsuit brewing, and it's contagious," he said.

"But on what basis?" It struck me that, at least as far as Vivos Indiana was concerned, Vicino had fulfilled his side of the bargain. I told him: "He's provided what people have paid for, and the bunker looks pretty sick, to be honest."

Blake pushed a tomato around with his fork. "Let's just say, if you signed a deal at a car dealership for a Mustang with red paint, tinted windows, and some nice exhaust pipes, and the salesman pulls around the bottom-model green mustang, you'd be pretty pissed, wouldn't you?"

He sighed. "Robert's sales guy said this bunker could be underwater for three months, for instance. Where's the air system for that? It's a solid bunker, it's two-foot-thick concrete. It'll withstand earthquakes, environmental pollution, sure, whatever. But I want a fifteen-foot fence with razor wire and foxholes and sniper towers to kill anyone who comes near the property. 'The fence,' man, it rhymes with 'dee-fence' and I can't get these guys to understand this."

So even here, in a functional facility, residents seemed cranky, doubtful it would stand the test. It appeared to reinforce Larry Hall's point about people wanting luxury but only being prepared to pay economy. Even if the facility would hold, I thought, it sounded like the people inside might well kill each other before any outside threat emerged. And this also backed up Hall's contention that the secret of bunkered living lay in social dynamics.

In any event, it looked like I could stop asking to see Vivos Asiana, Vivos Europa, or the bunker in New Zealand he'd told the media he was scoping out. Vicino had a track record of "trying things on" before committing to the projects, in contrast to Larry's "build it and they will come" approach. This was the best the Vivos Group had to offer. I thought it was impressive, but then, I didn't live in it.

"Look, man, I understand this isn't Survival Condo," Blake was saying, "we don't have a climbing wall or pool, and no one expects one. It's enough to survive, but to call this a luxury bunker just isn't accurate." I wasn't so sure. Based on what I'd seen on my journeys, Vivos Indiana was relatively plush.

"Anyway, I'm glad I'm in," he said, as if to draw a line under his own worries. "I'm worried about what happens when the grid goes down and the four prisons in this area let all those motherfuckers into the streets. The cops are already the bad guys. They're not here to protect the public, they're killing us. You can quote me when I say the government is going to fuck us good, they've got it all figured out. We're all going to FEMA concentration camps, and it's the kids they want, the rest of us will be labor or Soylent," Blake concluded, slamming down his empty bottle.[2]

Back at the bunker we got on the phone with Vicino. Apparently, the security cameras had gone down—because, it transpired, the WiFi had cut out, and with it the video stream to Vicino's house in the California beach city of Del Mar two thousand miles away. It struck me as ridiculous that Vivos Indiana was reliant on existing infrastructure of the sort that would be knocked out during an event. "Robert?" I inquired. "Are you saying that if the internet goes down the cameras won't work?"

"Just go check the box with the phone line connection, fuckers," came the tinny voice over the speakerphone. We walked around the bunker once and found the phone box. It was intact.

"Well, I'll have to call the internet provider and see what's going on," Robert snapped. "But let me ask you, Brad: You've seen the bunker, you like breaking into places, do you think it's secure?"

I took the question seriously. "Honestly? Knowing what I know now, I'd just cut the phone line outside the building to kill the cameras and then either take a plasma torch to the blast door hinges or smoke you out by throwing something down the vent shaft. I think Blake is right, you need a better first line of defense."

There was a pause at the other end of the line, then Vicino's overconfident voice. "You hear that, Blake? Brad's a security expert now. You guys have fun tugging each other tonight." There was a click and the line went dead. Blake found my mild takedown of Vivos security hilarious: he doubled over with tears in his eyes, laughing hysterically. It seemed I'd won Blake over, at least. We eventually reset the router and then, as the underground night wore on, proceeded to get drunk—assuming, naturally, that Vicino was monitoring our progress on the CCTV.

"I'm not really worried about it all, to be honest," Blake told me, endless beers later, prostrate in a leather recliner staring at the ceiling and snacking on vile food from the #10 cans. "The military guys living here are confident they can defend this place. I couldn't be in a better bunker.

"In fact, you know what? I've been sneaking around every house around here at night and I know what they've got," he said in a conspiratorial whisper. I got the sense that he was getting worked up again. "Once we cross the line, I'm going to behead those people and put their heads on the fence and bring all their shit back here. No one is coming near this bunker after that. I know it sounds harsh, but we all have to have somewhere to go, we all have to have somewhere to run to, and I'm not going to have people running here looking for a handout." I thought of those survivalist communities of the past—Waco and so on—and how they almost all imploded after some loose cannon fired off.

"I know that in the after time, I'll just kill, which is why I don't want to shoot this pistol, I can't break that seal yet," Blake said, pulling it from the shoulder holster. "When the time comes, though, I won't feel remorse, I won't feel bad, I'll kill anybody that gets in my way, I'll kill anybody that tries to get in this facility, and I won't think twice about it. There won't be any conversation, just action.

The only thing stopping me doing that now are the consequences—in the after time there will be no consequences. What there will be is survival."

After the event, according to Blake, Vivos Indiana would become a free-floating impregnable island of autonomy in an archipelago of spaces taken over from the state. In Blake's eyes, the Earth's subsurface would be a political battleground, a territory to be controlled. From his redoubt, Blake was ready to hold his ground against the government. He assured me that, in a state of civil breakdown, four or five people could hold the territory for years.

Sometime after midnight, Blake and I stumbled up out of the bunker to get some fresh air. Being underground was giving me a headache. We hung out next to Blake's bug-out vehicle, the cream-colored RV. It was sticky and quiet outside. The fireflies from Tennessee had followed me here. Their soft illuminations seemed to signal a sea change in Blake: slowly, his drunken anger bled into paranoia. He explained to me that when it snowed, the snow no longer melted: if examined under an electron microscope, the snow would reveal a structure full of tiny cyborgs made from red blood cells. These bots, he continued, were crafted by the government from donated blood and are sometimes visible as a shimmer in clouds at dusk. Their movements were apparently controlled by the High Frequency Active Auroral Research Program (HAARP) relay in Alaska. (HAARP, a $290 million installation built by the US Air Force and Navy to study the ionosphere, has been at the center of a lot of theories. In 2010, the late Venezuelan president Hugo Chavez claimed that HAARP had triggered the Haitian earthquake of that year.)

Blake divulged that he was, like the homestead preppers, a devout evangelical. Despite dropping out of Christian school in the tenth grade, he was fully invested in the idea that the seven seals of the Book of Revelation were being broken. He wondered whether fires and flooding and earthquakes and other cataclysmic environmental catastrophes attributed to the climate crisis were an indication of the breaking of the sixth seal. The breach of this seal, according to Revelation, is meant to bring about a great earthquake, the sun becoming "black as sackcloth of hair," and the moon turning bloodred. Mountains and islands would be shifted when the seal was broken, and the "kings of the earth, and the great men, and the rich men" would hide "in the dens and in the rocks of the mountains." Not so far removed from bunkers, perhaps. Picking at his beer label, Blake explained that the breaking of the seventh seal is meant to produce silence, with the death of nonbelievers and the rapture, and the devout are received into heaven.

I wondered aloud if the seventh seal was the end of the brief Anthropocene, the age dominated by our species, and the beginning of what the maverick centenarian scientist James Lovelock has called the Novacene: the machine age, when believers in a point of machine/human singularity have their consciousness uploaded.[3] Or maybe it's when we're all murdered by Blake's "tiny cyborgs." The end result may be the same: silence.

"Fuck, I don't know, bro, that's dark," Blake said, as he threw his last empty beer bottle into the dark forest beyond the chain-link fence. "But until the time comes, we'll just be two guys in a bunker, waiting for something to happen."

The Last Plan

"It's the end of the world every day, for someone. Time rises and rises, and when it reaches the
level of your eyes you drown."
    —Margaret Atwood, *The Blind*
    Assassin, 2000[1]

I remained in touch with Jim O'Connor, the CEO of Trident Lakes
near Dallas, over the course of a few years, but there didn't seem
to be much forward momentum with the project. O'Connor asked
me not to return to the site, explaining that they were redrafting
the plans. Eventually, my curiosity got the best of me and I went
out there anyway.

When I pulled up to the site, it was clear that no one had been there for a long time. An emaciated steer grazed lazily in front of the fifty-foot fountain, which was filled with stagnant puddles covered by thick lime-green tendrils of algae. Vandals had chipped the lion head plaques from the fountain and made off with them. Stretchy plastic, once wrapped around such ornamental details to keep them clean, now sagged into the stinking water, which had become a breeding ground for mosquitos.

The only new addition I could see as I walked the main drag into the compound were two rows of life-sized marble Roman statues flanking the road in wooden crates. The statues wore rose crowns and victory laurels. Some disconcertingly appeared to be reaching toward the sun. I had the urge to break the crates and free them.

When I got to the main house, where O'Connor had shown me the site plans during the snowstorm years earlier, I climbed up on an air-conditioning unit and peeked inside. Someone had left the TV on to lend the illusion of occupancy. There were folders and papers everywhere, some haphazardly piled, some strewn across the floor. Wandering behind the building, I came to a garage containing a couple of stripped-down vehicles, wonky filing cabinets, and broken light fixtures. A pair of dusty suits of armor with pikes in hand guarded a John Deere riding mower with a mouse-eaten seat. The suits of armor faced off with another set of stone statues lined up against the opposite wall, including one of Julius Caesar. As a monument to the folly, greed, and vanity of bunker projects, Trident Lakes seemed complete.

The final time I spoke to Jim O'Connor, he'd advised me that John Eckerd, Paul Salfen, and Rob Kaneiss, whom I'd met on my last visit, were no longer involved with the project, that it was down to him alone. He assured me this wouldn't affect the plans going forward.

It would be a few months before I'd get the full story of what had happened, but when I did, it verified what I'd always suspected about Trident Lakes: it was a scam. The founder, John Eckerd, and a "co-conspirator" named Anthony Romano had been arrested by federal agents after accepting a $200,000 wire transfer that they thought was coming from a Colombian drug cartel. The charges against them suggested that Eckerd had intended to launder the money through Trident Lakes.[2]

According to the criminal complaint, Eckerd faced two counts of money laundering and one count of conspiracy to commit money laundering.[3] He was also being sued privately by a man in Dallas who'd invested $13 million in an Australian tire-hauling business and claimed his investment had been funneled into Trident Lakes instead.[4] Eckerd was eventually sentenced to fifteen months in federal prison. He also filed for bankruptcy. It seemed a fitting end for someone who'd sought to build a fortress to keep the world outside—now he had one, without ever having broken ground. These revelations triggered further research into the places I'd visited.

I began with the most obvious, or at least the issue at the fore of my mind—the "contagious" lawsuit against Vivos that Blake had mentioned was brewing when I was in Indiana. I could find no record of it online, so I emailed Vicino directly. He said that there was no lawsuit pending but did write back with another story.

"We had one woman back in 2012 that attempted to take over the Indiana shelter. Huge ego!" he wrote, in his usual overwrought manner. "That suit was dismissed, and she ended up settling a countersuit from Vivos for libel and slander. She may have bought into Larry Hall's shelter. I wish him luck with her!" He accepted that Indiana was not as luxurious as Larry Hall's silo conversion but made the point that the fees were a fraction of what residents of Survival Condo were paying. And as I knew, for that price it was still, in Blake's words, "a serious motherfucking bunker."

I tried to follow up with Blake but never heard back from him. Vicino finally let me in on the fact that Blake was "up for foreclosure by the association"—meaning he was being voted off the island. Vicino also suggested that Blake had been dealing with some mental health issues. I obviously couldn't verify this, but I recalled Blake's anxiety about the "tiny cyborgs"—which, at the time, I'd found quirky and interesting—with a heavy heart.

Next, I paid for access to court documents filed with the state of Kansas that documented how a Survival Condo resident named Peter Ziegler had made a $3 million loan in February 2013 to LAH

Cubed LLC, a company run by Hall.[5] Ziegler had died in a tragic accident in 2017, leaving it to his heirs to collect on the loan. When relatives sent a letter demanding payment, the suit alleged that Hall began transferring assets into a newly created entity called Raven Ten Development. In his response filed with the court, Hall suggested this was all a misunderstanding. A settlement for an undisclosed amount was reached before the case went to trial.

I also managed to dig up details of a class-action lawsuit that had been filed against Wise Company for "unlawful, unfair, and deceptive advertising and business practices," alleging that on its website and packaging, apparently, Wise Co. had made misrepresentations and omitted material information concerning how long its food would last and how many people it would feed.[6] The company settled the lawsuit in a distribution of cash payments.

Like so many other things, these issues became trivial when the COVID-19 pandemic roiled through the United States, and I watched Robert Vicino, Drew Miller, and Larry Hall pull residents into their respective fortresses with relative confidence. As the media spun out stories of Saudi royals and Silicon Valley elites taking to their yachts and private jets—some en route to New Zealand—Amanda and I were holed up in South Los Angeles with my mom, a good stockpile of food, and bug-out bags at the ready. We had a bunker waiting for us in South Dakota, but no willingness to go because we couldn't take our families with us. I imagined Auggie at Sanctum shaking his head at this lack of foresight, until I emailed him to ask his advice and learned that he was trapped on a ship off the coast of Burma where he'd been working, unable to get home to his wife and daughter after the Thai government curtailed international travel in an attempt to slow the spread of the virus in the country.

Hunkered down in self-isolation for months as I read through these cases, I began to feel the now familiar prickle of sinister portents. I recalled my looming dread, years ago, in the B-207 bunker at Vicino's xPoint in South Dakota as I meditated on the brittleness of global trade networks and the resources required to keep them afloat. I thought about how uncomfortable I felt at Moorish Blue in Sydney when the twitchy bodyguard Manny Ray took the gym bag to his car under the eye of the hookah-smoking restaurant owners. I remembered Drew Miller's body-burning pit in West Virginia and the shooter-proof children's backpacks at PrepperCon in Utah. I remembered my psychic dissociation in the Survival Condo.

I was apprehensive about being hounded by these wealthy dread merchants if they became unhappy with my account. But I also worried I'd gotten too cozy with them. I kept imagining FBI agents listening to tapes of me telling John Eckerd I would "pen the story of Trident Lakes for posterity"; surely, his house had been bugged. These bunkers I'd scoured the underworld to locate were supposed to be sanctuaries from the world's noise, but the more I learned about them, the more I saw that they were just as full of hokum, hustle, and avarice as any other business.

Despite the dubious claims Rising S had made about delivering bunkers to New Zealand, they continued to do steady business as we ticked over into the second decade of the century, and then sales increased exponentially during the pandemic. Ron Hubbard from Atlas Survival Shelters, clearly viewing Rising S as his primary competitor, launched a campaign against them on his YouTube channel.[7] In one video, Hubbard alleges that Rising S reported a client's illegal weapons cache to the FBI, sending the client to prison for thirty-three months. In a different video, Hubbard tours what he suggests is a $200,000 Rising S bunker that buckled under the weight of topsoil and was flooded with water, destroying everything inside. In yet another upload, a woman in Minnesota took Hubbard on a tour of what looked very much like a Rising S bunker installed on her property. The video claimed that the bunker was put in the ground only eight months previous, but it already looked dilapidated.

Each of these videos had garnered tens of thousands of views and provided the viewer with a link to the official Atlas Survival Shelters YouTube merchandise store, where you could purchase Atlas-branded coffee mugs and iPhone cases. So just another tendril of doomsday capitalism.

Meanwhile, the Los Angeles Better Business Bureau (BBB), a nonprofit established more than a hundred years ago to enhance consumer trust, requested that Atlas Survival Shelters "substantiate, modify, or discontinue claims on the company's website" that authorities found to be breaching the BBB's codes of advertising, including assertions that it "was a dominate [*sic*] supplier [of bunkers] during the Cold War Era," that they operate "the largest fall-out shelter factory in the world," and that they've provided "37 years of award-winning service." The bureau notes in the alert that Atlas Survival Shelters failed to respond to their request as of December 2019, suggesting to would-be bunker buyers that Ron Hubbard was unable to verify those claims. The web page was also littered with customer complaints, some of which an Atlas representative suggested were posted by Rising S.

Heidi, Sonya, and Carey from Tennessee Readiness kept in touch to let me know the store was still ticking along, and that they were all very worried about the rollout of 5G mobile phone towers in the area, which they thought were going to cause cancer, infertility, and even autism. If I wanted to get the "real news" on this, Heidi suggested I watch a film on YouTube called *5G Apocalypse—the Extinction Event*. I had a look, briefly, and then probed the film's provenance instead.

The director of the video is a Californian named Sacha Stone. On his website, a pixelated image of him with wooden beads in his hair and aviator sunglasses floats over a rambling "About" page filled with new-age conspiracy theories. In other words—in fact, in Heidi's own words from the time I met with her—Sacha didn't "pass the sniff test." I later discovered that RT News, which is funded by the Kremlin, had aired more than a dozen segments warning that dire health risks would result from people being near 5G towers, including cancer. Like the Yellowstone evacuation "broadcast" Carey had played for me on her phone, this hysteria was a result of a misinformation campaign probably propagated by a hostile goverment to stoke confusion. After the outbreak of COVID-19, internet sources began suggesting that the newly installed 5G towers were spreading the virus. In the UK, this led to towers being lit on fire, which looked to me like pagan rituals to banish the plague.

As the years passed, xPoint actually seemed to be succeeding as an intentional community. Since I'd last been there, National Geographic, HBO, Vice, the BBC in the UK, and ARD from Germany had all made shows or segments about xPoint, publicity that had helped add a few souls to the steadily growing bunker city. This included people who saw buying a bunker as an investment in their own celebrity.

Vicino had equipped a "show bunker" specifically for media tours, and the last time I visited the community I slept there. Inside, the bunker was reminiscent of the one I'd seen in Indiana: veneer paneling, modern kitchen appliances, and cozy interior touches including a piece of art by Vicino's son Dante. The living room was draped with warm-temperature bare lightbulbs, like a hipster brewery. Many of the camera crews who traveled to xPoint were incredulous regarding the bunkers' livability, which of course Vicino took in stride.

"You know," Vicino told me, "I had a reporter here the other day and I took him into the show bunker, and I asked him if he thought it was nice. He says yes. Then I asked him, 'Is it nicer than your house?' He says yes. Then I ask him if his wife would be happy there and he tells me no. So then, I asked him whether his wife would be happier in the bunker with me instead of him." As usual, Vicino laughed heartily at his own joke.

Vicino's childhood friend Jerry was equally undaunted. "These reporters come here and they think it all looks so grim," he said, "and I tell them when shit goes wrong this is going to look like the goddamn Hilton."

Milton, who'd rebranded himself "South Dakota Milton"—even making his own hats and T-shirts—continued to be the only person living full-time at xPoint. Over time his hair and beard grew wild, and he started to look like an old-school Luddite wilderness survivalist. Except he wasn't, at all. He spent a lot of his time stoned and locked in his bunker roaming around inside a PC-based virtual reality simulator that he ran off the diesel generator. It made sense to game inside the bunker, he said, "because when you've got the goggles on, you're super vulnerable."

In mid-2019, a delegation of Milton's friends arrived from his hometown in Chicago. They seemed keen to help him with homemaking projects, but Milton insisted they were trying to convince him to return to his job at the Department of Veterans Affairs. "They say they're here to help me but they're really staging an intervention," he told a camera crew from the German broadcaster ARD. "Everyone wants to tell me I'm crazy, but they're just jealous because I'm free."

In the spring of 2020, during the COVID-19 pandemic, Vicino sent a letter to the entire xPoint community stating that Milton hadn't made his rent payments and that he was "slandering" xPoint, Vivos, and Vicino himself. Milton angrily locked up his bunker and left, just as everyone else was arriving at the pandemic's peak to button up the blast doors and wait it out. When I contacted Vicino to ask if he'd kicked Milton out of the community, Vicino wrote back to assure me that it wasn't an executive decision, that "Milton has pissed a lot of members off for his never-ending reach for internet stardom."

The friction could have been due to the fact that a handful of more low-key residents had moved into xPoint, including Brett, an Alaskan knife manufacturer, and "Bunker Bob," a Californian in the Coast Guard. Bob's bunker was fantastic: it had a bar splitting the kitchen from the living room and a delicate etched entryway cresting a hall that stretched back through the bedrooms to the mechanical room for the diesel generator. Stained pine stairs with a bannister led to a loft where Bob planned to stash a couple years' supply of food. I had fond memories of Bob's very drunk girlfriend excitedly demonstrating their freshly installed dimmer switches for the interior lighting just before she blacked out and had to be carried upstairs over Bob's shoulder.

Sadly, Bunker Bob was never able to test out his creation; within a year of buying the bunker, he perished in a fire in Deadwood, South Dakota, where he was staging construction materials. I can't imagine the frustration he must have felt in his final moments, having prepared for so many potential disasters, only to die of something so commonplace as an electrical short.

Tom and Mark, egged on by their respective wives, Mary and Susan, continued to work diligently on their concrete "Igloos" until they eventually put them to use in 2020, just as planned. Other bunkers along the block were in less advanced states of construction, useless during the crisis. Piles of concrete blocks, wood, and bags of cement were piled outside the blast doors. Some had been fenced off with barbed wire to keep the cows out. Others began to be buried in cow shit again. But the point is: F-Block was sold out, there were water mains, and—as Vicino had promised years earlier—xPoint was indeed blooming.

In the final months of the 2010s, nuclear anxieties continued to escalate around the spin-up of Iran's nuclear program and development of military equipment used in launching long-range missiles in North Korea. Elon Musk's SpaceX began launching strings of internet satellites into space as part of Starlink, its space-based internet communication system that would allow for almost limitless surveillance of the Earth's surface, while the Chinese state ramped up production of techno-authoritarian tracking systems like facial recognition cameras run by artificial intelligence, emboldened by the pandemic. I left Sydney as it burned, only to land back home in Los Angeles into a haze of smoke. By the time I arrived, statistics were released by the Gun Violence Archive that there had been 419 mass shootings in the United States in 2019, a new record.

News of catastrophic floods came from all corners of the globe, but it was often overlooked because of the outbreak of the COVID-19 coronavirus. In the background to all of this, misinformation was being taken at face value while actual news continued to be labeled as "fake." As the calendar ticked over to 2020, the things people were prepping for in 2017 that had seemed distant and speculative had suddenly become everyday life. Even acknowledging that the calamity howling of dread merchants is, for the most part, a sales strategy, the desire to burrow grew with each passing day. I have always been, and will remain, a militant atheist, but there was no doubting the feeling that we were living through end times.

Subterranean space is an ancient sanctuary; the underground has been our place of protection for thousands of years. Never before in recorded history has humankind faced such grave, and myriad, existential threats. We've also never had such a clear window into those threats, or so much personal capacity to take shelter against them. Retreating into our bunkers, even just as a metaphor for confronting our dread of the unknown, will be necessary to escape the traps we've laid for ourselves. The survivors of the next catastrophe might very well end up being a peculiar mix of government officials, Mormons, self-sufficient indigenous communities, off-gridders, doomsday preppers, and people who happened to be at sea or in space.

The human story to date is that we're smart enough to dominate our habitat and then engineer our own destruction. The next chapter of that story will be about whether we're smart enough to engineer our survival. Looking past the dread wrought by dangers like atomic weapons, runaway technological advancement, and climate change is our greatest challenge. But there's hope to hang on to. Human beings, collectively, are living longer than at any time in history, and high-casualty global wars haven't been fought in decades.[8] Many diseases—including other coronavirus strains like SARS (2003) and MERS (2012)—that could have been catastrophic have been caught early and quarantined or quelled because of international cooperation. For the first time in history food is abundant, even if it is, like wealth, unevenly distributed owing to a lack of political will. The connectivity and speed of the modern age is still paying dividends in terms of quality of life, even if an aging, technologically dependent, and largely urban population is a double-edged sword for the planet and our psyche.

As an ethnographer—a culture writer—I can't help but feel that as adaptation overtakes mitigation in the debate over future crises, preppers may play an important role in understanding how people will respond to rising frustration and despair.

In my own search for answers to this sluggish apocalypse, I've been forced to be realistic in confronting notions of perishing, finitude, and fragility. This process has filled me with at least as much wonder as dread, and more political energy than resignation. And it's forced me to realize that prepping is practical, communities are crucial, and disasters aren't ends but irreversible transitions. Significant events are sometimes catastrophic, sometimes tragic and cruel, and sometimes generative. However, they're always something less than an extinction. Catastrophe, by its very nature, falls short of finality. It's the end of something but never *the* end.

As Robert Vicino once told me, "This is not a story about concrete or steel or a giant fountain, it's a story about survival and rebirth." It's also a story that has played out repeatedly over human history. Though the threats we face may have changed, hunkering down to chart a course through turbulent times remains a vital practice for survival, a lesson I learned in my journeys with preppers. The most *valuable* lesson they taught me, however, was about the futility of succumbing to despair. Their preparations may have appeared irrational only a short time ago, and we may still query their motivations, but we no longer have the luxury of being dismissive of their concerns. The time to hunker down and outthink extinction is upon us. Again.

CODA

Stalking the Apocalypse at Chernobyl

"The sharper our consciousness of the world's infinity, the more acute our awareness of our own finitude."

—E. M. Cioran, *On the Heights of Despair*, 1934[1]

Popping the hatch at the top of the stairwell on the fifteenth floor of the abandoned tower block, we were greeted with a rare spectacle: lightning forking over the most dangerous place on Earth. We were at the center of the doomed city of Pripyat, an hour's walk from the Chernobyl nuclear reactor that exploded in 1986. The red

269

lights along the spine of the new sarcophagus encasing that seeping radioactive tragedy seemed to dance with the bolts streaming down from the ether, performing an atmospheric ballet.

"Is this what the world would look like after the apocalypse?" I asked my fellow trespassers.

Aram panned the ruins. "Yeah, that's the world without us." Every window, in a city built for just under fifty thousand people, was dark, with trees waggling from rooftops like hair. Tidy human time had given way to rapacious vegetable time. Visiting Chernobyl was a chance to look on a postapocalyptic world; to see what hope had taken up residence in the ruins of our failed ambitions as a species. It was a stress test of the prepper's fantasies of life after a "hard reset."

"It's not empty, though," Kirill said, sweeping his beer can across the horizon. "There are dozens of stalkers out there." We hadn't seen them because they didn't want to be seen. Once the lights go off, the world becomes a place for those willing to take great risks for little reward. Stalkers—as the guides for illegal trips into the Chernobyl Exclusion Zone are known—were the explorers after the end of the world, temporarily repopulating the abandoned landscape in methodical raids. Local knowledge and stealth were their greatest assets.

Four of us—Darmon, Wayne, Aram, and me—had paid Kirill to take us into the Zone. I'm reluctant to call our four-day walk a death march, given how much radiation we absorbed trespassing into the Zone, but by the time we reached the rooftop in Pripyat, we were all pretty worn down.

From this height, the disaster felt proximal. It wasn't malice that produced these ruins, as in so many apocalyptic fictions, but the flick of a switch, a thirty-second error, an exercise gone wrong. When Reactor No. 4 overheated on April 26, 1986, a super-heated fuel fire chewed through the concrete-and-steel containment shell, collapsing the floor and melting a twelve-hundred-ton core full of radioactive isotopes that exploded like spores, blowing the four-million-pound roof off and seeding almost every country in the Northern Hemisphere with stardust: fissioned nuclear material.

The explosion released four hundred times more radioactive

material than the bomb dropped on Hiroshima. Nearly one hundred thousand residents were evacuated, half of them from Pripyat, and all of them too slowly, while Soviet officials tried to spin the story. But when radiation sensors went off as far away as Sweden, there was no possibility of toning down the severity of the calamity.

After a stream of remote-controlled bulldozers had their circuitry fried by radiation while trying to clean it up, the Soviet Union sent more than half a million citizens in to battle the disaster. The liquidators, as they were called, were tasked with putting out fires, shoveling radioactive soil, and burying cars, machinery, furniture, and food—all the trappings of the once-wealthy city of Pripyat—in massive concrete-capped pits.

With the Soviet Union already sliding into collapse, the liquidators were not provided with necessary equipment, despite being bombarded with alpha, beta, and gamma particles being disgorged from the reactor daily. Many of them slept in the open and wrapped their boots with plastic tape that they changed daily, since they couldn't afford to throw the boots away, regardless of contamination.[2]

Ground zero had to be contained. Over 206 horrific days, the first sarcophagus was constructed over Reactor No. 4 using four hundred thousand cubic meters of concrete and 7,300 tons of metal framing. This was, however, a wholly inadequate quick fix. A second vault called the "New Shelter," finished just before we arrived in the Zone, has been superimposed over the first, both to contain the original container and eventually to pull apart the old one, continuing the process of cleaning up the perpetual decay of 180 tons of radioactive material within it. This is the best plan human beings have come up with so far: to layer sarcophagi like murderous Matryoshka dolls, stacked encasements that will dismantle the older structures they contain. At the center of this perpetual activity sits the most dangerous object in the world: the "Elephant's Foot," a solid mass made of corium nuclear fuel mixed with concrete, sand, and graphite that's been melting since 1986. Just pausing next to the still-hot foot for three hundred seconds would offer up a lethal dose of radiation.

The second sarcophagus is expected to last for a hundred years before it, too, begins to leak. So, barring some radical advancement in containment technology, the vault will need to be rebuilt by generation after generation, potentially for thousands of years. Reactor No. 4 will be a managed disaster until the money runs out, or the human will, at which point its horrors may again escape into the world—a literal Pandora's box.

People have largely been excluded from the Zone of Alienation since 1986. It's a sixteen-hundred-square-mile area, containing two rings of exclusion at a six- and eighteen-mile radius from ground zero. As a consequence of keeping humans out, an area the size of Luxembourg has turned into what science fiction author Bruce Sterling calls an "involuntary park"—an accidental nature preserve now bristling with wild fruit, boar, wolves, deer, lynx, beavers, elk, bears, even a herd of rare Mongolian horses.[3]

We undertook the twenty-five-mile journey in the Zone on foot. Milky skins of birch had herded us, single-file, into the unknown. Night pressed in as we waded through the soft sand of the trail, stumbling over unseen patches of grass. The forest canopy interwove over the path in places, blocking out what little assurance the stars offered. I progressed almost wholly by the swishing sound of Aram's trousers in front of me, aurally measuring pace and direction, supplemented by ghostly images I wasn't sure I could trust. Branches smacked and scraped our arms and legs. Clearings would periodically open where I could just make out Kirill's tall silhouette stroking tall grass, his infrared headlamp a bobbing beacon among pulsing green fireflies. Negotiating space with little visual reference was a skill I suppose most people lost with the invention of electric lighting. Despite having spent a decade as an urban explorer sneaking around in dark corners of cities, it had really never occurred to me to go hiking in the wilderness at night without a light.

On the other side of the Uzh River, Kirill flipped on his dosimeter, which measured the biological risk of exposure to radiation, for the first time. He showed us that the reading was a relatively negligible 12 millisieverts (mSv)—about twice the exposure the average American soaks up in a year, most of which is accumulated during medical procedures. The leap of faith we'd taken by crossing into the Zone was that we had the right genes and would be subjected to low enough doses of radiation that we wouldn't develop cancer. But of course, even with science beeping assurance at us, we were confronting the unknown minute by minute. We did by choice what everyone might one day have to do by necessity, should great disaster strike.

We slept in the abandoned houses of evacuated residents, climbing in through empty window frames and clearing broken glass and debris from the floor in rooms filled with splintered furniture and rusting box springs with tattered yellow fabric hanging from them. We rolled sleeping bags out onto black garbage bags laid over an ominous patina of dust I imagined was deadly. The background reading showed only 15 mSv, but it was impossible not to coat your hands in the stuff. And washing them wasn't an option. Water was too precious.

The days of walking were dominated by private struggles—adjusting to the weight of a heavy pack, kicking free of vines, rubbing at sweaty nettle burns. Fruit dropped from trees in irregular thuds as we passed them. The Zone felt dangerously fecund, wild and overripe.

Taking a break near an apple tree, Kirill plucked one and ate it greedily. "Delicious! A little radiation is good for you!" He smiled at us through blue gums.

Kirill Stepanets had the mannerisms of someone who—at twenty-eight—had spent a great deal of time alone. A lithe machine trapped in a soft body, with boundless stamina and appetite—for dense bread, sweets, rehydrated fare, chocolate, cans of raw corn, and whatever else was at hand. When you live out of a backpack in an irradiated landscape for most of the year, you make do. In his perpetually smudged, delicate frameless glasses, he was the only person in the group without hiking boots. Instead, he wore floppy, filthy faux Adidas. He paired camouflage pants with a snow-white tank top that screamed from the forest. His army backpack was often draped with a lime-green sweater. With a sitting pad strapped to it and the sweater arms dangling, the backpack looked like a modern-day totemic standard, leading us to our doom.

Kirill navigated us through dozens of kilometers without ever referring to a map, phone, or GPS, while clearing spiderwebs from our path with a stick, waving it like he was casting a spell. He would periodically stop and point out a feature: a depression in the tall grass where a giant boar had slept, wolf shit with hair in it, or a distant moose mating call. At other moments, he seemed to use superhuman senses to navigate us over areas where police patrolled. He heard the sound of rubber on tarmac long before anyone else, a critical skill cultivated during more than a hundred illegal visits into The Zone.

As we crossed the threshold from the eighteen-mile Exclusion Zone into the six-mile Exclusion Zone, where we anticlimactically stepped over a downed barbed-wire fence, Darmon told us about new techniques being developed to hasten the radioactive waste cleanup.

"Mycologists found that some fungi actually absorb radiation," he said. "The research is still in its early days, but if that's true, maybe someday we'll develop spore bombs full of mycelium that can be shot into radioactive danger zones by autonomous vehicles. Let the fungus do its job, scrape it off, then ship it to safe storage." Mushrooms were among the first organisms to return to the Hiroshima blast zone as well.

"It seems more realistic than some technical solutions," Aram said. "Mushroom bombs are about as analog as it gets."

"It's worth a try. That reactor's going to be dangerous for more than ten thousand years," Darmon replied. "There might be a sarcophagus over Reactor 4 for longer than the pyramids at Giza have existed. That's a long time to brainstorm alternative solutions. Imagine it . . . the sarcophagus is going to be an ancient structure someday. One of the wonders of the world, a metal tomb taller than the Statue of Liberty. It's going to fascinate future civilizations. Let's just hope they remember why it mustn't be opened."

Soon we came to the Duga-1 Radar System (also known as the "Russian Woodpecker"): a giant, mysterious antenna array that had emitted a powerful anonymous signal between 1976 and 1989 somehow meant to detect a ballistic missile launch from the United States. It had also had the unfortunate effect of disrupting global radio and television stations during those years, with a pecking sound. This had spawned all sorts of conspiracy theories involving weather—or even mind—control. The five-hundred-foot-high wall of plaited metal seemed to lean against the sky as we approached it. It made disconcerting creaking noises. The others hung back while I crept from tree to tree to get a closer photo of it. When I returned, they were debating various theories about the military object.

"There were going to be twelve reactors in all. Some people believe they were all being built to power the Duga," Aram was saying.

"Even if it was designed to do more than just detect incoming missiles, maybe those extra functions never worked," Darmon commented. "At least, that's what some people reckon. . . . There's a whole conspiracy theory about how the disaster was a cover-up to hide the Duga's design failures." Darmon told us about a slightly dubious new documentary that claimed that Vasily Shamshin, the Communist Party bureaucrat who commissioned the Duga, had pressured the head engineer of Reactor 4 to sabotage it, deliberately engineering the crisis as a cover-up.[4]

Kirill was picking his teeth with a dirty fingernail. "I can't believe you guys don't want to climb it," he said, staring up at the tower of metal.

Our next stop was an abandoned rocket base inside a massive bunker with a blast door two stories tall. If the Duga was built to detect a launch, this was the Soviet surface-to-air response system. Stalkers had been camping inside the bunker, evidenced by the tagging on the walls from various groups including "Dark Stalk" and "Geo Stalk." Waving the dosimeter over the remains of a recent fire, it pinged at 1,500 mSv.

"Those idiots committed suicide burning radioactive wood here last night," Kirill said. The dosimeter's alarm would not stop going off, so he eventually took out the batteries.

Thousands of dark tourists every year fly to the Ukraine and pay to tramp around the site. Their numbers only grew after the Fukushima meltdown in 2011, almost exactly twenty-five years later, the only other Category 7 nuclear disaster in human history. In 2017, fifty thousand tourists entered the Chernobyl Exclusion Zone on official tours. Each of them forked over good money for a satisfying illusion of freedom. Many of them swanned around staged sets of the tragedy set up by guides and photographers who'd preceded them, thinking they were snapping photos of the "untouched" remains of the evacuation.

The photographer Andy Day, a friend who was meant to join us on this excursion, had taken one of these tours previously and felt that the overwhelming drive to see the place dovetailed with the doomsday fantasies of preppers. He wrote that we all "harbour a secret desire for our own apocalypse. . . . Quietly we crave a future where man's capacity for self-sabotage undermines this regime, bringing both liberation and destruction, finally providing that conclusive, fundamentally authentic and terminal experience that creates the ultimate story and, fatally, allows us to know truly who we are. With apocalypse comes meaning."[5]

Meaning at Chernobyl is more than a reflection on the disasters lurking in the fragility of our creations. Cosmological and scriptural references were seemingly fulfilled by the explosion of Reactor No. 4. The word "disaster," originating in the Greek for "bad star," comes from an imagining of an astrological calamity triggered by the position of planets, not unlike Robert Vicino's nefarious Planet X. A supernova, or exploding star, within fifty light-years of Earth could saturate us with radiation, just as the explosion of No. 4 did. In fact, the word "Chernobyl," translated from Ukrainian, means "wormwood"—this is also the name of a star prophesied to fall to Earth in the Book of Revelation (8:10–11), poisoning a third of the Earth's fresh water.

And then there are the science-fiction-come-to-life prophecies. In 1972, almost fifteen years *before* the disaster, the Russian Strugatsky Brothers wrote *Roadside Picnic*, a sci-fi novel in which an ambiguous disaster creates "The Zone." In the novel, The Zone is a ruined landscape patrolled by armed guards around a secure perimeter filled with weirdly mutated, if not alien, creatures, and magical, often deadly, artifacts—including one which will apparently grant wishes to whoever finds it at the center of The Zone.[6]

According to Andrei Tarkovsky's 1979 film *Stalker*, adapted from *Roadside Picnic* and made less than a decade before the Chernobyl explosion, the magical artifact at the center of The Zone is located in "Bunker Four." Reactor No. 4 is now the epicenter of the sixteen-hundred-square-mile Zone of Alienation, and at the center of Reactor No. 4 stands the Elephant's Foot, the solid mass of corium nuclear fuel that has been melting since 1986. In the film, one of the Stalkers has a dream in which that sixth seal from the Book of Revelation is read out. The Stalkers themselves are apocalypse fantasy characters come to life. One of the Stalkers in the book, who meets a grisly end by backing into a spiderweb, is named Kirill. Living out these fictions on the ground was, by far, the most surreal experience I'd ever had. As was the later realization that the paranoia about contaminated surfaces that developed on our journey through the Exclusion Zone had trained me well for the future global disaster that awaited us: the COVID-19 pandemic. Radiation and viruses are cousins in disaster.

After sunset, we'd make the final push into Pripyat. The only viable path to do so was down the central road, through the highly irradiated Red Forest. Half an orange moon hung over the asphalt. As we tromped, we got our first glance of the sarcophagus, a pulsing red speck on the horizon.

Three times Kirill sent us into the woods—twigs scraping our limbs and faces—as vehicles passed by. The first was a truck heading toward the reactor, the second was the police, and the third, he reckoned, was an illegal logger. During this third dodge, in an unfortunate area of the Red Forest, he estimated we sopped up 500 mSv apiece.

As we entered Pripyat, gorgeous specimens of Soviet modernist architecture with zigzagging exterior concrete stairwells emerged like exoplanetary ruins, slowly replacing the clusters of pines. After the terrifying exposure of the central road, the buildings afforded a comforting sense of enclosure. To fully apprehend the empty sprawl of the city, however, we took to the rooftops.

"This has been like a dream," Aram said to no one in particular, as we watched lightning bolts dance around Reactor No. 4 from on top of the abandoned tower, "like walking through a lost civilization, except it's our own." We'd survived traversing the ruins of the future; we'd followed the performance of the bug out to its logical terminus.

Before leaving the Zone, the last thing I saw from the backseat of an SUV driven by a smuggler whom we'd paid to extract us was a giant concrete egg in the middle of an intersection.

"Oh, that," Darmon said, noticing it had caught my eye. "That's the 'Chernobyl Egg.' It's by an artist called Armin Kölbli—he filled it with letters and mementos, sealed inside a radioactive waste storage drum. The egg's not supposed to be cracked until the year 3000."

"A time capsule?" I asked.

"Yeah, like a cocoon waiting for the future," Darmon said as he stared out the window.

Acknowledgments

Writing *Bunker* has been my life's greatest joy. It's required a lot of support, hard work, and (frankly) good luck to get this book into print. I wasn't cut out for this kind of opportunity. I had a rocky childhood in California. School authorities told my parents I had attention deficit hyperactivity disorder (ADHD). I told my parents I was just bored and proceeded break everything. I eventually got kicked out of middle school and then high school. Whatever the underlying neuroses and external factors that led to my rebellion, my parents, Marcia and Erpel, let me learn from my mistakes. It was just what I needed. My disrespect for authority and skepticism about social and political norms made me hungry for knowledge produced on my own terms, and higher education suited me quite well. I now have an arrest record in four countries and yet have been able to work with some of the most venerable institutions on the planet. The light-touch support my parents offered is what enabled me to carve this wonky but fruitful path through life. Erpel and Marcia—you created the perfect amalgam of encouragement, order, and freedom. Thanks.

This isn't to say writing *Bunker* wasn't taxing, or that I dealt with the pressures of the project well. I've been courting my partner, Amanda, since middle school—from California to the UK to Ireland to Istanbul to Las Vegas—and when we finally both ended up in the same place in 2017 (Sydney), she had to suffer me being absent for long periods on fieldwork, was subjected to me talking about depressing things endlessly, and was on the hook to herd me through long hours, sometimes literally propping me up while I wrote to deadline. Amanda, thank you for your love and support. I promise I've learned some valuable lessons and that next time it will be easier on both of us!

Our reunion came about because Kurt Iveson at the University of Sydney sent me an email in May 2016 asking me if I had any interest in applying for a Sydney Fellowship. By 2017, I had full funding to work on the project that became *Bunker*. Kurt, it was a pleasure to work with you and watch you fight the good fight over those three years. And of course, if you hadn't sent that email, this book wouldn't exist—I'm forever in your debt. Thank you also to my colleagues in the School of Geosciences and the Sydney Environment Institute for the encouragement and feedback and, in particular, to everyone in the Urban Crew for being a lifeline out of my writing den.

The heads of the Sydney Society of Fellows, Ofer Gal and Madeleine Beekman, did a remarkable job of putting together a group of interdisciplinary scholars at the University of Sydney. It was a golden age that I took great pride in being a part of. Ofer, you've been a wonderful mentor to me. The conversations we had on campus, at your kitchen table, and sitting under trees in the park had an enormous influence not just on this book but on my career path. You're a mensch.

Rebecca Carter, my UK agent at Janklow & Nesbit, met me at the British Library café in London after the publication of my first book and reminded me recently that one of my shoes was wrapped in duct tape at the time. After rescuing me from post-PhD poverty, Rebecca waited patiently for the right idea to emerge that we could pitch. It wasn't a short wait. Rebecca, thank you for your patience, persistence, and careful navigation. Without you, I would've inevitably drifted down endless detours without ever arriving anywhere in particular. I don't know what I'd do without you.

When Rebecca and I pitched *Bunker*, we went on a whirlwind multiday black-cab crawl of London, touring publishing houses. When we found the right match, it was pretty obvious. Thomas Penn, my eventual editor at Penguin, had just the right mix of brilliance and savvy to know what to do with my half-baked plans. I'm delighted to have been picked up by an editor that I respect so much. Tom, thanks for fighting my corner, for your steady hand, and for that mad dash pre-pandemic night tour around historic London that seems like a lifetime ago now.

Rick Horgan, my editor at Simon & Schuster, changed my life

with a phone call. Over the past three years, with patience and generosity, Rick has done his utmost to cultivate my inner writer, getting me to distill my academic jargon and philosophical ramblings into a more carefully crafted and accessible form. Rick, thank you for helping me understand the worth of grace, pace, and style. You haven't just changed the way I write, but the way I think.

Emma Parry, my New York–based agent at Janklow & Nesbit, has the coolest head in the business and has had to use it to talk me down from a ledge on more than one occasion. Emma, thank you for knowing just when to deploy that legendary diplomacy.

My publicists, Matthew Hutchinson at Penguin and Clare Maurer at Simon & Schuster, have been tireless in their work on my behalf. I don't know what keeps you both motivated, but I appreciate it. My deepest thanks also to Liz Parsons, Etty Eastwood, Brian Belfiglio, and Ashley Gilliam for your keen eyes, thoughts, ideas, and encouragement. Beckett Rueda at Simon & Schuster, you've been an absolute star, thanks for your focus and dedication. Richard Duguid at Penguin, thank you for leaning in when we needed it—I needed that push. Thanks to Elisa M. Rivlin and Victoria Simon-Shore for careful and generous legal navigation. I am grateful to have had Laura Wise as a production editor; thanks for your careful attention to the manuscript, Laura, especially in the eleventh hour. And throughout this process I was blessed by two fantastic copy editors: Jane Robertson and Rick Willett—you deserve my utmost gratitude for the cracking job and your estimable patience with my processual ignorance and inane queries.

I owe a great deal to Thomas Dekeyser. Thomas, thanks for helping me with the references, for working though the architecture of dread over Goldsmiths Café breakfasts and edgeland walks, and for keeping me criminal when I needed it most. What a journey we embarked upon from our first rendezvous for Last Breath! I still wish we'd stayed on the sea fort.

Wayne advised me to be a trunk not a branch, which inspired me to cut the tree down. Brother, I think I buried much of your vast influence over this work in the process, but I don't think you'll care, because gifting is your modus operandi. We've driven continents, plumbed depths, ascended terrifying heights, walked the old ways and the new, shot guns, dunked in waterfalls, and broke into the most dangerous place on earth for fun. And that was all in the last five years. Here's to another five of heady adventure and rich interior life. I've got a lot of respect for you, and even more love. You're one of a kind.

Adam Fish, my first mentor and "field corruptor," found me in the jungle of the Yucatán Peninsula seventeen years ago. Since then, we've danced at Burning Man, written articles for newspapers and academic journals, built and crashed drones, made documentaries for TV and film festivals, navigated university jobs in three countries, and undertaken countless spiritual, deeply embodied, and psychoactive journeys. Adam, thanks for making that third flight from Sikkim, and for being there for my birth and death. Along the journey, Robin and Moxie came into our lives and only added to the chaotic splendor—I love you all.

I first encountered Will Self on stage at the Barbican in London back when I was doing a postdoc at Oxford University. We hit it off straight away. In the years since, we've worked together, walked together, entertained large audiences together, and conspired together. Will, I've never met anyone who gives me more faith in the intellectual project. You taught me to live my philosophy, and I aim to never let you down.

My humble appreciation is also owed to the following people. My stepfather Major General John "Jack" Kulpa, who passed away in 2018, for being the most intelligent and accomplished man I've ever met whom I wholeheartedly disagreed with about almost everything. The late Denis Cosgrove for selflessly setting me on the path to a PhD in the last months of his life. Robert Macfarlane for teaching me that being an adventurer and an academic are not mutually exclusive projects. Leo Hollis for pulling me from my cloister into the world of publishing. Tim Cresswell for being a superb PhD supervisor and asking for so little in return. Ian Klinke for the walks, decadent dinners, pints, and good conversation—you're the best of Oxford, my friend. Alison Young for offering friendship and steady support navigating the liminal space between the academy and public life. Andy Day and Zofia for bringing me to Bulgaria on the slow train and showing me how to keep bullshit work at arm's length while we climbed rocks. Edgar Gomez-Cruz and Leila for enduring friendship and the inspiration to keep creativity paramount—Edgar, that day with the drone and the six pack on the beach was so good! Darmon and Aram for that dumb thing we did in Ukraine. I really needed that. Candice Boyd for seeking me out and showing me the importance of pursuing dreams. Ben Nathan and Stephen Walter for making art come alive through adventure. Triin, Rob, Sofia, and Helena for being awesome friends and for taking care of our pigs while we roamed. Marilu Melo for our shared love of the subterranean world and the important periodic reminders that work isn't everything. Barny Lewer for finally getting us to the jump rock to watch the pandemic cruise into port. Naama Blatman-Thomas for keeping my critical edge honed and helping me find my next job! Theo Kindynis for never losing sight of priorities and for the tacit late-night escapades in between drafts. Anna Minton for keeping me brave. And Mark O'Connell for almost agreeing to be my new arch nemesis.

The writing of this book began and ended in the Big Bear, California, cabin of Christine and Arthur Robles. Thanks to you both for giving me the space to write. The magic of the mountain cabin solitude clearly did the trick! Your share of the royalties is under the wood pile outside. Thanks to the rest of the fam too: Kristin, Damon, Colton, Kendall, Bonnie, Pip, Oliver, Charlotte, Robert, Lacey, Riley, and Layla and Trent, the last of whom can't read yet but might one day see this.

I wrote the bulk of this book in dozens of beautiful libraries around the world, but specific recognition is due to the Friends Room at the New South Wales State Library. Staff let me essentially live there for years, nestled amongst eleven hundred editions of Miguel de Cervantes's *Don Quixote*. I couldn't have asked for a more inspiring and peaceful place to write. You'll find a signed copy of *Explore Everything* cached in the shelves in thanks. Cheers to everyone who came to write with me there!

Cheers, as well, to all the people and institutions who invited me to speak about my research. I feel very fortunate to have such a community. Thanks also to the tribe of urban explorers who first piqued my interest in bunkers.

Finally, it goes without saying that I couldn't have written this

ACKNOWLEDGMENTS

book without invitations from the preppers featured within and my biggest thanks goes to them. You've all taught me a great deal. I hope this book can serve as a worthy record of living through the end of an age together. I don't know what's on the other side, but I now share your hope in rebirth.

Notes

Introduction: Private Arks of the Underground

1 C. Wright Mills (1958), *The Causes of World War Three* (New York: Simon & Schuster), p. 90.

2 Ömer Aydan and Reşat Ulusay (2003), "Geotechnical and Geoenvironmental Characteristics of Man made Underground Structures in Cappadocia, Turkey," *Engineering Geology* 69 (3): 245–272.

3 Xenophon (1960), *III Anabasis*, Books I-VII (Cambridge, MA: Harvard University Press), p. 307.

4 Geoff Manaugh (2016), *A Burglar's Guide to the City* (New York: FSG Originals), p. 192.

5 Adam Fish and Bradley Garrett (2019), "Resurrection from Bunkers and Data Centers," *Culture Machine* 18.

6 Lisa Fletcher and Ralph Crane (2015), *Cave: Nature and Culture* (London: Reaktion Books).

7 John Beck (2011), "Concrete Ambivalence: Inside the Bunker Complex," *Cultural Politics* 7: 79–102.

8 Mark O'Connell (2017), *To Be a Machine: Adventures Among Cyborgs, Utopians, Hackers, and the Futurists Solving the Modest Problem of Death* (London: Granta Publications), p. 36.

9 Lewis Dartnell (2014), *The Knowledge: How to Rebuild the World from Scratch* (London: Penguin Books).

10 Anya Bernstein (2019), *The Future of Immortality: Remaking Life and Death in Contemporary Russia* (Princeton: Princeton University Press).

11 Peter Thiel (2011), "Foreword," in Sonia Arrison, *100 Plus: How the Coming Age of Longevity Will Change Everything, from Careers and Relationships to Family and Faith* (New York: Basic Books), pp. 13–14.

12 Mark Duffield (2011), "Total War as Environmental Terror: Linking Liberalism, Resilience, and the Bunker," *South Atlantic Quarterly* 110 (3): 757–769.

13 Naomi Klein (2017), *No Is Not Enough* (London: Allen Lane), p. 351.

14 Lieven De Cauter (2004), *The Capsular Civilization: On the City in the Age of Fear* (Rotterdam: Nai Publishers), p. 69.

15 Sharon Weinberger (2007), "Tom Cruise's \$10M Survival Bunker," *Wired*, October 1, https://www.wired.com/2007/10/tom-cruises-10m.

NOTES

16 Evan Osnos (2017), "Doomsday Prep for the Super Rich," *New Yorker*, January 30, https://www.newyorker.com/magazine/2017/01/30/doomsday-prep-for-the -super-rich.

17 CBS News (2011), "LA Porn Studio Begins Construction on 'Post-Apocalyptic' Underground Bunker," CBS Los Angeles, September 14, https://losangeles.cbslo cal.com/2011/09/14/la-porn-studio-begins-construction-on-post-apocalyptic-un derground-bunker.

18 Tom Junod (2007), "Trump," *Esquire*, January 29, https://www.esquire.com /news-politics/a1571/lessons-simple-humanity-donald-trump-0300.

19 Michael Havis (2017), "Donald Trump's Secret Bomb Shelter: Apocalypse Bunker on Golf Course Revealed," *Daily Star*, April 12, https://www.dailystar.co.uk /news/latest-news/604830/donald-trump-secret-golf-course-bomb-shelter-bunker -nuclear.

20 Tom Vanderbilt (2002), *Survival City: Adventures Among the Ruins of Atomic America* (New York: Princeton Architectural Press), pp. 142–144.

21 Carly Stec (2015), "The Doom Boom: Inside the Survival Industry's Explosive Growth," HubSpot, https://blog.hubspot.com/marketing/survival-industry -growth.

22 Richard J. Mitchell (2012), *Dancing at Armageddon: Survivalism and Chaos in Modern Times* (Chicago: University of Chicago Press), p. 156.

23 Bulletin of the Atomic Scientists (2019), "A New Abnormal: It Is Still Two Minutes to Midnight," *Bulletin of the Atomic Scientists*, January 24, pp. 2–3, https:// media.thebulletin.org/wp-content/uploads/2019/01/2019-Clock-Statement -Press-Print-Version.pdf.

24 Jurriaan M. De Vos, Lucas N. Joppa, John L. Gittleman, Patrick R. Stephens, and Stuart L. Pimm (2014), "Estimating the Normal Background Rate of Species Extinction," *Conservation Biology* 29 (2): 452–462.

25 Damian Carrington (2017), "Arctic Stronghold of World's Seeds Flooded After Permafrost Melts," *Guardian*, May 19, https://www.theguardian.com/environ ment/2017/may/19/arctic-stronghold-of-worlds-seeds-flooded-after-permafrost -melts.

26 Decca Aitkenhead (2008), "James Lovelock: 'Enjoy Life While You Can: In 20 Years Global Warming Will Hit the Fan,'" *Guardian*, March 1, https://www.the guardian.com/theguardian/2008/mar/01/scienceofclimatechange.climatechange.

27 Glenn Albrecht, Gina-Maree Sartore, Linda Connor, Nick Higginbotham, Sonia Freeman, Brian Kelly, Helen Stain, Anne Tonna, and Georgia Pollard (2007), "Solastalgia: The Distress Caused by Environmental Change," *Australasian Psychiatry* 15: S95–S98.

28 Peter Brannen (2017), *The Ends of the World: Volcanic Apocalypses, Lethal Oceans and Our Quest to Understand Earth's Past Mass Extinctions* (New York: HarperCollins Publishing), pp. 103–140; Annalee Newitz (2013), *Scatter, Adapt, and Remember: How Humans Will Survive a Mass Extinction* (New York: Doubleday).

NOTES

29 Anthony J. Martin (2017), *The Evolution Underground: Burrows, Bunkers, and the Marvelous Subterranean World Beneath Our Feet* (New York: Pegasus Books).

30 Donald McNeill (2019), "Volumetric Urbanism: The Production and Extraction of Singaporean Territory," *Environment and Planning A: Economy and Space* 51 (4): 849–868.

31 H. P. Lovecraft (1926), "The Call of Cthulhu," *Weird Tales*, February.

32 James Bridle (2018), *The New Dark Age: Technology and the End of the Future* (London: Verso Books), p. 185.

33 Immanuel Kant (1987 [1790]), *Critique of Judgment* (Indianapolis: Hackett Publishing).

34 Kevin Killeen (2018), *Thomas Browne: Selected Writings* (Oxford: Oxford University Press), p. 784.

35 Josh Jones (2015) "In 1704, Isaac Newton Predicts the World Will End in 2060," *Open Culture*, October 14, 2015.

36 Stephen Hawking (2018), "Will Robots Outsmart Us? The Late Stephen Hawking Answers This and Other Big Questions Facing Humanity," *Sunday Times Magazine*, October 14.

37 John R. Hall (2013), "Apocalyptic and Millenarian Movements," in David Snow, Donatella della Porta, Bert Klandermans, and Doug McAdam (eds.), *Wiley-Blackwell Encyclopedia of Social and Political Movements* (Oxford: Blackwell Publishing), p. 1.

38 Casey Ryan Kelly (2016), "The Man-Pocalpyse: Doomsday Preppers and the Rituals of Apocalyptic Manhood," *Text and Performance Quarterly* 36: pp. 2–3, 95–114.

39 For those with more patience than I, there are two books you can read to get a sense of the message: Jim Bakker (1998), *Prosperity and the Coming Apocalypse* (Nashville: Thomas Nelson Inc.), and Jim Bakker (2013), *Time Has Come: How to Prepare Now for Epic Events Ahead* (Nashville: Worthy Books).

40 Michael Mills (2019), "Obamageddon: Fear, the Right, and the Rise of 'Doomsday' Prepping in Obama's America," *Journal of American Studies*, pp. 1–30.

41 Situationist International (2007), "The Geopolitics of Hibernation," in Ken Knabb (ed.), *Situationist International Anthology* (Berkeley: Bureau of Public Secrets), pp. 100–107.

42 Arthur Schopenhauer (2007), *Counsels and Maxims* (New York: Cosimo Classics), p. 89.

Chapter 1 The Dread Merchants: Selling Safe Space

1 Maurice Blanchot (1986), *The Writing of the Disaster* (Lincoln: University of Nebraska Press).

2 The American television journalist Tom Brokaw even lived there for a few years as a young boy.

NOTES

3 Steven Cuevas (2010), "San Diego Businessman Selling Spaces in Mojave Dooms-day Bunker," *Southern California Public Radio*, June 10, https://www.scpr.org/news/2010/06/10/16004/doomsday-bunker.

4 Everett Rosenfeld (2014), "Apocalypse Later: Largest Bunker Scrapped," CNBC, July 3, https://www.cnbc.com/2014/07/03/apocalypse-later-largest-bunker-scrapped.html.

5 "If It's the End of the World as We Know It . . . New Survey Reveals Ameri-cans Are Not Prepared! National Geographic Channel Releases Survey Timed to New Series *Doomsday Preppers*," *PR Newswire*, February 7, 2012, https://www.prnewswire.com/news-releases/if-its-the-end-of-the-world-as-we-know-it-new-survey-reveals-americans-are-not-prepared-national-geographic-channel-releases-survey-timed-to-new-series-doomsday-preppers-138865199.html.

6 Melanie Randle and Richard Eckersley (2015), "Public Perceptions of Future Threats to Humanity and Different Societal Responses: A Cross-National Study," *Futures*, 72: 4–16.

7 Setha Low (1997), "Urban Fear: Building the Fortress City," *City and Society* 9 (1): 53–71.

8 Søren Kierkegaard [publishing under the nom de plume Vigilius Haufniensis] (1844), *The Concept of Dread: A Simple Psychological Deliberation Oriented in the Direction of the Dogmatic Problem of Original Sin* (Copenhagen: Bianco Luno Printing Press). A later philosopher in the existential school, Martin Hei-degger, wrote that "what anxiety is about is indefinite." Martin Heidegger (2010 [1953]), *Being and Time* (New York: SUNY Press), p. 509. Sigmund Freud called fear without an object "neurotic fear." Sigmund Freud (1920), *A General Intro-duction to Psychoanalysis* (Dodo Collections), pp. 689–690. Mikhail Bakhtin referred to it as "cosmic terror." Mikhail Bakhtin (2009 [1968]), *Rabelais and His World* (Bloomington: Indiana University Press).

9 Marta Jewson and Charles Maldanado (2015), "The Myths of Katrina," *Slate*, August 28.

10 Rebecca Solnit (2011), *A Paradise Built in Hell: The Extraordinary Communities That Arise in Disaster* (London: Penguin), p. 262.

11 Reed Richardson (2013), "The Doomsday Prepper Caucus," *Nation*, April 2.

12 Nick Bostrom (2003), "Are You Living in a Computer Simulation?," *Philosophi-cal Quarterly* 53 (211): 243–255.

13 Andrew Culp (2016), *Dark Deleuze* (Minneapolis: University of Minnesota Press), p. 17.

14 Nassim Nicholas Taleb (2007), *The Black Swan: The Impact of the Highly Improbable* (New York: Random House), p. xxii.

15 Paul Virilio (1999), *The Politics of the Very Worst* (Cambridge, MA: MIT Press), pp. 37–38.

16 Hannah Arendt (1973), *The Origins of Totalitarianism* (New York: Harcourt).

17 Robert G. Gunderson (1940), "The Calamity Howlers," *Quarterly Journal of Speech* 26 (3): 401–411.

NOTES

18 Donna Haraway (2016), *Staying with the Trouble* (Durham, NC: Duke University Press), p. 28; Frank White (2014), *The Overview Effect: Space Exploration and Human Evolution* (Washington, DC: American Institute of Aeronautics).

19 Carl Sagan (1994), *Pale Blue Dot* (New York: Ballantine Books), p. 39.

Chapter 2 Geological Deterrence: Prepping Like a State

1 Hans J. Morgenthau (1961), "Death in the Nuclear Age," *Commentary*, September 1.

2 Benjamin Phelan (2004), "Buried Truth: Debunking the Nuclear 'Bunker Buster,'" *Harper's*, December.

3 Fred Coleman (1997), *The Decline and Fall of the Soviet Empire: Forty Years That Shook the World, From Stalin to Yeltsin* (New York: St. Martin's Press).

4 Tyler Headley (2018), "China's Djibouti Base: A One Year Update," *Diplomat*, https://thediplomat.com/2018/12/chinas-djibouti-base-a-one-year-update/.

5 Krishna N. Das and Mukesh Gupta (2019), "India Builds Bunkers to Protect Families along Pakistan Border," London: Reuters, https://www.reuters.com/article/us-india-kashmir-border/india-builds-bunkers-to-protect-families-along-pakistan-border-idUSKCN1QG20Y.

6 "Life on the Newsfronts," *Life*, March 1, 1954, p. 40.

7 See Garret M. Graff (2017), *Raven Rock: The Story of the U.S. Government's Secret Plan to Save Itself—While the Rest of Us Die* (New York: Simon & Schuster).

8 Scott MacFarlane (2015), "Mt. Weather: Top Secret Government Facility Activated for Power Outage in April," News4 I-Team, June 24.

9 Xavier Poez (2019), "FEMA, Mount Weather, Conspiracy Theory Literature," https://www.insideedition.com/headlines/24133-inside-the-secret-bunkers-designed-to-house-thousands-in-the-event-of-nuclear-war.

10 Garrett M. Graff (2017), "The Secret History of FEMA," *Wired*, September 3.

11 Ted Gup (1992), "The Ultimate Congressional Hideaway," *Washington Post*, May 31.

12 *Review of the Federal Relocation Arc* (College Park, MD: National Archives and Records Administration), Record Group 396, Declassified P-95 Records, Accession # 66A03, Box 3, Untitled Binder.

13 Robert M. Gates (1996), *From the Shadows: The Ultimate Insider's Story of Five Presidents and How They Won the Cold War* (New York: Simon & Schuster), p. 114.

14 David Hoffman (1998), "Cold-War Doctrines Refuse to Die," *Washington Post*, March 15.

15 Swedish Civil Contingencies Agency (2018), "If Crisis or War Comes," https://www.dinsakerhet.se/siteassets/dinsakerhet.se/broschyren-om-krisen-eller-kriget-kommer/om-krisen-eller-kriget-kommer---engelska.pdf.

NOTES

16 Henrik Pryser Libell and Christina Anderson (2020), "Finland, 'Prepper Nation of the Nordics," Isn't Worried About Masks," *New York Times*, April 5, https://www.nytimes.com/2020/04/05/world/europe/coronavirus-finland-masks.html.

17 Daniele Mariani (2009), "Bunkers for All," Swiss Broadcasting Corporation, July 3, https://www.swissinfo.ch/eng/prepared-for-anything_bunkers-for-all/995134.

18 Matan Shapiro and Nurit David-Bird (2017), "Routinergency: Domestic Securitization in Contemporary Israel," *Environment and Planning D* 35 (4): 637–655.

19 Benjamin Phelan (2004), "Buried Truth: Debunking the Nuclear 'Bunker Buster,'" *Harper's*, December.

20 Kyle Mizokami (2020), "North Korea's Underground Bunkers and Bases Are a Nightmare for America," *National Interest*, January 10.

21 Peter Hayes (1990), *Pacific Powderkeg: American Nuclear Dilemmas in Korea* (Lanham: Lexington Books).

22 See Ian Klinke (2018), *Cryptic Concrete: A Subterranean Journey into Cold War Germany* (Oxford: Wiley-Blackwell).

23 Herman Kahn (2007 [1960]), *On Thermonuclear War* (New Brunswick, NJ: Transaction Publishers), p. 213.

24 Daniel Wojcik (1996), "Embracing Doomsday: Faith, Fatalism, and Apocalyptic Beliefs in the Nuclear Age," *Western Folklore* 55 (4), Explorations in Folklore and Cultural Studies: 298.

25 Rachael Squire (2016), "Rock, Water, Air and Fire: Foregrounding the Elements in the Gibraltar-Spain Dispute," *Environment and Planning D: Society and Space* 24 (3): 551.

Chapter 3 Living with the Bomb: A Cultural History of Prepping

1 Garret Keizer (2016), "Solidarity and Survival," *Lapham's Quarterly* IX (2), Disaster: 205.

2 Timothy Egan (1990), "Thousands Plan Life Below, After Doomsday," *New York Times*, March 15, https://www.nytimes.com/1990/03/15/us/thousands-plan-life-below-after-doomsday.html.

3 David Monteyne (2011), *Fallout Shelter: Designing for Civil Defense in the Cold War* (Minneapolis: University of Minnesota Press), p. xix.

4 Paul Starrs and John Wright (2005), "Utopia, Dystopia, and Sublime Apocalypse in Montana's Church Universal and Triumphant," *Geographical Review* 95 (1): 97–121: 109; John Wright (1998), *Montana Ghost Dance: Essays on Land and Life* (Austin: University of Texas Press).

5 Kathy Webber (2008), *Sean Prophet on Church Universal & Triumphant*, KULR-TV, Billings, Montana.

6 Elizabeth Clare Prophet (1990), *The Astrology of the Four Horsemen: How You Can Heal Yourself and Planet Earth* (Gardiner, Montana: Summit University Press).

NOTES

7   Philip Lamy (1996), *Millennium Rage: Survivalists, White Supremacists and the Doomsday Prophecy* (New York: Springer), p. 5.

8   Hans J. Morgenthau (1961), "Death in the Nuclear Age," *Commentary*, September 1.

9   Paul Starrs and John Wright (2005), "Utopia, Dystopia, and Sublime Apocalypse."

10 Waters et al. (2016), "The Anthropocene Is Functionally and Stratigraphically Distinct from the Holocene," *Science* 351(6269).

11 George H. Gallup, "July 16, 1956," "July 18, 1956," "December 19, 1956," in *The Gallup Poll: Public Opinion, 1972–1977*, Vol. 2 (New York: Random House), 1972, p. 929.

12 John F. Kennedy (1961), "Radio and Television Report to the American People on the Berlin Crisis," July 25, Washington, DC, https://www.jfklibrary.org/archives /other-resources/john-f-kennedy-speeches/berlin-crisis-19610725.

13 Andrew Szasz (2007), *Shopping Our Way to Safety* (Minneapolis: University of Minnesota Press), p. 17.

14 "Amway Offering Provided Shelter from Nuclear Fallout," *Amway Corporation*, January 16, 2019.

15 Warren R. Young (1962), "Group Shelters Are a Start—the Facts Require Much More," *Life*, January 12, p. 40.

16 "Civil Defense, The Sheltered Life," *Life*, October 20, cited in Alison McQueen (2018), *Political Realism in Apocalyptic Times* (Cambridge: Cambridge University Press), p. 161.

17 James Coates (1987), *Armed and Dangerous: The Rise of the Survivalist Right* (New York: Hill and Wang).

18 Michael Mills (2017), *Witness to the American Apocalypse? A Study of 21st Century "Doomsday" Prepping*, unpublished PhD dissertation, University of Kent, UK, p. 38.

19 Andrea Luka Zimmerman (2017), *Erase and Forget* (London: LUX).

20 Stephen Stuebner (1998), "Patriot Leader Bo Gritz Shoots Himself Under Troubling Circumstances," *Intelligence Report*, December 15, https://www.splcen ter.org/fighting-hate/intelligence-report/1998/patriot-leader-bo-gritz-shoots -himself-under-troubling-circumstances.

21 Rebecca Boone (2004), "Almost Heaven Almost Gone? 'Patriot' Haven Silent a Decade Later," *Casper Star-Tribune*, August 27, www.casperstartribune.net/arti cles/2004/08/27/news/regional/.

22 Malcolm Gladwell (2014), "Sacred and Profane: How to Negotiate with Believers," *New Yorker*, March 31.

23 Jen Percy (2018), "Fear of the Federal Government in the Ranchlands of Oregon," *New York Times*, January 18.

24 See https://www.splcenter.org/fighting-hate/extremist-files/ideology/antigovern ment.

25 Richard J. Mitchell (2012), *Dancing at Armageddon: Survivalism and Chaos in*

Modern Times (Chicago: University of Chicago Press), p. 34; Tom Vanderbilt (2002), *Survival City: Adventures Among the Ruins of Atomic America* (New York: Princeton Architectural Press), p. 111.

26 *Home Is Where the Bunker Is: Extremist, Survivalist, and Fringe Housing Developments* (New York: Anti-Defamation League, 2013).

Chapter 4 Pipes in the Ground: Burying Secret Spaces

1 Louis Wilson (1994), "Cyberwar, God and Television: Interview with Paul Virilio," *CTHEORY*, www.ctheory.net/articles.aspx?id=62.

2 Joseph Bruchac and Michael J. Caduto (1991), "Four worlds: The Dine Story of Creation," in *Native American Stories* (Golden, CO: Fulcrum Publishing).

3 Lawrence James (2003), *Warrior Race: A History of the British at War* (London: Hachette), p. 623.

4 Robert Macfarlane (2019), *Underland: A Deep Time Journey* (London: Hamish Hamilton), p. 100.

5 C. A. Davis and J. P. Bardet (2000), "Responses of Buried Corrugated Metal Pipes to Earthquakes," *Journal of Geotechnical and Geoenvironmental Engineering* 126 (1): 28–39.

6 Richard Ross (2004), *Waiting for the End of the World* (New Jersey: Princeton Architectural Press), p. 14.

7 Trump's election also caused a record number of background checks for gun purchases by liberals. See: Brian Wheeler (2016), "Why US Liberals Are Now Buying Guns Too," BBC News, December 20, https://www.bbc.com/news/magazine-38297345.

8 My stepfather, Major General John E. Kulpa Jr., who passed away in 2018, was one of the pioneers of space surveillance technology, having put some of the first spy satellites into orbit as part of the CIA's P-11 Program.

9 Adam Fish (2019), *Technoliberalism and the End of Participatory Culture in the United States* (London: Palgrave Macmillan), p. 123.

10 James Bridle (2018), *The New Dark Age: Technology and the End of the Future* (London: Verso Books), p. 210.

11 Ryan Bishop (2011), "Project 'Transparent Earth' and the Autoscopy of Aerial Targeting: The Visual Geopolitics of the Underground," *Theory, Culture & Society* 28 (7–8): 283.

12 Ellen Nakashima and Craig Whitlock (2011), "With Air Force's Gorgon Drone 'We Can See Everything,'" *Washington Post*, January 2. Also see Stephen Graham (2018), *Vertical: The City from Satellites to Tunnels* (London: Verso Books).

13 David Morris (2016), "Baltimore's All-Seeing 'Eye in the Sky' Will Stay in Service," *Fortune*, October 8.

14 Brandon Soderberg (2020), "Baltimore Defense Attorneys Claim Surveillance Plane Footage Contradicts Law Enforcement Account of Police Shooting," *Davis Vanguard*, February 18.

NOTES

15 Hugh G. Evelyn-White (1914), *The Theogony of Hesiod* II, "Hesiod, the Homeric hymns, and Homerica" (Harvard: Loeb Classical Library), pp. 270–294.

16 Stephen R. Wilk, *Medusa: Solving the Mystery of the Gorgon* (Oxford: Oxford University Press), p. 95.

17 Caroline Alexander (2017), "The Dread Gorgon," *Lapham's Quarterly* X (3), Fear: 187–192.

18 Judith Scott-Clayton (2018), "The Looming Student Loan Default Crisis Is Worse Than We Thought," *Evidence Speaks Reports* 2 (34), Brookings Institution, January 10.

19 Tim Luke and Gearóid Ó Tuathail (2000), "Thinking Geopolitical Space: The Spatiality of War, Speed and Vision in the Work of Paul Virilio," in Mike Crang and Nigel Thrift (eds.), *Thinking Space* (London: Routledge), p. 361.

20 Michael Mills (2017), *Witness to the American Apocalypse? A Study of 21st Century "Doomsday" Prepping*, unpublished PhD dissertation, University of Kent, UK, p. 38.

Chapter 5 Texas Redoubt: Tribulation in Style

1 Aristotle [1935], *Politics: A Treatise on Government*, William Ellis (trans.) (London: J. M. Dent and Sons Ltd.).

2 DEFCON stands for "Defense Condition" and ranges from 1 to 5. DEFCON 1 means "Nuclear war is imminent."

3 Some of this information can be found in Eckerd's cringeworthy autobiography, *Blood, Sweat and Cheers*, https://johneckerd.com/book.

4 Kezia Barker (2019), "How to Survive the End of the Future: Preppers, Pathology and the Everyday Crisis of Insecurity," *Transactions of the Institute of British Geographers* 45 (2): 483–96.

5 Geoff Manaugh (2016), *A Burglar's Guide to the City* (New York: FSG Originals), p. 188.

6 Lieven De Cauter (2004), *The Capsular Civilization: On the City in the Age of Fear* (Rotterdam: Nai Publishers), p. 117.

7 See https://www.coelux.com/en/home-page/index.

8 Félix Guattari (2000), *The Three Ecologies* (London: The Atholone Press), p. 66.

9 Evgeny Morozov (2013), *To Save Everything Click Here: The Folly of Technological Solutionism* (New York: Allen Lane).

10 Paul Virilio (2012), *The Administration of Fear* (New York: Semiotext(e)), p. 50.

11 Rawles writes his name in this way, apparently, to separate his "Christian" name from his given names.

12 Hatewatch Staff (2019), "Far-Right Survivalist and Icon of 'Patriot' Movement Predicts Religious Civil War," Southern Poverty Law Center, January 9.

NOTES

13 William Strauss and Neil Howe (1997), *The Fourth Turning* (New York: Broadway Books), p. 22.

14 John R. Hall (2009), *Apocalypse: From Antiquity to the Empire of Modernity* (Cambridge, UK: Polity Press), pp. 2–3.

15 Paul Virilio (1999), *The Politics of the Very Worst* (Cambridge, MA: MIT Press), pp. 17–18.

16 I told my friend Will Jennings about this at the pub soon after learning it. "But Shaq has made his living with a sphere . . . ," he responded, clearly disappointed.

Chapter 6 Preps Down Under: Bugging Out of Cities

1 Franz Kafka (1999 [1931]), *The Complete Short Stories* (London: Random House), p. 352.

2 Clive Williams (2020), "Government-Approved Bushfire Bunkers Could Help Protect Homes, Lives," *Sydney Morning Herald*, January 1.

3 Ben Smee (2019), "Queensland School Runs Out of Water as Commercial Bottlers Harvest Local Supplies," *Guardian*, December 11.

4 Climate Institute of Australia (2007), "Bushfire Weather in Southeast Australia: Recent Trends and Projected Climate Change Impacts," pp. 2–6, https://publi cations.csiro.au/rpr/pub?list=BRO&pid=procite:5910842c-f62e-4006-b88f -1055d8e981fa.

5 Elizabeth Povinelli (2016), *Geontologies: A Requiem to Late Liberalism* (Durham: Duke University Press), p. 126.

6 These material manifestations of inconceivable scale are also called "hyperobjects." See Timothy Morton (2013), *Hyperobjects: Philosophy and Ecology After the End of the World* (Minneapolis: University of Minnesota Press).

7 Gwendolyn Audrey Foster (2014), *Hoarders, Doomsday Preppers, and the Culture of Apocalypse* (London: Palgrave MacMillan).

8 Neville Shute (1957), *On the Beach* (London: Penguin).

9 Cited in James T. Sparrow (2011), *Warfare State: World War II Americans and the Age of Big Government* (Oxford: Oxford University Press), p. 23.

10 Zygmunt Bauman (2006), *Liquid Fear* (Cambridge, UK: Polity Press).

11 Nick Clark (2012), "Doomsday Cult Link," *Cult Education*, January 20, https:// culteducation.com/information/8109-doomsday-cult-link.html.

12 Emile Corian (1960), *History and Utopia* (New York: Arcade Publishing), p. 98.

Chapter 7 Escape from California: Boltholes at the Bottom of the World

1 Arthur Schopenhauer (2007 [1851]), *Counsels and Maxims* (New York: Cosimo Classics), p. 89.

2 Jim Hickey (2011), "Underground Bunkers Are Big Business," ABC News, March

24, https://abcnews.go.com/Business/underground-bunkers-big-business/story?id
=13212546.

3 If you want to forestall the climate apocalypse, by the way, adopting a vegan diet
is the single most important decision you can make right now.

4 Joseph L. Flatley (2011), "Condo at the End of the World," *Verge*, November 1,
https://www.theverge.com/culture/2011/11/1/2525857/2012-survival-condo-at
-the-end-of-the-world.

5 "What's Inside Kim Dotcom's Panic Room?," *Observer*, February 16, 2012,
https://observer.com/2012/02/whats-inside-kim-dotcoms-panic-room.

6 Steve Braunias (2018), "Spending Doomsday with Kim Dotcom," *New Zealand
Herald*, December 28, https://www.nzherald.co.nz/nz/news/article.cfm?c_id=1&
objectid=12180577.

7 Eleanor Ainge Roy (2017), "Billionaires' Bolthole: How New Zealand Became an
Escapee's Paradise," *Guardian*, February 17, https://www.theguardian.com/world
/2017/feb/17/billionaires-bolthole-new-zealand-preppers-paradise.

8 Evan Osnos (2017), "Doomsday Prep for the Super Rich," *New Yorker*, January
30, https://www.newyorker.com/magazine/2017/01/30/doomsday-prep-for-the
-super-rich.

9 Olivia Carville (2018), "The Super Rich of Silicon Valley Have a Doomsday
Escape Plan," Bloomberg, September 5, https://www.bloomberg.com/features
/2018-rich-new-zealand-doomsday-preppers/.

10 Jo McKenzie-McLean and Joanne Carroll (2018), "Mystery Surrounds Secret
Kiwi Survival Bunker Claims," *Stuff*, September 14, https://www.stuff.co.nz
/national/106980695/mystery-surrounds-secret-kiwi-survival-bunker-claims.

11 Kevin Roose (2018), "His 2020 Campaign Message: The Robots Are Coming,"
New York Times, February 10.

12 James Dale Davidson and Lord William Rees-Mogg (1997), *The Sovereign Individual: Mastering the Transition to the Information Age* (New York: Simon &
Schuster).

13 Tom Stoppard (1994), *Arcadia* (London: Faber and Faber).

14 Naomi Klein (2008), *The Shock Doctrine: The Rise of Disaster Capitalism* (London: Penguin Books).

15 Mark O'Connell (2018), "Why Silicon Valley Billionaires Are Prepping for the
Apocalypse in New Zealand," *Guardian*, February 15, https://www.theguard
ian.com/news/2018/feb/15/why-silicon-valley-billionaires-are-prepping-for-the
-apocalypse-in-new-zealand.

16 Oliver Price (2019), "The Brexit Millionaires," *Channel 4 Dispatches*, Monday
March 11.

17 Nadine Gordimer (1999), *The House Gun* (London: Bloomsbury), p. 6.

18 *World's Fair Information Manual* (New York: World's Fair Publication, 1965).

19 John Treanor (2018), "Cryogenics: Can a Company Really Help You Live For-

NOTES

ever?," 3 News Las Vegas, February 3, https://news3lv.com/news/local/after-the -game-cryogenics.

20 Brian Massumi (2015), *Ontopower: War, Powers, and the State of Perception* (Durham, NC: Duke University Press), p. 240.

21 Gayle Spinazze (2020), "Press Release—It Is Now 100 Seconds to Midnight," *Bulletin of the Atomic Scientists*, January 23.

22 Friedrich Nietzsche [2008], *Man Alone with Himself* (London: Penguin), p. 7.

23 Steve Braunias (2018), "The Bodyguard at the End of the World," *New Zealand Herald*, November 17, https://www.nzherald.co.nz/nz/news/article.cfm?c_id= 1&objectid=12155198.

Chapter 8 Sustainable Security: Thailand's Eco-Fortress

1 Werner Herzog cited in Paul Cronin (2014), *Werner Herzog: A Guide for the Perplexed* (New York: Faber and Faber), p. 86.

2 Zygmunt Bauman (2006), *Liquid Fear* (Cambridge: Polity Press), p. 130.

3 Abraham Maslow (1943), "A Theory of Human Motivation," *Psychological Review* 50(4): 370–396.

4 Danny Dorling (2018), *Peak Inequality: Britain's Ticking Timebomb* (Bristol: Polity Press).

5 Stephen Graham (2018), *Vertical: The City from Satellites to Tunnels* (London: Verso Books), p. 314.

6 Roger Burrows (2018), "Mega-Basements of the Super Rich Are a Good Reminder of the City London Has Become," *The Conversation*, June 15.

7 Oliver Wainwright (2012), "Billionaires' Basements: The Luxury Bunkers Making Holes in London Streets," *Guardian*, November 9, https://www.theguardian .com/artanddesign/2012/nov/09/billionaires-basements-london-houses-archi tecture.

8 Rowland Atkinson and Sarah Blandy (2017), *Domestic Fortress: Fear and the New Home Front* (Manchester, UK: Manchester University Press).

9 Martin Heidegger (1949), "What Is Metaphysics?," republished in Werner Brock (ed.), *Existence and Being*, (Chicago: Henry Regnery Company).

Chapter 9 Captain Paranoid: Fortitude Ranch

1 Bryan Walsh (2019), *End Times: A Brief Guide to the End of the World* (New York: Hachette).

2 Drew Miller (1985), *Fortifications and Underground Nuclear Defense Shelters for NATO Troops*, Unpublished PhD Thesis, Harvard University.

3 Drew Miller (2017), *Rohan Nation: Reinventing America After the 2020 Collapse* (Responsibility Press).

4 Drew Miller (2016), "The Age of Designer Plagues," *The American Interest*, November/December Issue.

5 Arundhati Roy (2020), "The Pandemic Is a Portal," *Financial Times*, April 3.

6 Alexander Koch, Chris Brierley, Mark M. Maslin, and Simon L. Lewis (2019), "Earth System Impacts of the European Arrival and Great Dying in the Americas After 1492," *Quaternary Science Reviews* 207: 13–36.

7 Tom Chivers (2019), *The AI Does Not Hate You: Superintelligence, Rationality and the Race to Save the World* (London: Weidenfeld & Nicolson), p. 54.

8 Jasmin Fox-Skelly (2017), "There Are Diseases Hidden in Ice, and They Are Waking Up," BBC, May 4, http://www.bbc.com/earth/story/20170504-there-are-diseases-hidden-in-ice-and-they-are-waking-up.

9 James Woolsey and Vincent Pry (2017), "How North Korea Could Kill 90 Percent of Americans," *The Hill*, March 29, https://thehill.com/blogs/pundits-blog/defense/326094-how-north-korea-could-kill-up-to-90-percent-of-americans-at-any.

10 William R. Forstchen (2009), *One Second After* (New York: Tom Doherty Associates), p. 12.

11 Robert Beckhusen (2014), "The Pentagon Is Building a $44-Million EMP Bunker in Alaska," *Medium: War Is Boring*, May 22, https://medium.com/war-is-boring/the-pentagon-is-building-a-44-million-emp-bunker-in-alaska-5a37dee2bcd8.

12 Sigmund Freud (1920), *A General Introduction to Psychoanalysis* (Dodo Collections), pp. 689–690.

13 Martin Rees (2003), *Our Final Hour: Will Civilisation Survive the Twenty-First Century?* (London: Arrow Books), p. 91.

14 For more on this, see Douglas Rushkoff (2018), "Survival of the Richest," *Medium*, July 5, https://medium.com/s/futurehuman/survival-of-the-richest-9ef6cddd0cc1.

15 Donna Haraway (2016), *Staying with the Trouble: Making Kin in the Chthulucene* (Durham, NC: Duke University Press), p. 184.

16 Lawrence W. Gross (2003), "Cultural Sovereignty and Native American Hermeneutics in the Interpretation of the Sacred Stories of the Anishinaabe," *Wicazo Sa Review* 18(2): 127–134.

17 Germaine Greer (1984), *Sex and Destiny: The Politics of Human Fertility* (New York: Harper & Row).

18 Yuval Noah Harari (2014), *Sapiens: A Brief History of Humankind* (London: Harvill Secker).

19 Annalee Newitz (2013), *Scatter, Adapt, and Remember: How Humans Will Survive a Mass Extinction* (New York: Doubleday), p. 20.

20 John Hawks, Keith Hunley, Sang-Hee Lee, and Milford Wolpoff (2000), "Population Bottlenecks and Pleistocene Human Evolution," *Molecular Biology and Evolution* 17(1): 2–22.

NOTES

Chapter 10 The Antibunker: Bloom Where You're Planted

1 Ursula K. Le Guin (2001), *The Lathe of Heaven* (London: Gollancz), p. 120.

2 Jessica Stapf (2017), "Preparing for 'The Big One,'" FEMA, Department of Homeland Security report, June 2.

3 Garrett M. Graff (2017), "The Doomsday Diet," *Eater*, December 12, https://www.eater.com/2017/12/12/16757660/doomsday-biscuit-all-purpose-survival-cracker.

Chapter 11 Community Nourishment: Utah's Mormon Citadel

1 Lucius Annaeus Seneca [1917], *Epistles*, Volume I: *Epistles 1–65* (Cambridge, MA: Harvard University Press), p. 74.

2 Thomas S. Monson (2014), "Are We Prepared? First Presidency Message," *The Church of Jesus Christ of Latter-Day Saints*, September, https://www.lds.org/study/ensign/2014/09/are-we-prepared?lang=eng.

3 Gordon B. Hinckley (2005), "If Ye Are Prepared Ye Shall Not Fear," *The Church of Jesus Christ of Latter-Day Saints*. October, https://www.lds.org/general-conference/2005/10/if-ye-are-prepared-ye-shall-not-fear?lang=eng.

4 Mette Ivie Harrison (2015), "Confessions of a Former Mormon Doomsday Prepper," *Huffington Post*, September 24, https://www.huffingtonpost.com/entry/confessions-of-a-former-mormon-doomsday-prepper_b_8170504.

5 The DHS web page https://www.ready.gov/food is a clear US government mandate to prep.

6 Mark Hamm (1997), *Apocalypse in Oklahoma: Waco and Ruby Ridge Revenged* (Boston, MA: Northeastern University Press), p. 223.

7 Peggy Fletcher Stack (2015), "Some Mormons Stocking Up Amid Fears That Doomsday Could Come This Month," *Salt Lake Tribune*, September 15, http://archive.sltrib.com/article.php?id=2935776&itype=CMSID.

8 Amanda Little (2017), "Business Is Booming for America's Survival Food King," *Bloomberg Businessweek*, November 22, https://www.bloomberg.com/news/features/2017-11-22/business-is-booming-for-america-s-survival-food-king.

9 Tim Murphy (2013), "Preppers Are Getting Ready for the Barackalypse," *Mother Jones*, January–February.

10 Isabelle Stengers (2015), *In Catastrophic Times: Resisting the Coming Barbarism* (London: Open Humanities Press), p. 65.

Chapter 12 PrepperCon: The Business of Survival

1 Carl Sagan (2007), *The Varieties of Scientific Experience: A Personal View of the Search for God* (New York: Penguin), p. 125.

2 National Academy of Sciences (2008), *Severe Space Weather Events: Understand-*

ing Societal and Economic Impacts (Washington, DC: The National Academies Press).

3 Kevin Liptak (2018), "Trump Opposes 'Active Shooter Drills,' References His Own Son," CNN, February 22, https://www.cnn.com/2018/02/22/politics/donald-trump-active-shooter-drills/index.html.

4 Adam K. Raymond (2018), "How Active Shooter Drills Became a Big (and Possibly Traumatizing) Business," *Medium*, September 12, https://medium.com/s/youthnow/the-response-to-school-shootings-may-be-a-misfire-active-shooter-drills-teachers-students-6acb56418062.

5 Philip Bump (2018), "The NRA's Solution for School Shootings: Make Schools Battle Ready," *Washington Post*, February 23, https://www.washingtonpost.com/news/politics/wp/2018/02/23/the-nras-solution-for-school-shootings-making-schools-battle-ready/?utm_term=.074ae285b88a. The full National School Shield report can be found at https://assets.documentcloud.org/documents/673448/nss-final-full.pdf.

6 James Tennent (2018), "To Keep Students Safe, Oklahoma Is Using Bullet-Proof Storm Shelters at Elementary and Middle Schools," *Newsweek*, February 28, https://www.newsweek.com/oklahoma-schools-storm-shelters-shooting-824328.

7 Matt McKinney (2019), "Indiana Teachers Hit with Pellets During Active Shooter Training, ISTA Says," RTV4 Indianapolis, March 21.

8 Allie Nicodemo and Lia Petronio (2018), "Schools Are Safer Than They Were in the 90s, and School Shootings Are Not More Common Than They Used to Be, Researchers Say," *Northeastern University News*, February 26.

9 David Ropeik (2018), "School Shootings Are Extraordinarily Rare, Why Is Fear of Them Driving Policy?," *Washington Post*, March 8.

Chapter 13 Rolling Territory: The Mobile Bunker

1 The Invisible Committee (2004), *The Call* (New York: US Committee to Support the Tarnac 9), pp. 13, 17.

2 Rebecca Solnit (2011), *A Paradise Built in Hell: The Extraordinary Communities That Arise in Disaster* (London: Penguin), p. 262.

3 Stephen Graham (2010), *Cities Under Siege: The New Military Urbanism* (London: Verso); Naomi Klein (2008), *The Shock Doctrine: The Rise of Disaster Capitalism* (London: Penguin Books).

4 Laura Cozzi and Apostolos Petropoulos (2019), "Growing Preference for SUVs Challenges Emissions Reductions in Passenger Car Market," (Paris: International Energy Agency).

5 The first armored car used to ferry around a US president was a 1928 Cadillac 341A Town Sedan that was seized from Al Capone. After Pearl Harbor, the Secret Service cleaned the car up so they could drive Franklin Roosevelt around in it. See Garret M. Graff (2017), *Raven Rock: The Story of the U.S. Government's Secret Plan to Save Itself—While the Rest of Us Die* (New York: Simon & Schuster).

NOTES

6 Federal Civil Defense Administration (1955), *Four Wheels to Survival* (Washington, DC: GPO).

7 Douglas E. Campbell (2016), *Continuity of Government: How the U.S. Government Functions After All Hell Breaks Loose* (New York: Lulu Publishers), p. 66.

8 FEMA (2013), *FEMA Director Battle Book*, https://info.publicintelligence.net/FEMA-BattleBook.pdf, p. 32.

9 Garret M Graff (2017), *Raven Rock: The Story of the U.S. Government's Secret Plan to Save Itself—While the Rest of Us Die* (New York: Simon & Schuster).

10 Tom Vanderbilt (2002), *Survival City: Adventures Among the Ruins of Atomic America* (New York: Princeton Architectural Press), p. 163.

11 John Armitage (2000), "*Ctheory* Interview with Paul Virilio: The Kosovo War Took Place in Orbital Space," *Ctheory*, October 18.

12 Garret Keizer (2016), "Solidarity and Survival," *Lapham's Quarterly* 9 (2), Disaster: 200–205.

13 Hanan al-Shaykh writes beautifully about "tank vision" in her 2004 book *Beirut Blues* (New York: Putnam), p. 67.

14 Phil Patton (2003), "A Proud and Primal Roar," *New York Times*, January 12, https://www.nytimes.com/2003/01/12/style/cultural-studies-a-proud-and-primal-roar.html; Andrew Garner (2000), "Portable Civilizations and Urban Assault Vehicles," *Techné: Journal of the Society for Philosophy and Technology* 5(2): 1–7; Peter Rowe (2015), "Tank Rampage: A Symbolic Story Turns 20," *San Diego Union-Tribune*, May 16, https://www.sandiegouniontribune.com/lifestyle/people/sdut-tank-rampage-story-symbol-2015may16-htmlstory.html.

15 Mike Davis (2007), *Buda's Wagon: A Brief History of the Car Bomb* (London: Verso Books).

16 Sheldon Rampton and John Stauber (2003), *Weapons of Mass Deception: The Uses of Propaganda in Bush's War on Iraq* (London: Robinson). Also see Stephen Graham (2004), Stephen Graham (ed.), "Cities as Strategic Sites: Place Annihilation and Urban Geopolitics," in *Cities, War, and Terrorism: Towards an Urban Geopolitics* (Oxford: Blackwell), pp. 31–53.

17 Eduardo Mendieta (2005), "The Axle of Evil: SUVing Through the Slums of Globalizing Neoliberalism," *City* 9 (2): 195.

18 Phil Patton (2003), "A Proud and Primal Roar"; Andrew Garner (2000), "Portable Civilizations and Urban Assault Vehicles."

19 Zygmunt Bauman (1992), "Survival as a Social Construct," *Theory, Culture and Society* 9: 10.

20 Carly Stec (2017), "The Doom Boom: Inside the Survival Industry's Explosive Growth," *HubSpot*, November 5, https://blog.hubspot.com/marketing/survival-industry-growth.

21 David Campbell (2005), "The Biopolitics of Security: Oil, Empire and the Sports Utility Vehicle," *American Quarterly* 57(3): 943–972.

22 Cited in Tom Vanderbilt (2002), *Survival City: Adventures Among the Ruins of Atomic America* (New York: Princeton Architectural Press), p. 108.

Chapter 14 Life in a Geoscraper: The Survival Condo

1 Lieven De Cauter (2004), *The Capsular Civilization: On the City in the Age of Fear* (Rotterdam: Nai Publishers), p. 189.

2 The costs to the taxpayer today, adjusted for inflation, would be $300 million US.

3 Stephen L. Schwartz (1998), *Atomic Audit: The Cost and Consequences of U.S. Nuclear Weapons Since 1940* (Washington, DC: Brookings Institution Press), p. 3.

4 Tom Vanderbilt (2002), *Survival City: Adventures Among the Ruins of Atomic America* (New York: Princeton Architectural Press), pp. 166–172.

5 Rosalind Williams (2008), *Notes on the Underground: An Essay on Technology, Society and the Imagination* (Boston: MIT Press), p. 2.

6 Stephanie Buck (2017), "What the Government Didn't Mention About Fallout Shelters," *Medium*, April 18, https://timeline.com/fallout-shelter-psychology -f04085f41654.

7 John A. Hammes (1964), "A Summary of the Final Report, Shelter Occupancy Studies at the University of Georgia," p. 12, https://apps.dtic.mil/dtic/tr/fulltext /u2/615005.pdf.

8 Edward J. Murray (1960), "Adjustment to Environmental Stress in Fallout Shelters," in *Human Problems in the Utilization of Fallout Shelters*, George W. Baker and John H. Rohrer (eds.) (Washington, DC: National Academy of Sciences), p. 67.

9 See Garret M. Graff (2017), *Raven Rock: The Story of the U.S. Government's Secret Plan to Save Itself—While the Rest of Us Die* (New York: Simon & Schuster), p. 301.

10 Tea Krulos (2019), *Apocalypse Any Day Now: Deep Underground with America's Doomsday Preppers* (Chicago: Chicago Review Press), p. 123.

11 Evan Osnos (2017), "Doomsday Prep for the Super Rich," *New Yorker*, January 30, https://www.newyorker.com/magazine/2017/01/30/doomsday-prep-for-the -super-rich.

12 Lieven De Cauter (2004), *The Capsular Civilization: On the City in the Age of Fear* (Rotterdam: Nai Publishers), p. 83.

13 Joshua Foer and Michel Siffre (2008), "Caveman: An Interview with Michel Siffre," *Cabinet* (30).

14 Michel Siffre (1964), *Beyond Time* (London: McGraw-Hill), pp. 1, 217, 228.

15 Kisho Kurokawa (1972), *The Concept of Metabolism* (Tokyo: Architectural Foundation).

16 David Pinder (2005), *Visions of the City: Utopianism, Power and Politics in Twentieth-Century Urbanism* (Edinburgh: Edinburgh University Press).

NOTES

17 Le Corbusier (2000 [1929]), *The City of Tomorrow and Its Planning* (London: Dover Publications).

18 The biomes were agriculture, human, ocean, rain forest, savannah, marsh, and desert.

19 Abigial Alling (1993), *Life Under Glass: The Inside Story of Biosphere 2* (Santa Fe: Synergetic Press).

20 Roger Dunbar (1992), "Neocortex Size as a Constraint on Group Size in Primates," *Journal of Human Evolution* 22 (6): 469–493.

Chapter 15 The Concrete Cave: Vivos Indiana

1 Douglass Rushkoff (2018), "Survival of the Richest," *Medium*, July 5, https://medium.com/s/futurehuman/survival-of-the-richest-9ef6cddd0cc1.

2 This is in reference to the 1973 film *Soylent Green*. The primary food in the film, called Soylent, is *spoiler alert* made from human cadavers.

3 James Lovelock (2019), *Novacene: The Coming Age of Hyperintelligence* (London: Penguin).

Conclusion: The Last Plan

1 Margaret Atwood (2000), *The Blind Assassin* (New York: Anchor Books), p. 478.

2 Kristen Weaver (2018), "Man Behind Fannin County's Trident Lakes Development Files for Bankruptcy," KX12 News, July 16.

3 The federal complaint alleges that: "on or about February 23, 2018, CC-1 [Co-conspirator 1], ECKERD, and UCE-1 [Under Cover Enforcement] met at a location in Texas. UCE-1 had a backpack containing $100,000 in purported narcotics proceeds. During this audio and video-recorded meeting, UCE-1 told ECKERD that UCE-1 and CC-1 had opened up the backpack and noticed that the bundles of cash from the supposed Colombian drug traffickers contained some twenty-dollar bills. CC-1 noted that it would be easier to transport cash in higher denominations, and, ECKERD also noted, 'That's a lot of conversion.' [CC-1] later accepted from UCE-1 $100,000 in cash contained inside the backpack. In exchange, ECKERD provided a check in the amount of $90,000."

4 Melia Robinson (2018), "A Doomsday Shelter for the 1% Is Being Investigated by the FBI as a Possible Front for a Colombian Money Laundering Scheme," *Business Insider*, July 7, https://www.businessinsider.com.au/apocalypse-development-trident-lakes-fbi-investigation-2018-7?r=US&IR=T.

5 James Dornbrook (2019), "Suit: Developer of Luxury Doomsday Survival Condos Defaulted on Loan," *Kansas City Business Journal*, February 4.

6 Information on the class-action settlement can be found at http://www.wisefoodsettlement.com/.

7 The Atlas Survival Shelters YouTube channel can be easily found through the site's search function. As of March 2020, the channel had 182,000 subscribers and more than 23 million views.

NOTES

8 Steven Pinker (2011), *The Better Angels of Our Nature: Why Violence Has Declined* (New York: Viking).

Coda: Stalking the Apocalypse at Chernobyl

1 Emil Cioran (1992 [1934]), *On the Heights of Despair* (Chicago: University of Chicago Press).

2 Kate Brown (2013), *Plutopia: Nuclear Families, Atomic Cities, and the Great Soviet and American Plutonium Disasters* (Oxford: Oxford University Press), p. 283.

3 Bruce Sterling (ND), "The World Is Becoming Uninsurable, Part 3," *Viridian Note* 23, http://www.viridiandesign.org/notes/1-25/Note%2000023.txt.

4 Chad Gracia (2015), *The Russian Woodpecker* (London: Roast Beef Productions).

5 Andy Day (2017), "Is Every Photograph from Chernobyl a Lie?," *Fstoppers*, December 26, https://fstoppers.com/documentary/every-photograph-chernobyl-lie-204470.

6 Arkady Strugatsky and Boris Strugatsky (1972), *Roadside Picnic* (Chicago: Chicago University Press).

Index

INDEX

INDEX

INDEX

dialectic philosophy, 31
disaster
  benefits of, 37, 158
  communities and, 37, 44–45
  ideology of, 18, 37
  as natural human environment, 168–69
  nonfinal nature of, 266
  place and, 20
disaster capitalism, 133, 136, 219–20
Disaster Response Team (DRT), xiv, 206–7
disaster solidarity, 37–38
Dispatches, 133–34
DIY (do it yourself), xiv
DNA, xiv, 6, 27, 101, 135–36
Docheff, Cody, 215
Doctrine and Covenants, 182
Donne, John, 66
doomsday capitalists. *See* dread merchants
Doomsday Clock, 10–11, 140
Doomsday Preppers, 90
doomsday vaults, 12
Dorling, Danny, 150
Dotcom, Kim, 130, 131, 137
dread, 10
  author's meditations on, 45–46
  author's skepticism and, 260–61
  bug-out vehicles and, 218
  fiction as catalyst for, 120
  formlessness and, 14, 15, 122
  Freud on, 164–65
  Heidegger on, 153
  Kierkegaard on, 33–34, 153
  Lovecraft on, 14–15, 16
  natural disasters and, 176–77
  nuclear threat and, 64–66, 68, 120, 121
  ongoing anxieties, 265
  private bunkers and, 18
  promotion of, 16–17, 44, 68
  school shootings and, 200
  self-alienation and, 86
  sources of, 88
  trickle-down, 132
dread merchants, 3, 16
  author's skepticism and, 261
  Camden, 126, 140, 239, 240
  Clarry, 125–29, 136–37, 138, 140–41, 151
  government abdication of responsibility and, 17–18
  Gritz, 70–72, 73
  Lynch, 82–85, 88–89, 90–91, 131
  O'Connor, 93–100, 104–5, 106, 257, 258
  as scam artists, 258–59
  success of, 29–30, 265
  See also elusiveness of dread merchant

products; Hall, Larry; Miller, Drew; safe space marketing; Vicino, Robert
drone technology, 86
Dr. Strangelove, 53
DRT. *See* Disaster Response Team
DUMBS. *See* deep underground military bases
Dunbar, Robin, 242–43
Dunbar's number, 242–43

Eckerd, John, 94–95, 96, 99, 106–8, 219, 258, 259
ecological sustainability, 96, 99–100
economic inequality, 7
  bug-out vehicles and, 218
  dread merchants and, 25
  gated communities and, 29, 44, 144–45, 217
  Hardened Structures and, 127
  secrecy and, 150
  techno-libertarian philosophy and, 132, 133–34, 136
  Thailand and, 144
  Trident Lakes and, 106
Eisenhower, Dwight D., 52, 67, 155
ELE. *See* extinction level event
elite panic, 207
elusiveness of dread merchant products, 257–61
  author's skepticism, 247
  Fortitude Ranch, 161–62, 247
  Hardened Structures, 126, 129, 136–37, 140–41, 239–40, 247
  media and, 139–40, 161
  scams and, 258–59, 261–62
  Trident Lakes, 247, 257–58
  Vicino, 40, 247, 251, 252, 259
  xFest, 30–31, 40, 161
emergency food stores
  Brexit and, 135
  disaster solidarity and, 38
  Fortitude Ranch, 162
  government guidelines, 17
  LDS Church, 184, 186–89
  private industry, 16, 189–91
  Survival Condo, 224
  Vivos Indiana, 248–49
EMPs (electromagnetic pulses)
  defined, xv
  Jones on, 163, 194–95, 196
  Miller on, 163–64
  nuclear war close calls and, 54
  in postapocalyptic fiction, 157
  shields for, 28, 234
end of the world as we know it, the (TEOTWAWKI), xvii, 3

308

INDEX

INDEX

INDEX

311

INDEX

INDEX

INDEX

Vicino, Robert (*cont.*)
  Burlington Bunker and, 3, 16, 24
  as dread merchant, 16, 40
  Hall on, 239
  Kansas salt quarry, 27
  on life assurance solutions, 3, 16, 218
  Miller on, 166, 167
  on Oppidum, 139
  on Planet X, 24, 42, 129, 166, 276
  on preparation, 182
  PrepperCon and, 192
  product elusiveness, 40, 247, 251, 252, 259
  on rebirth, 267
  on ripple effect, 117
  safe space marketing and, 25–28, 39–40, 131, 139
  unfinished projects, 26–28
  Vivos Group CEO, 26
  Vivos Indiana and, 243, 247, 249, 251, 252–53, 259
  xFest and, 23, 30–32, 44
  See also xPoint
violence
  mass shootings, 128, 147, 153, 200–202, 265
  perceptions of, 202
Virilio, Paul, 43, 44, 77, 90
Vivos Asiana, 27, 28
Vivos Europa One, 27–28
Vivos Indiana, 245–55
  elusiveness of, 251, 259
  evangelical Christianity and, 254–55
  food stores, 248–49
  Hall on, 239
  internet dependence, 252–53
  psychological environment in, 251–52
  sleep and waking in, 245–46

Waco siege (1993), 73, 213
Wahlberg, Donnie, 104
Walsh, Bryan, 155
War Games, 53
War of the Worlds, The (Wells), 120
War Plan UK (Campbell), 85
wealth. *See* economic inequality
Weaver, Randy, 72–73, 90
Welles, Orson, 120
Wells, H. G., 120
Wever, Rütger, 232
wildfire disasters, 11, 19, 110, 111, 121

Wildfire Safety Bunkers, 110–11
Wilson, Louis, 77
Wired, 8
Wise Company, 189, 219, 260
without rule of law (WROL), xviii, 70, 115
Wool (Howey), 230
Woolsey, R. James, 163
World Health Organization (WHO), xviii, 169
World Made by Hand, 178
World War II structures, 22–23, 48, 58, 113–14
Writing of the Disaster, The (Blanchot), 21
Wydeveld, Jae, 138, 139

Xenophon, 4
xFest, 23, 30–31, 38, 40, 44, 139, 192, 196, 199
xPoint, 38–40
  Almost Heaven and, 70, 71, 72
  author's sleep in, 33–34
  community ethos and, 35, 36–37
  elusiveness of, 30–31, 40, 161
  friction with Milton at, 263–64
  gender and, 145
  government abdication of responsibility and, 38
  marketing of, 26, 39–40, 44, 46, 72
  media coverage, 38, 39, 262–63
  ownership of, 25–26
  progenitors of, 74
  progress of, 44–45, 131–32, 202–3, 264–65
  promotion at PrepperCon, 192, 194, 196, 199
  secrecy and, 90
  site of, 22–24
  struggles of, 82
  technological dependence of, 237

Yang, Andrew, 132
Yeltsin, Boris, 54
You're on Your Own (YOYO), xviii, 207, 270

Zamrazil, Jakub, 129, 137, 138, 139, 140
ZetaTalk conspiracy website, 129
Zhao, Zhiye, 13–14
Ziegler, Peter, 259–60
Zimmerman, Andrea Luka, 71
Zuckerberg, Mark, 133